Question
&Answer
Encyclopedia

Question & Answer Encyclopedia

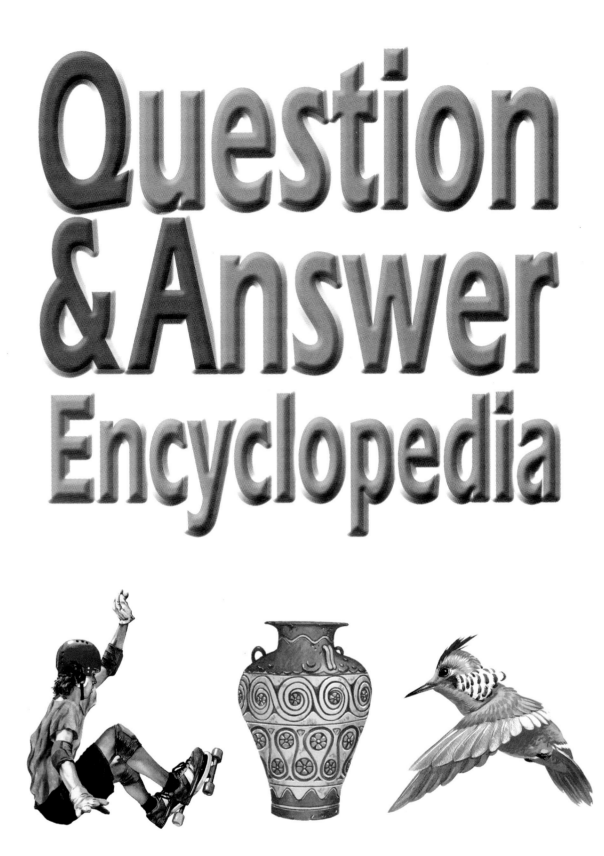

Steve Parker & Brian Williams

Miles Kelly

PUBLISHING

First published in 2004 by Miles Kelly Publishing Ltd
Bardfield Centre Great Bardfield Essex CM7 4SL

2 4 6 8 10 9 7 5 3 1

British Library Cataloguing-in-Publication Data
A catalogue record for this book is available from the British Library

ISBN 1-84236-417-0

Printed in India

Publishing Director Anne Marshall
Senior Editor Jenni Rainford
Assistant Editor Teri Mort
Copy Editor Rosalind Beckman
Design Concept John Christopher
Designers Jo Brewer, Michelle Cannatella,
Louisa Leitao, Debbie Meekcoms
Cover Design Debbie Meekcoms
Picture Researcher Liberty Newton
Indexer Helen Snaith
Colour Separation DPI Colour Digital Ltd

www.mileskelly.net
info@mileskelly.net

All statistics used in this book are accurate at the time of going to press.

CONTENTS

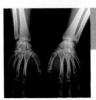

The Universe is where we live – all the stars we can see, and billions more besides. Scientists think the early Universe was very small, but still contained all the matter and all the energy there is today. And, to make it more amazing, scientists also think the original Universe lasted for less time than it takes to blink your eye. Then it began to grow. They call this theory the 'Big Bang'.

When did the Universe begin?

Many scientists believe that the Universe began between 13 and 18 billion years ago but no one is quite sure exactly when. What was there before remains a mystery. Some scientists think our Universe began as a 'bubble', which split off from another universe! Others think that in the beginning, all the matter in the Universe was squeezed into a tiny, incredibly hot, incredibly massive ball. When the ball began to get bigger, like a balloon being blown up, all the matter in the Universe started to explode outwards.

What holds things in place in space?

All the matter in the Universe – stars, planets, clouds of gas, tiny particles of dust – is held together by four invisible forces. These forces are gravity, electromagnetism, and two forms of nuclear force, strong and weak, which hold the particles of every atom together. Gravity is the attraction between all matter in the Universe. It keeps the Moon in orbit around the Earth, and the Earth in orbit around the Sun. The more matter a body has, the stronger its 'pull' on other bodies.

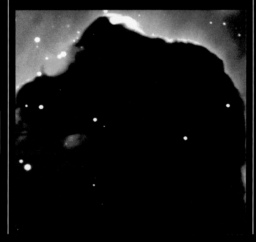

⬇ *This is the Horsehead Nebula, one of many 'star factories' in space where new stars are born.*

What is the fastest thing in the Universe?

Nothing in the Universe travels faster than light (see page 175). Light is given off by stars, such as our Sun, and it travels through space at roughly 300,000 km/sec. Yet because the Universe is so large, even at this speed, light from the Sun takes more than eight minutes to reach us on Earth.

Measuring **space and time**

Light years and parsecs

Earth distances are measured in miles or kilometres, but these units are too small to be useful in space. Scientists measure the Universe in light-years and parsecs. Light is the fastest thing in the Universe, so by measuring in light-years scientists are able to get a better idea of such great distances. A light-year is the distance that light travels in one year – about 10 million million km. A light-year is roughly 3.25 parsecs. Light from even the closest stars takes years to reach us. The nearest star is over four light-years away, so this means that when astronomers look at it through a telescope, they are actually looking back into the past – seeing the star as it was four years ago. Light from the most distant galaxies takes about 10,000 million years to reach us.

➡ *The Universe may go on expanding for ever. Or it may eventually stop and begin collapsing in on itself to possibly even start all over again.*

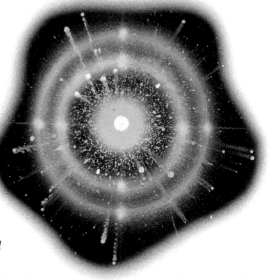

Is the Universe getting bigger?

Yes. Scientists can tell that groups of stars, known as galaxies, appear to be moving away from us. The galaxies themselves are not moving, but the space between them is stretching. By measuring how fast this distance is increasing, scientists can work out how long it has taken for everything to get where it is now. So they have a rough idea when the Big Bang set everything off.

← *Scientists can detect background radiation spread throughout space, probably left over from the Big Bang. In the 1920s, astronomer Edwin Hubble (1889–1953) discovered that there were other galaxies apart from our own Milky Way. The distance between Earth and each of these galaxies is increasing at unbelievable speeds.*

← *Scientists have calculated that the hot ball before the Big Bang must have swelled at a much faster rate than even the speed of light. The hot ball would have grown to the size of a galaxy within a fraction of a second!*

Is space empty?

Not really. Matter was created almost as soon as the Universe began. Space is littered with stars and gas clouds, made almost entirely of two elements: the gases hydrogen and helium. There are other elements too, such as iron, carbon and oxygen, but these are rare. The space between stars and planets is full of bits of space debris, including very tiny specks of dust and larger pieces of rock. Some of this space-dust forms clouds, called nebulae. These vast clouds of matter are the 'factories' inside which new stars and planets are made.

↑ *Galaxies are giant groups of up to trillions of stars, and there may be as many as 20 trillion galaxies in the Universe.*

Telescopes and radio dishes

Early astronomers could only see stars visible with the unaided eye. Today, scientists use light-collecting telescopes and radio dishes that pick up radio and other waves to scan and photograph the most distant objects in outer space. Scientists depend mostly on these photographs to study space.

→ *With the help of his sister Caroline, William Herschel (1738–1822) discovered Uranus in 1781. He later identified two of the moons of Uranus and Saturn.*

↑ *Johannes Kepler (1571–1630) became the great Danish astornomer Tycho Brahe's assistant and took over his work when Brahe died.*

Amazing **Universe**

• In the first micro-seconds of the Universe, matter did not exist. There was just very hot space.

• Anti-matter is equal and opposite to matter: when the two collide, they eliminate one another.

• Hydrogen is the the most common element found in the Universe.

• Some scientists think there may be lots of 'parallel' universes, like a pack of cards – each 'card' separated by a fraction of time.

Astar is a massive ball of hot hydrogen gas. To people on Earth, a star looks like a tiny pinpoint of light in the night sky. Stars look small because they are so far away. In fact, many stars are enormous, many times bigger than our Sun – our nearest star. The Sun glows fiercely because it is a star that is still hot and active. That is why we see it shining in the sky.

Binary system with one star larger than the other

➜ *Stars are born inside vast gas clouds. Some old stars die as exploding supernovae. Others swell up and become giants, which then fade and dim.*

True binary stars orbit the same centre of gravity together

➜ *About half the stars in our own galaxy are binary stars. They orbit around the same point, or centre of gravity.*

4 A nebula formed from cloud and dust

What are twin stars?

Some stars, like our Sun, are alone in space, but others, called binary stars, have companions or twins, which are held together by gravity. Eclipsing twin stars appear to 'dance' around each other in space. Binary stars move faster the closer together they are, but some may be so far apart that they take millions of years to orbit one another. When one star is hidden behind the other, its light is dimmed. When the star reappears, the pair of dancing stars shine brightly once more.

Where is a star born?

Stars are born inside giant dust and gas clouds called nebulae. There are nebulae in every galaxy across the Universe. Nebulae are 'star factories', as clouds of dust and gas shrink under the pull of gravity, the mass of matter becomes immensely hot and begins to give off energy as light and heat. A new star starts to shine.

1 A star is born when nuclear reactions begin

2 A star burns steadily

3 Dust swirling around a new star may form planets

Starry **facts**

Countless stars

We know what stars are made of: 75 per cent hydrogen, 22 per cent helium and traces of other elements. But no one knows how many stars there are. Space seems to be full of stars and there are too many for one person to count in a lifetime! Star facts are mind-boggling. The Sun is more than 100 times bigger than the Earth, yet the Sun is a very ordinary star. Even huge stars look tiny in space because they are such vast distances away from us. The biggest stars are 700 times larger than our Sun.

Are all stars the same size?

No, they vary in size and heat. Our Sun is a medium-sized hot yellow star. The biggest stars are called supergiants and there are many supergiant stars that are hundreds of times bigger than our Sun.

⬆ *This is a globular star cluster, made up of millions of stars of different ages and sizes.*

How long do stars last?

A star's lifetime may be up to millions of years. During their lives, stars burn up energy, sending out light and heat. Some grow into blue giants and explode as supernovae. Other smaller stars swell up as their fuel starts to run out and become vast glowing red giants. They then shrink into white dwarfs, which are very small, tightly compressed stars. White dwarfs are so small that they are hard to detect in the sky. The surface of a white dwarf can reach 8,000°C.

➲ *A cluster of ancient stars, or stellar swarm, is one of 147 such clusters in our galaxy. Every star in this cluster is older than our Sun.*

Where does a star get its energy from?

A star's energy comes from nuclear fusion, in which most of the hydrogen changes to helium, but enough hydrogen is left over to produce huge amounts of energy. The light from stars streams out across space in a range of colours (blue, orange-red, yellow and white).

⬇ *A star can shine for millions of years before it swells up to become a red giant, then shrinks to a small white dwarf.*

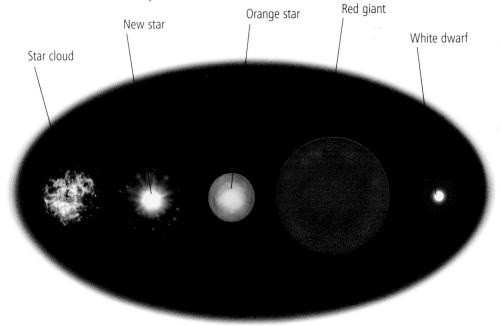

Star cloud   New star   Orange star   Red giant   White dwarf

➲ *The largest telescopes can see about 100 billion galaxies. A galaxy can have up to 100 billion stars in it. Astronomers call this galaxy NGC 4214 and it is about 13 million light-years from us.*

Amazing **facts**

Brightest star: Sirius in the constellation Caris Majoris.
Smallest stars: Neutron stars are only 20 km across.
Nearest star (excluding the Sun): Proxima Centauri, 4.22 light-years away.

Star type	Temperature (°C)
Blue	up to 40,000
Blue-white	11,000
White	7,500
Yellow	6,000
Orange	5,000
Red	3,500

There are 88 'star patterns' visible in the night sky. These are the constellations. When the first astronomers in ancient Babylonia, Egypt, China and Greece began looking at the stars, they saw patterns and shapes, formed by stars that appear close together in the sky. They named each constellation after an animal or a character from myth and legend – such as Taurus (the bull) and Perseus (a Greek hero). Later, more constellations were discovered and given names, such as Telescopium (the telescope).

The star-groups seen in the Northern Hemisphere (below) are not the same as those seen south of the Equator, in the Southern Hemisphere (right). Stars are best seen on a clear, moonless night away from the glare of city lights.

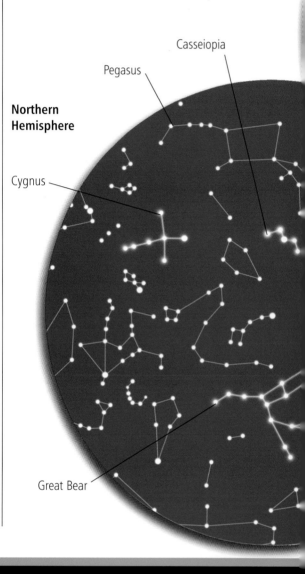

Northern Hemisphere

Casseiopia

Pegasus

Cygnus

Great Bear

When did people first see constellations?

Many constellations were first seen by astronomers living in China and Babylon more than 2,000 years ago. Stars fascinated early scientists, but the scientists had no telescopes, so could only name the star-groups that they could see with the unaided eye. Constellations are all different shapes and sizes, and it is not always easy to recognize the animal or object they are named after without a drawing showing an outline around the stars. Some star-groups have more than one name.

The ancient Greeks, called Orion the Hunter, but the ancient Egyptians called it the god Osiris.

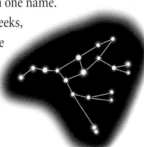

Does everyone see the same stars?

No. Different constellations can be seen in the Southern Hemisphere (south of the Equator) and in the Northern Hemisphere (north of the Equator) (see page 44). Many of the constellations were named before 2000 BC by astronomers in Babylonia. By AD 150, the Greek scientist Ptolemy was able to list 48. No new ones were added until European explorers sailed to the Southern Hemisphere and saw stars that are invisible to people in the Northern Hemisphere. Constellations are not easy to pick out because the night sky looks so crowded with stars. It helps to concentrate on the brightest stars.

This is Ursa Major, the Great Bear, a constellation in the Northern Hemisphere. Its other names include the Plough and the Big Dipper.

Astrological **signs**

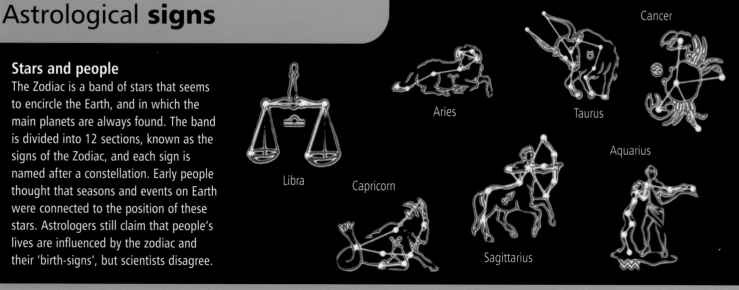

Stars and people
The Zodiac is a band of stars that seems to encircle the Earth, and in which the main planets are always found. The band is divided into 12 sections, known as the signs of the Zodiac, and each sign is named after a constellation. Early people thought that seasons and events on Earth were connected to the position of these stars. Astrologers still claim that people's lives are influenced by the zodiac and their 'birth-signs', but scientists disagree.

Cancer

Aries

Taurus

Libra

Capricorn

Aquarius

Sagittarius

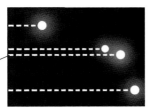

Southern Hemisphere

Same star pattern seen side on

Scorpion

View from Earth

Great Dog

Southern Cross

⬆ *Seen from the Earth, the stars making up the Southern Cross look the same distance away, but they are, in fact, scattered.*

What is Orion's Belt?

Orion's Belt is the name given to three bright stars in the constellation Orion (the Hunter). Orion can be seen from anywhere on Earth and because it is bright and easily seen, it makes a good star-guide. The Belt points in one direction to the star, Aldebaran, and in the other to the star, Sirius.

What is the Southern Cross?

The Southern Cross is the smallest of the constellations, but is well known because its stars are so bright. Some constellations contain very few bright stars and so are hard to see. Hydra, the Water Snake is the biggest constellation, but it is very dim and so incredibly difficult to spot.

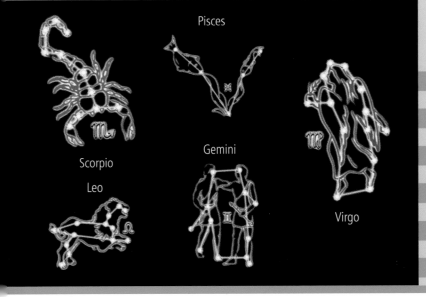

Pisces

Gemini

Scorpio

Leo

Virgo

Signs of the **Zodiac**

22 December–19 January	Capricorn, the Goat
20 January–18 February	Aquarius, the Water Carrier
19 February–20 March	Pisces, the Fish
21 March–19 April	Aries, the Ram
20 April–20 May	Taurus, the Bull
21 May–20 June	Gemini, the Twins
21 June–22 July	Cancer, the Crab
23 July–22 August	Leo, the Lion
23 August–22 September	Virgo, the Virgin
23 September–22 October	Libra, the Scales
23 October–21 November	Scorpio, the Scorpion
22 November–21 December	Sagittarius, the Archer

A galaxy is a vast group of stars, like a stellar city, which can contain as many as a trillion stars. Galaxies are found in clusters, some with fewer than 50 galaxies, others with hundreds. There are many millions of galaxies, each of which began as a cloud of gas when the Universe was formed and new stars are still being born inside them. As the Universe expands, the galaxies fly apart.

➔ Hubble proved that the Universe was much larger than anyone had believed, by discovering that there are many other galaxies.

Do all galaxies look the same?

No. The main shapes are spirals, ovals and irregular. Two kinds of galaxy look like whirling spirals with 'arms'. Spiral galaxies either have several arms of stars around a central core or, like our Milky Way galaxy, have arms that start from bars – this is a 'barred spiral'. Elliptical galaxies are oval or egg-shaped. Irregular galaxies have no set shape. Elliptical galaxies send out stars in all directions, like sparks from a huge firework.

Who realized there is more than one galaxy?

American astronomer Edwin Hubble first realized there was more than one galaxy in 1924. Until then, people thought there was just one mass of stars – making one very big galaxy. Hubble detected a winking variable star beyond the Milky Way. He realized that the Andromeda Nebula he was studying was not a gas cloud within our Milky Way galaxy, but was in fact another galaxy. All the stars that we can see with the unaided eye belong to our galaxy, but there are millions more beyond it.

➔ The four main kinds of galaxies are spiral, irregular, elliptical and barred spiral.

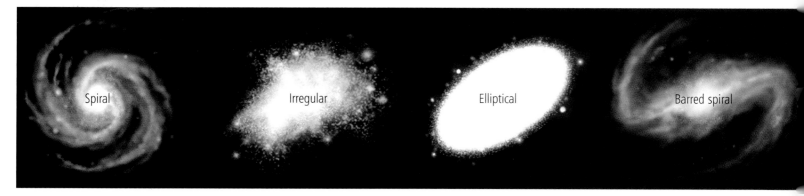

Spiral   Irregular   Elliptical   Barred spiral

Facts about our **galaxy**

Heavenly milk
The word 'galaxy' comes from the ancient Greek word for milk, *gala*. The Greeks saw a hazy belt in the night sky, which reminded them of a trail of spilt milk. They made up a story to explain that the heavenly milk had been spilt by the baby Heracles (Hercules). The galaxy came to be known as the 'road of milk', or Milky Way. The centre of the Milky Way is the core or nucleus of the galaxy, with a dense mass of stars.

The Sun is about halfway out from the centre, on one of the spiral arms of the galaxy.

Galaxies visible from **Earth**

The Large Magellanic Clouds	160,000 light-years away
The Small Magellanic Clouds	180,000 light-years away
The Andromeda Galaxy	2 million light-years away

⊕ *The Milky Way spins extremely quickly, moving the Sun and all the stars in it at up to 100 million km/h.*

Which galaxy do we live in?

Our galaxy is the Milky Way. There are about 200,000 million stars in the Milky Way galaxy, and one of them is our Sun. The Sun is moving around the galaxy, but in the last 200 million years it has only done this once as the galaxy is so big.

What is dark matter?

Galaxies look like bright clouds of starry matter, but around them is a swirling mass of invisible 'dark matter'. Astronomers believe that nine-tenths of all the matter in the Universe is dark and know about the existence of it because its gravity pulls on stars and galaxies in the Universe. Dark matter could be the remains of ordinary matter, such as stars, which burnt out early in the life of the Universe.

⊕ *This is an irregular galaxy, In ten days in 1995, the Hubble Space Telescope took photographs of almost 2,000 galaxies in one small area of sky.*

How big are galaxies?

Unbelievably vast. Even travelling at light-speed, a spacecraft would take 100,000 years to cross the Milky Way. A very ordinary galaxy contains a million stars, while the super-galaxies are giants with as many as a billion stars.

⊕ *The Milky Way looks different seen from 'above' (showing the spiral arms) and from sideways on, when it looks like a flying saucer (right).*

Our galaxy is amazingly big: two billion stars, 100,000 light-years across. But it is just one of millions of similar galaxies. As well as stars, there are other faraway objects in space: black holes, supernovae, nebulae and quasars. No one knows how many galaxies there are, all speeding away from us. The Big Bang expansion may go on forever. Or the Universe may slow down and contract, like a deflating balloon – a theory that scientists call the 'Big Crunch'.

What is the biggest object in the Universe?

The most gigantic object detected so far is a wall of galaxies, appropriately called the Great Wall. This stretch of stars is 500 million light-years long and 16 million light-years wide. However, size does not really matter in the Universe, because there are such a lot of giants out there.

Why did scientists put a telescope into space?

The Earth's atmosphere obscures our view of the stars, so the Hubble Space Telescope was launched in 1990 from the space shuttle, to give scientists a clearer view of space. It now circles in an orbit high above the Earth, where the view is unobscured. Hubble gave scientists their first unhazy view of the stars, and even though at first the telescope did not work as planned (it had to be repaired by astronauts), the results were astounding.

The Great Wall is a vast string of galaxies, like this spiral galaxy (photographed from the Hubble Space Telescope).

The Hubble Space Telescope weighs 11 tonnes and has a mirror 2.5 m across. When first launched in 1990, the mirror was the wrong shape and a replacement had to be taken up in 1994.

Nebulae and neutron stars

Clouds of dust and gas

Nebulae are huge clouds of dust and gas. These clouds are made mostly of hydrogen and helium – the raw materials of star-building, and it is inside nebulae that new stars are made. It is intensely cold inside a big nebula, only 10° above absolute zero. Clumps of gas are pulled together by gravity, and the more the atoms are squeezed, the warmer they become. The clumps do not all become new stars – some never get hot enough, but the bigger ones get hotter and hotter. We can see some nebulae through telescopes, some because they glow faintly and others because they reflect light from stars and so 'shine'. There are other nebulae that are dark, veiling the stars being born inside them.

The word nebula was once used to describe any patch of light in the night sky. Many nebulae are now galaxies instead.

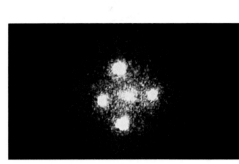

⬆ *Quasars send out vast amount of energy, in the form of radiation such as light, X-rays and radio waves. Studying these objects helps astronomers discover more about the early Universe, since the radiation from a quasar probably left it billions of years ago.*

What are the most distant objects?

Quasars, which look like stars, but actually are not. A quasar is much smaller than a galaxy (a mere light-year or two across), but up to a thousand times brighter. Quasars give off radio waves and would be invisible if they were not so incredibly luminous. Quasars are at least 10–13 billion light-years away from Earth, making them the most distant objects in the Universe.

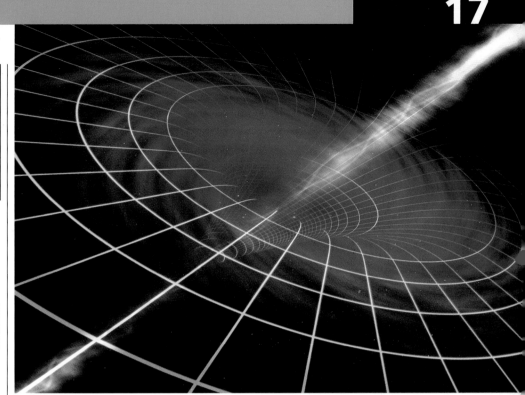

⬆ *This is an artist's impression of a black hole. Black holes suck up any type of matter. Some scientists think there may be a black hole at the heart of every galaxy.*

What is a supernova?

A supernova is a vast explosion of light, brighter than millions of suns, that happens when an old giant star collapses into itself. The collapse sets off a nuclear reaction and the explosion can be seen far across the Universe. In 1987, a supernova was visible from the Earth – a rare event.

⬅ *When a supernova explodes, star-debris is flung far out into space.*

Debris expands

Supernova explodes

What goes into a black hole?

Anything within reach. Nothing that goes into a black hole can come out. A black hole is all that is left of a collapsed star. It is invisible because it has such a strong gravitational pull that no matter and no light can escape from it. A black hole sucks up vast amounts of matter into an incredibly tiny space. To travel through interstellar space (between galaxies), astronauts in the future may have to use 'wormholes' – cosmic tunnels, which avoid black holes – if such tunnels exist.

⬇ *A photo of the Horsehead Nebula, taken with a telescope on Earth. This nebula is in the constellaton Orion.*

Neutron stars

Neutron stars may be the smallest stars known, but they are incredibly dense. They form when a big star uses up all its fuel and collapses under its own gravity. All its matter gets squashed together, then the star explodes as a supernova and all that is left is a spinning core, called a neutron star. Neutron stars were first spotted as fast-spinning 'pulsars' in 1967.

➡ *A neutron star may be only 20 km across but it contains more matter than the Sun.*

Space missions involve travelling vast distances, either around or away from the Earth. To send people into space costs a lot of money and effort. So far, the only way to get into space is by using a big rocket. Rockets have sent people to the Moon and probes to the planets. Astronauts live and work in space stations, which orbit the Earth. For exploring the distant planets, a robot probe is best: it needs no air, water or food – and it never gets bored!

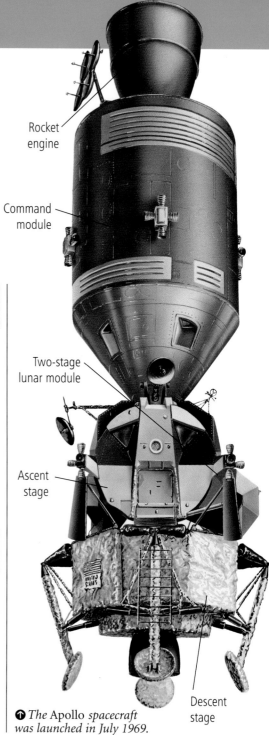

Rocket engine

Command module

Two-stage lunar module

Ascent stage

Descent stage

⊕ *The Apollo* spacecraft *was launched in July 1969.*

⊕ *The US Pathfinder landed on Mars with the roving vehicle* Sojourner. *The rover stopped working after three months on Mars.*

What makes rockets the best engines for space flight?

A rocket needs no air (unlike a jet engine) – indeed, air slows it down. Most rocket engines get their thrust from the reaction between a fuel, such as liquid hydrogen, and an oxidant (liquid oxygen), which allows the fuel to burn.

How many people have stood on the Moon?

Since the astronauts of *Apollo 11* first landed on the Moon in 1969, a total of 12 astronauts have stood on the Moon. From 1969 to 1972, the Americans sent seven Apollo missions to the Moon. One mission, *Apollo 13*, failed to land but returned safely after an explosion on board. The other six missions each landed two astronauts.

When did scientists land craft on the planet Mars?

Two US *Viking* spacecraft visited Mars in 1970–76. The craft orbited the planet and robot landers took samples of the soil and sent data and TV pictures back to Earth. In 1997, the US *Pathfinder* craft landed a rover called *Sojourner*, and in 2004 the US *Express Orbiter* craft sent two rovers to different sides of Mars to explore the surface.

Pioneers of **spaceflight**

Space activity
In 2003, *Voyager 1* became the first spacecraft to leave the Solar System. This small robot craft is one of the most remarkable pioneers of space flight. In 2004, the USA landed two golf-buggy sized rovers, *Spirit* and *Opportunity*, at different sites on Mars. Europe's *Mars Express Orbiter* craft surveyed the planet but could not spot the small rover *Beagle 2*, which disappeared after landing in December 2003.

⊕ *Unmanned robots can go on sending back data for years. The two* Voyagers *have been in space for more than 25 years.*

Message for aliens
So far no astronauts have travelled farther than the Moon. Since the Apollo missions ended, humans have been confined to flights in Earth orbit.Two unmanned probes called *Voyager 1* and *Voyager 2* left the Earth in 1977. They carried messages for any aliens that might find the tiny spacecraft somewhere in the vastness of space. The aim was to let any aliens know where in the Universe the small spacecraft had come from. Not every scientist thought this a good idea. What if the aliens are unfriendly? Fortunately, the chances of anyone finding the *Voyagers* lost in space is very remote!

Why do astronauts float in space?

Once in orbit, a spacecraft and the people inside it are freed from the full effects of Earth's gravity and so they feel weightless. Anything inside the spacecraft that is not fixed in place floats about. This takes a bit of getting used to, but most astronauts enjoy the experience of weightlessness. Exercises must be done to keep their muscles and bones in good shape.

❶ *An astronaut wearing a MMU (manned manoeuvring unit) can move safely about outside the spacecraft.*

❷ *The Shuttle is lifted off the launch pad by the thrust of its three main engines and two booster rockets. It must reach a speed of 28,000 km/h to be able to go into orbit and not fall back down to Earth.*

How is a spacecraft launched?

There are two kinds of launch systems for spacecraft: multi-stage rockets and reusable shuttles. The American space shuttle began its missions into orbit in 1981. It is launched with the aid of two solid-fuel rocket boosters, which fall off after two minutes and fall to the ground to be reused. After eight and a half minutes, the main fuel tank also drops away and the shuttle flies into orbit. On its return, the shuttle glows red-hot due to friction as it re-enters the atmosphere. It uses its wings to glide down to land.

Which spacecraft first explored the giant planets?

The US probe *Pioneer 11,* launched in 1973, flew past Jupiter and then on to Saturn in 1979 before heading out towards the edge of the Solar System. A later US space probe called *Voyager 2* flew past Jupiter in 1979, Uranus in 1986 and Neptune in 1989. The *Galileo* spacecraft visited Jupiter in 1995. Some long-range probes will probably go on travelling through space for ever, far beyond the Solar System.

❷ *Valentina Tereshkova became the first woman cosmonaut in 1963.*

Key dates

1926 First liquid-fuelled rocket.
1957 First artificial satellite launched by Russians: *Sputnik 1.*
1958 First US satellite: *Explorer 1.*
1961 First person in space: Russia's Yuri Gagarin.
1965 Russian *Venera* spacecraft hits Venus.
1965 First 'space walk' in orbit by Russia's Aleksei Leonov.

1969 America lands two *Apollo 11* astronauts on the Moon.
1970 Russian *Venera 7* soft-lands on Venus.
1971 Russian *Salyut* is first space station in orbit.
1976 Two US *Viking* robot craft land on Mars.
1977 *Voyager 1* and *Voyager 2* probes leave Earth for the distant planets.
1981 First flight of US Space Shuttle – two are later lost in accidents.
1997 *Sojourner* rover explores Mars.
2003 *Voyager 7* enters 'interstellar space'.
2004 *Spirit* and *Opportunity* explore Mars.

The astronomers of the ancient world had no telescopes, but had to rely on their eyes to observe the stars, and on mathematics to try and make sense of what they could see. They named five of the nine planets and gave names to many stars. The use of the telescope in the 1600s revolutionized the science of star-gazing. For the first time, scientists could see details such as the craters on the Moon.

Why are telescopes put on mountain peaks?

Optical telescopes need a clear view of the night sky but the air above cities is just too 'fogged up' by air pollution, heat, gases and bright lights. Therefore telescopes are sited in observatories on high mountain peaks, where the air is thinner and clearer. Stars are best viewed from space.

Astronomers use large telescopes like this one, located at the Kitt Peak National Observatory in Arizona, USA, to study the night sky. With such powerful lenses, experts are able to see and study stars that are too far away for us to see with the naked eye.

How does a telescope study the stars?

Early telescopes were refracting (light-bending) telescopes, with a lens to collect light. In 1671, the English scientist Sir Isaac Newton built a telescope that had a mirror to collect light – this was the first reflecting telescope. Today, most optical (light-collecting) telescopes used by astronomers are reflectors, linked to computers that enhance the images of distant objects. Optical telescopes are still in use, even in the era of radio telescopes and space probes.

Telescope moves around to capture the best image

Main mirror to catch light from distant objects

Axle tilts the telescope

Secondary mirror

Platform for observation

Mount swings around

The largest telescopes can see about 100 billion galaxies. Most modern optical telescopes are reflectors, and the bigger the mirror, the more light is collected. The same goes for radio dishes – big ones or lots of little ones see furthest.

Seeing **stars**

Famous telescopes
The Hale Observatories on Mount Wilson and Mount Palomar in California, USA, has a 5-m reflector. Even bigger is the 6-m reflector at Zelenchukskaya in Russia.

Jodrell Bank in Cheshire, England has a 76-m diameter radio-dish.

The biggest optical telescope is the Keck telescope in Hawaii, which has 36 mirrors forming a light-collector 10 m across.

The world's biggest radio telescope is the Very Large Array (VLA) in New Mexico, USA. This multi-dish instrument has 27 dishes, each measuring 25 m across.

Effelsberg Radio Observatory in Germany has a 100-m dish.

Telescopes have come a long way since they were first used in the 1600s. People can now enjoy space observation at home with the use of personal telescopes.

What do radio telescopes detect?

Radio telescopes do not collect light, but pick up different forms of radiation (rays) from stars, such as radio waves and X-rays. Such telescopes can detect these rays, invisible to the eye, which can reveal, for example, the magnetic field around a planet or allow us to see through clouds of space dust.

Who first looked into space through a telescope?

The first scientist to use a telescope or 'spyglass' to look at the heavens was the Italian Galileo Galilei about 1609. With a telescope he had made himself, he saw four moons circling the planet Jupiter and also got the first close-up view of the craters on the Moon.

Radio telescopes have large dish antennae to collect rays reaching the Earth from distant space objects. Radio telescopes are linked to an array of other dishes, which together provide a clearer picture of space.

Who made the first catalogue of the stars?

A Greek named Hipparchus, who lived more than 2,000 years ago. He was the first to notice that stars change their position in the night sky (this is called the precession of the equinoxes). Hipparchus made a list of the stars, showing their brightness and position. Hipparchus' writings on astronomy were lost, but his ideas were preserved by later astronomers such as Ptolemy.

Hipparchus recorded the stars he could see with the naked eye – he had no telescope.

Galileo made his own telescope. What he saw astonished scientists of the day.

Key **dates**

1300s BC	Chinese astronomers map the constellations.
100 BC	Hipparchus makes a catalogue of stars.
500 BC	Pythagoras states that the Earth is round.
250 BC	Aristarchus proves that the Sun must be farther away from us than the Moon.
1540s	Nicolaus Copernicus demonstrates that the Earth moves around the Sun, not the other way round.
1608	Hans Lippershey of the Netherlands uses a telescope, though others probably invented it before him.
1609–10	Galileo makes a telescope to look at the skies and finds that the Sun has spots.

1668	Isaac Newton makes the first reflecting telescope, though the idea was suggested five years earlier by Scottish scientist James Gregory.

Polish astronomer Nicolaus Copernicus's theories were so shocking to the people of the day that it was more than 100 years before his theories became widely accepted.

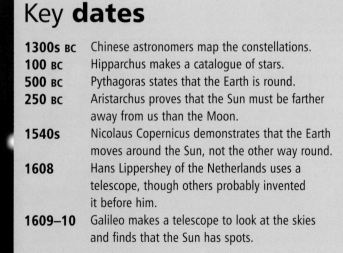

The Sun is the centre of the Solar System. It is a star like the millions of other stars in the Universe. It is the 'offspring' of an older, bigger star, which, after it blew up, left clouds of gas behind. The Sun is a nuclear furnace inside, which hydrogen atoms are turned into helium – crushed by the enormous pressures. During this nuclear reaction, vast amounts of energy are created.

The chromosphere is a layer of gas. Bursts of heat-light energy called spicules flame through it

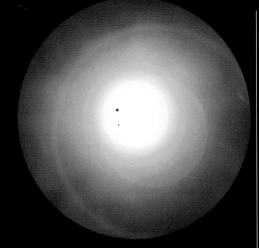

What makes the Sun an unusual star?

Only the fact that it is nearer to us than any other star – only 150 million km away. In all other respects, the Sun is a very ordinary star. It is middle-sized and middle-aged. But without the Sun, the Earth would be a dark, cold, lifeless world. You should never look at the Sun directly as its intense brightness could damage your eyes.

What is inside the Sun?

The Sun is not solid, but a very dense mass of gas. It has an outer surface called the photosphere and an inner layer known as the convection zone, and below that is the hottest part of the Sun – the centre or core, where the nuclear reactions take place. Energy moves from the core, through the many layers, such as the chromosphere and photosphere, to reach the surface and out into space. Without solar energy, the Earth would be lifeless.

The Sun's outer 'skin' is the corona, a halo-like layer of boiled-off gases

➔ *This cutaway of the Sun shows its different parts. The energy that is created inside the core takes ten million years to pass through its many layers and reach the surface.*

Giant tongues of hot gas, known as prominences, burst out from the chromosphere

Sun **worship**

The Sun's importance
Ancient people did not know what the Sun was, but they knew how important its warmth and light were to life. The ancient Egyptians, Greeks and Mayan people, among others, thought of the Sun as a god. They made up stories about the gods to explain the movement of the Sun across the sky. They were alarmed when there was an eclipse of the Sun, fearing that the Sun god must be angry. People also used the Sun as a means of telling the time and making calendars. Stonehenge, a ring of 4,000-year-old stones in England, is a Sun calendar that indicates the time from the shadows cast by the stones. The Aztecs of Mexico sacrificed human victims to the Sun god, believing it would win his favour and therefore ensure the world's survival.

➔ *The Ancient Egyptians believed their Sun god Ra sailed a boat in the sky from east to west every day.*

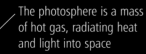

The photosphere is a mass of hot gas, radiating heat and light into space

Radiating zone

The core of the Sun reaches 15 million°C

➔ Sunspots look darker because they are cooler than the rest of the Sun's surface.

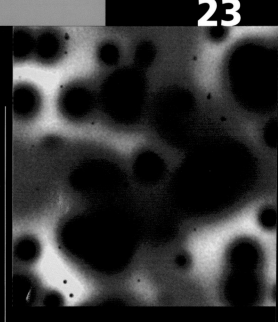

Why does the Sun have spots?

The photosphere or surface of the Sun is covered in dark blotches – sunspots – which are caused by changes in the Sun's magnetic field. They can be up to thousands of kilometres across. The number of sunspots we see varies from anything up to 100, over an 11-year cycle.

What are solar flares?

There are sometimes storms on the Sun, which send bursts of hot gas, called solar flares, into space. They shoot out light, heat and cosmic rays far beyond the Sun's atmosphere or chromosphere, and can break up radio communications on Earth.

What happens during a solar eclipse?

A solar eclipse occurs when the Moon blocks out light from the Sun, causing a shadow to pass across the Earth (see page 27). Usually, most places on Earth see only a partial eclipse, but when the disc of the Moon blots out the Sun completely, day turns to night for about seven minutes. The Sun's corona can then be seen from Earth.

⬇ Solar flares contain vast bursts of energy and coil out 100,000 km into space.

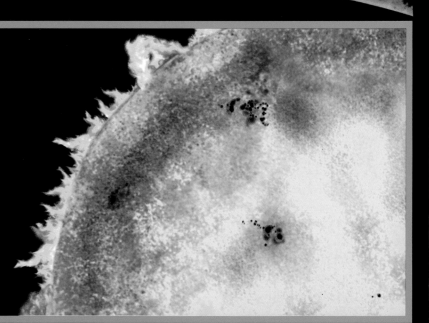

Amazing **Sun facts**

• Sunlight takes 8 mins 20 sec to reach us.

• The Sun's diameter is about 1,392,000 km – that's more than 100 times bigger than the Earth.

• The Sun is 400 times farther away from us than the Moon.

• The Sun is thought to be 4.6 billion years old, about the same age as the Earth.

• 98.8 per cent of all matter in the Solar System is in the Sun.

• The temperature at the surface of the Sun is about 5,500°C.

• The temperature at the core is much hotter, about 15 million°C.

The Earth is the planet we know best, but the first time we got a complete view of it was in 1968, when the *Apollo 8* astronauts flew around the Moon and saw the Earth floating in space. The Earth is just one of nine planets orbiting the Sun, all held in place by the Sun's massive gravity pull. Our world is a rocky ball, not quite round, with a belt of air around it like a protective blanket.

1 Dust and gas

2 Fiery Earth cools. Surface forms a crust

How was the Earth formed?

Scientists believe that the Earth began as a cloud of gas and dust, whirling around a new star – the Sun – before gravity forced the gas and dust together into a red-hot ball. Over millions of years it cooled and a rocky crust began to form. An atmosphere was formed from poisonous gases, such as methane, hydrogen and ammonia, which had risen from volcanoes on the surface of the Earth. Over billions of years, water vapour fell as rain from the clouds and the oceans began to form inside basins in the Earth's crust. The remaining landmasses formed the continents.

3 Gases and water vapour form the atmosphere

➲ *In the early stages of the Earth's formation lumps of rock called planetesimals formed from dust whirling around the Sun. Pulled together by their gravity, the planetesimals then formed the Earth and other planets.*

What does the Earth look like from space?

It is a beautiful blue-and-white globe, with patches of green and brown. Until about 500 years ago, most people were taught to believe that the Earth was flat. It is, in fact, round, though not a perfect sphere. It has a bulge around its centre, the Equator, and the poles are slightly flattened.

4 Oceans and landmasses are formed

➲ *It took about 4.5 billion years for the Earth to form as it is now.*

Where **are we?**

➲ *This is how Copernicus realized the Universe must work – with the Sun at the centre of the Universe. Earlier scientists had believed the theory of Ptolemy, a Greek living in Egypt, that the Earth was at the centre of the Universe.*

Plotting our position in the Universe

Until the 1500s most people thought the Earth was the fixed centre of the Universe. They believed the Sun and the other known planets moved around the Earth in a series of spheres. A Polish scientist named Nicolaus Copernicus (1473–1543) made the startling suggestion that the Sun was at the centre of the Universe, and that the Earth moved around the Sun, along with the other planets.

In 1762, two astronomers, Jacques Cassini and Jean Richer, worked out fairly accurately how far the Earth was from the Sun (between 147 and 152 million km), by first measuring the distance to Mars and then using geometry. Today, scientists measure the distance between planets by firing laser and radar beams at them.

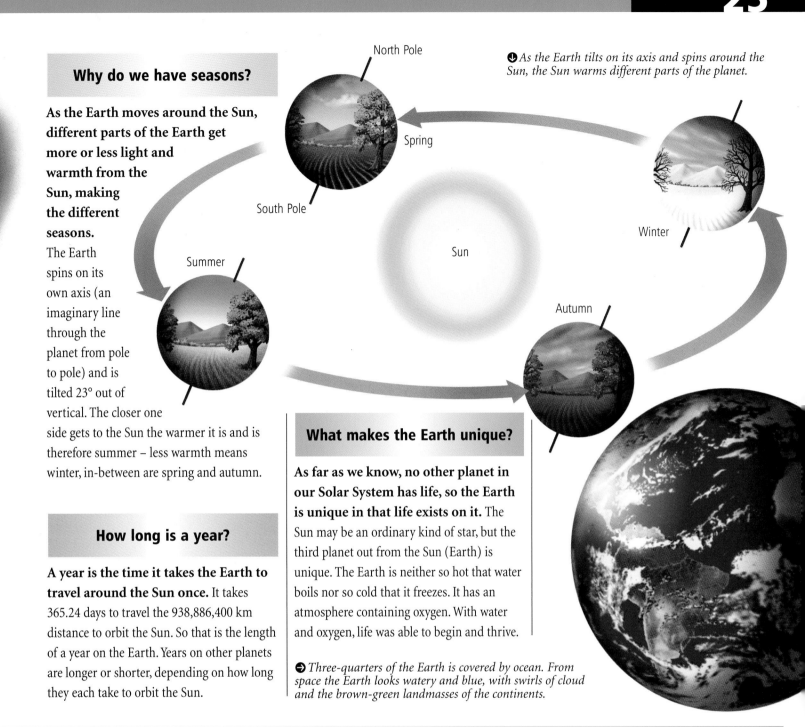

Why do we have seasons?

As the Earth moves around the Sun, different parts of the Earth get more or less light and warmth from the Sun, making the different seasons. The Earth spins on its own axis (an imaginary line through the planet from pole to pole) and is tilted 23° out of vertical. The closer one side gets to the Sun the warmer it is and is therefore summer – less warmth means winter, in-between are spring and autumn.

North Pole

Spring

South Pole

Summer

Sun

Autumn

Winter

⬇ *As the Earth tilts on its axis and spins around the Sun, the Sun warms different parts of the planet.*

How long is a year?

A year is the time it takes the Earth to travel around the Sun once. It takes 365.24 days to travel the 938,886,400 km distance to orbit the Sun. So that is the length of a year on the Earth. Years on other planets are longer or shorter, depending on how long they each take to orbit the Sun.

What makes the Earth unique?

As far as we know, no other planet in our Solar System has life, so the Earth is unique in that life exists on it. The Sun may be an ordinary kind of star, but the third planet out from the Sun (Earth) is unique. The Earth is neither so hot that water boils nor so cold that it freezes. It has an atmosphere containing oxygen. With water and oxygen, life was able to begin and thrive.

➡ *Three-quarters of the Earth is covered by ocean. From space the Earth looks watery and blue, with swirls of cloud and the brown-green landmasses of the continents.*

Earth layers

Scientists call planet Earth the geosphere. The outer rocky part on which we live is the biosphere. Surrounding this is the atmosphere, in layers. The inside of the Earth is also in layers. At the centre is a solid inner core made of an alloy of nickel and iron squeezed together under massive pressure. The rocks surrounding the core are hot and liquid.

Earth **facts**

Solar day	24 hrs
Spins on axis	23 hrs 56 mins and 4 sec
Orbits Sun (sidereal period)	365 days 6 hrs 9 mins and 10 sec
Velocity in orbit	29.8 km/sec
Rotation velocity at Equator	0.5 km/sec
Escape velocity	11.2 km/sec

⬅ *This telescope was used by the astronomer Sir William Herschel (1738–1822). His most famous discovery was the planet Uranus, in 1781. He was the first scientist to make a thorough study of the night sky.*

The Moon is the Earth's only satellite. Other planets have many more moons. Our Moon is the closest body to us in space, and has always fascinated people. Like the Sun, the Moon was thought by some ancient peoples to be a god. The Moon was probably hot when young, with volcanoes, but it has cooled down much faster than the Earth. It has also lost whatever atmosphere it may once have had.

People once thought the flat areas of the Moon were seas or dried-up seabeds. They gave them the Latin name mare (sea). They are in fact plains of very old volcanic lava.

The near side of the Moon, pock-marked with craters

How old is the Moon?

The Moon may be a little younger than the Earth, perhaps 4.5 billion years old. One theory about its birth is that a rocky mini-planet smashed into the Earth. Bits of rock from the collision were hurled into space and came together to form the Moon, which was then trapped in orbit by Earth's gravity.

The Moon may have been formed when a smaller, newly-formed planet collided with the Earth early on in the formation of the Solar System.

Can we see all the Moon from Earth?

No. The Moon orbits the Earth in the same time (27.3 days) as it takes for it to rotate once on its axis. This oddity keeps one side always facing away from us. Until the *Apollo 9* spacecraft flew around the Moon in 1968, no one had ever seen the far side, which actually turned out to look much the same as the near side.

What is it like on the Moon?

The Moon is very quiet and very still. It has no atmosphere, so there is no wind. It has no surface water either. The surface is dry and dusty. There are ancient craters measuring up to 1,000 km across and mountains as high as the highest mountains on Earth, such as Mount Everest, which measures 8,863 m above sea level.

Moon **facts**

An astronaut's footprint left on the Moon will remain there for centuries because there is no wind or erosion to disturb it.

Our Moon
The Moon has roughly the same surface area as the continent of Africa. It is about a quarter of the size of the Earth and has about one-sixth the gravity. This means that astronauts on the Moon weigh a sixth of what they weigh on Earth. So they can jump six times higher – although spacesuits makes acrobatics difficult and dangerous.

From the surface of the Moon, the Earth looks close, but is in fact 384,000 km away.

⊙ *When US astronauts raised the Stars and Stripes flag on the Moon, it had to be stiffened to 'fly' because there is no air on the Moon to move it.*

Why are there New and Full Moons?

The Moon is moving around the Earth and because one side of the Moon is always in sunlight, we see different amounts of the lit half as it moves. This means that the Moon seems to change shape during each month. These changes are known as the phases of the Moon. At New Moon, we cannot see any of the lit half. After a week, we can see about half a Moon (the Moon is waxing or getting bigger), and at Full Moon, we can see the whole lit disc. Then we see less of the Moon (it is waning) until by the last quarter, we again see only half the lit part, and finally a sliver of the 'old moon'.

What made the Moon's craters?

The craters on the Moon were created by space-rocks (meteors) smashing into it. The Moon is covered with craters, as if someone had been throwing stones into a ball of soft clay. The Moon has no atmosphere to burn up incoming space debris, and no weather to wear away the craters.

⊙ *Craters on the Moon are as well-defined as when they were first made, because the Moon has no wind or rain to smooth them away.*

⊙ *The changes from New to Full Moon and back again are called the phases of the Moon. The full cycle from New to Full and back to New again takes one month.*

Last Quarter

Crescent Moon (waning)

Gibbous Moon (waning)

New Moon

Full Moon

Crescent Moon (waxing)

Gibbous Moon (waxing)

First Quarter

Earth   Moon

Light rays passing from Sun to Earth

Sun

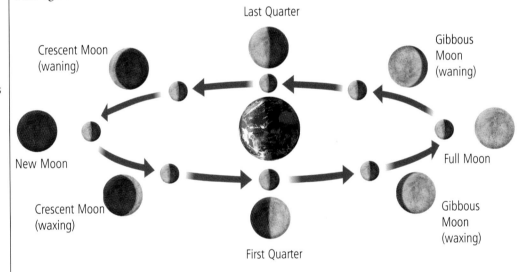

⊙ ⊙ *When the Moon passes between the Earth and the Sun, it causes a solar eclipse, that is, it blocks out the light from the Sun momentarily.*

Moon **facts**

Distance from Earth	384,399 km (average)
Diameter	3,476 km
Biggest crater (far side)	South Pole-Aitken – 2,500 km across and 12,000 m deep
Biggest crater (visible)	Bailly Crater – 295 km across and 4,250 m deep
Highest mountains	8,000 m near the Korolev Basin (far side)
Length of day	20 days 12 hrs and 44 mins
Mass	0.012 that of the Earth
Density	0.061 that of the Earth

The Solar System is the name for the 'family' of planets that orbit the Sun. In addition to the planets, there are millions of much smaller bodies travelling through space around the Sun. These include minor planets or asteroids, and comets that sweep close to the Sun and then travel out far beyond the outer planets.

Sun
Earth
Moon
Mars
Venus
Mercury
Jupiter
Saturn
Uranus
Neptune
Pluto

⬆ The planets orbit the Sun at different distances.

How many planets orbit the Sun?

Nine planets orbit the Sun, including the Earth. They were formed from material which about 4,600 million years ago was spinning around the Sun. Mercury, Venus, Mars, Jupiter and Saturn can be seen with the naked eye because they shine brightly with reflected sunlight. You need a telescope to see Uranus, Neptune and tiny Pluto.

Which planet is nearest the Sun?

Mercury is the planet closest to the Sun. It orbits the Sun at a distance of 58 million km. If you think of Mercury as one pace away from the Sun, the Earth is two and a half paces away. Mercury moves very fast around the Sun. One day on Mercury is equivalent to 59 Earth days, and a year lasts only 88 Earth days.

Where could an astronaut fly through a ring of snowballs?

Around Saturn, the planet with the biggest set of rings in the Solar System. Saturn has thousands of rings, which from far away look solid. However, close-up, an astronaut would see millions of icy particles, like hailstones and small snowballs, whirling around the giant planet. Some of Saturn's smaller moons hurtle around near the edge of the rings – these have been called shepherd moons because, like sheepdogs chasing sheep, they seem to be keeping the smaller particles in their orbits.

↩ Twice during its orbit, Mercury gets very close to the Sun and speeds up so much that the Sun seems to go backwards in the sky.

Planet **data**

Different worlds
The Sun's nine planets are the space worlds we know most about, even though it takes months or years to reach each of them by spacecraft because the Solar System is at least 20 billion km across. However, unmanned spacecraft have visited eight of the nine planets and actually landed on two of them.

Planet **record holders**

Hottest	Venus	462°C
Coldest	Pluto	Approximately −235°C
Fastest-moving	Mercury	172,000 km/h
Faintest	Pluto	Only visible through a telescope
Most dense	Earth	Five times denser than water

↩ The Sun's nine planets are seen here, accurate in terms of sequence and appearance, but not in terms of size.

What are the biggest planets made of?

The four biggest planets – Jupiter, Saturn, Uranus and Neptune – are vast balls of gas. There are two kinds of planet – rocky and gassy. Although the gassy planets are much bigger than the Earth, they are actually not very dense.

Do any other stars have planets?

It was once thought that the Solar System was unique, but scientists have discovered other stars with planets orbiting them. The distant star Upsilon Andromedae (44 light-years away) has three planets circling it. One of them is four times bigger than Jupiter. About 20 planets have been found orbiting other stars. But this is the only other Solar System spotted so far.

Which planets have been explored by spacecraft?

Robot spacecraft have been sent from the Earth to fly past Mercury, Jupiter, Saturn, Uranus and Neptune. Spacecraft have already landed on Mars and Venus, and mapped these planets from orbit. The 'easiest' planet to explore is Mars – at least its atmosphere does not crush or melt spacecraft landing on its surface.

The nine planets in our Solar System, in order from the Sun, are: Mercury, Venus, Earth, Mars, Jupiter, Saturn, Uranus, Neptune and Pluto

The **planets**

Name	Discovered	Distance from Sun (million km)	Diameter (million km)
Mercury	Ancient times	58	4,878
Venus	Ancient times	108	12,104
Earth	–	150	12,756
Mars	Ancient times	228	6,790
Jupiter	Ancient times	778	142,980
Saturn	Ancient times	1,427	120,536
Uranus	1781	2,870	51,120
Neptune	1846	4,504	49,528
Pluto	1930	5,900*	2,300

Pluto has an unusual orbit, which at times brings it closer to the Sun than Neptune.

The four inner planets, which include the Earth, are comparatively small. The other three are Mercury, Venus and Mars. We know more about them than we do about the outer planets, because exploration by spacecraft is possible, even though a journey to Mars takes six months – so planetary exploration is a very patient business.

What are the inner planets made of?

The four inner planets are made of rock and have hard surfaces. Each one has an outer crust enclosing a mantle of sticky-hot, semi-melted rock with, in the middle, a core of iron and nickel. They are also referred to as terrestrial (Earth-like) planets. Each of the four inner planets has some kind of atmosphere – a layer of gas – although Mercury has very little atmosphere to protect against the heat of its neighbour, the Sun. However the similarities with Earth and the inner planets end there.

⊕ *Robot landers have photographed the barren surface of Mars.*

Why is Mars called the red planet?

Mars looks reddish because its rocks contain a lot of iron dust. This dust has been oxidized by the carbon dioxide gas in the Martian atmosphere. This chemical reaction has in effect turned Mars rusty.

← *Mars has seasons and what are probably water-containing ice-caps. Rivers may have flowed across Mars millions of years ago.*

Which planet looks most like the Moon?

Mercury is a small rocky ball with craters all over the surface. It has hardly any atmosphere – all gases except traces of vaporized sodium are boiled off by the blazing heat of the nearby Sun. Without an atmosphere to burn up incoming debris, any rock flying through space towards the planet is able to impact on the surface – smashing new holes in the surface.

← *Mercury is the second smallest of the planets, and closest to the Sun.*

Earth and Mars compared

Earth and Mars

Mars is a very different planet from Earth. Mars is 228 million km away from the Sun, compared to Earth's 150-million-km distance. Due to this larger distance, Mars takes 687 days to orbit the Sun, whereas Earth takes only 365. The mass of Mars is only one-tenth that of the Earth and its diameter of 6,790 km is only half that of Earth's (12,756 km). Nights on Mars are chilly – as cold as the poles on Earth. Winter on Mars is colder than on Earth.

Temperatures on Mars can plunge to −125°C, cold enough to freeze carbon dioxide gas in the atmosphere. There is no oxygen on Mars, so no human could live there without the use of a spacesuit. Earth has one moon but Mars has two moons, Deimos and Phobos.

However, there are also some similarities between these two planets. Like the Earth, Mars has canyons and volcanoes on its surface. Its longest canyon, Valles Marineris, could contain the Grand Canyon, in the USA.

Mars is our nearest neighbour planet, and the world that most attracts scientists planning future space missions, perhaps even a manned landing on the planet.

Could you see the stars from Venus?

No, because this planet has a thick atmosphere of poisonous gas clouds that blot out the Sun and stars. The sky looks red and the clouds are so thick that it is impossible to see the surface of Venus from Earth. Venus also has rainfall of acid and is altogether unwelcoming. No space probe landed there so far has kept working for more than an hour.

Which planet is the hottest?

Venus is the hottest – even hotter than Mercury. The temperature on Venus reaches 470°C, which is hot enough to melt some metals. Venus has an atmosphere of carbon dioxide, which traps the heat from the Sun like a blanket. It is like the 'greenhouse effect' on Earth, only worse.

Which planet spins strangely?

Venus spins in the opposite direction to Earth. Unlike Earth, which spins in an anti-clockwise direction, Venus spins clockwise. If it were not for the clouds, someone on Venus would see the Sun rise in the west, and set in the east. Venus also spins very slowly, only once every 243 Earth days. Venus is almost exactly the same size as Earth at 12,000 km across, but weighs one-fifth less.

⊕ *Venus is shrouded in clouds of sulphuric acid, which hide the surface.*

The highest mountain on Mars is called Olympus Mons and is three times higher than Mount Everest. In 1976, a photo taken by a Viking probe showed what some people claimed was a giant stone face on Mars. Later photos showed it was a rocky hill.

In the late 19th century, Italian astronomer Giovanni Schiaparelli thought he had found another similarity between Earth and Mars. Looking through a telescope, he thought he saw canals on Mars. This caused great excitement. Did this mean there were, or had been, Martians? However, later observations proved there are no canals and it is believed that what he actually saw might have been shifting sand trails or wind-blown markings.

➔ *Unlike Mars, the appearance of Earth is very varied. Water and land can be seen all over the planet, and the atmosphere contains clouds and gases.*

The outermost planets from the Sun include the four gas giants – Jupiter, Saturn, Uranus and Neptune. These planets are all much bigger than the Earth, yet apparently with no solid surfaces at all. Their rocky cores are buried within masses of liquid and slushy, frozen gas. The fifth outer planet, Pluto, with its companion moon Charon, is a ball of rock-hard ice.

↑ Jupiter spins so fast that a day on Jupiter lasts only just under ten hours. The Great Red Spot is a violent whirling storm on the planet.

What is the biggest planet made of?

The biggest planet is Jupiter, but no spacecraft can land on it because there is no 'ground', it is just a whirling mass of gases, mostly hydrogen and helium. It spins faster than any other planet, so fast that the clouds in its atmosphere are whipped up into vast, swirling storms with winds of up to 500 km/h. The Great Red Spot visible on the surface of Jupiter is a huge storm, a giant gas-hurricane, which is as big as the size of two Earths.

Which planets have rings?

Jupiter, Saturn, Uranus and Neptune all have rings. Saturn's rings are the most brilliant, measuring 270,000 km from edge to edge. The rings are made of millions of blocks of ice whizzing around the planet. Saturn's rings can be seen from Earth through a telescope. When, in the 1980s, robot spacecraft flew close to Jupiter, Neptune and Uranus, their rings were seen for the first time.

→ Saturn's rings are one of the most spectacular sights in the Solar System.

Which planet has the most satellites?

Uranus has at least 21 moons (satellites). Saturn and Jupiter each have more than 18 moons – new tiny ones are still being discovered. Four of Jupiter's moons are bigger than Pluto. The biggest moon in the Solar System is Jupiter's moon Ganymede, which measures 5,276 km across. Saturn's biggest moon Titan is only a bit smaller than Ganymede. The planets with the least moons are Earth and Pluto, which only have one each.

Outer planet facts

Varied planets

The outer planets are very varied and different from our planet, Earth. Saturn's moon Titan is one of the few moons with an atmosphere. Its sky is a mass of yellowish clouds. Jupiter's moon, Europa, is interesting because it is covered by ice, and is very smooth. Could there be a cold, watery ocean underneath, maybe with some form of life in it? On Triton, the biggest of Uranus's 17 moons, it gets incredibly cold – as cold as Pluto.

Geysers on Triton shoot out plumes of frozen nitrogen gas. Neptune probably has a hard core and has violent storms raging on it. Uranus is calmer than Neptune, and probably cold inside as well as out.

→ Neptune and Uranus are gas giants, too. Neptune has a Great Dark Spot, similar to Jupiter's Great Red Spot, a whirling storm bigger than the Earth!

Uranus

Which planet may have had a near-miss?

Uranus is tilted on its side, perhaps because of a space collision that could have almost destroyed it. Scientists think that a giant asteroid may have smashed into Uranus and knocked it sideways. Miranda, one of Uranus's moons, looks as if it was blasted into chunks and then stuck back together again by gravity.

Which are the windiest planets?

Jupiter and Saturn are the windiest planets. Both spin so fast that all the gases in their atmosphere are whipped around at speeds of up to 500 km/h on Jupiter and even faster on Saturn, around 1,300 km/h – that is more than ten times faster than a hurricane on Earth!

Neptune

Which are the least known planets?

Hardly anything is known about Pluto and its moon-neighbour Charon. Both worlds are made mostly of ice with a thin nitrogen–methane atmosphere. Pictures taken by the Hubble Space Telescope show hazy markings and brighter areas around the poles. Pluto is the furthest planet from the Sun, and so takes 248 years to orbit the Sun, swinging out to a maximum 7.3 million-km distance away.

🔽 *Like Earth, Pluto only has one moon – Charon, visible from the surface of the planet. Pluto is the smallest of the planets.*

⬅ *Uranus and Neptune have rings, too. Both these blue-green worlds are shrouded in clouds of poisonous methane gas above a freezing chemical slush surface.*

Big and small

Jupiter is so big that 1,000 Earths could fit inside it. But the Sun is bigger: in fact 90 per cent of all the matter in the Solar System is contained in the Sun. Almost 900 Jupiters would fit into the Sun. Jupiter has the shortest day of all the planets. A day on Jupiter lasts just 9 hrs 55 mins.

➡ *The little Galileo space probe hit Jupiter's atmosphere in 1995. It lasted an hour in the stormy, freezing clouds before it was first crushed and then vaporized.*

Outer **planet facts**

Planet	Volume compared with Earth (Earth = 1)	Atmospheres
Jupiter	1,300	Thick atmosphere of gases, mainly hydrogen, with clouds of ammonia, sulphur and other chemicals
Saturn	766	Hydrogen and helium gases, and ammonia clouds
Uranus	63	Methane and other gases
Neptune	58	Methane and other gases
Pluto	0.0058	Nitrogen–methane

Travelling through space across the Solar System are other bodies, including asteroids, meteors and comets. They provide brilliant light-shows in the night sky from time to time, and also give scientists clues to the origins of the Universe.

Shooting stars flash across the night sky as meteors burn up in the atmosphere.

Asteroids sometimes stray close to the Earth, but most stay within the so-called asteroid belt, further out from the Sun. Comets travel far out across the Solar System, occasionally passing by the Earth.

What is a shooting star?

'Shooting stars' are the glowing tails of meteors, which heat up as they enter the Earth's atmosphere. Millions of tiny lumps of metal or rock called meteoroids whizz through space, orbiting the Sun. As they hit the thick atmosphere around the Earth – about 90 km away from the Earth's surface – they heat up and for a second or two leave glowing trails behind them. They flash through the sky like brilliant firework displays.

What are asteroids?

Asteroids are mini-planets that orbit the Sun in a 'belt' between Mars and Jupiter. Most big asteroids look like rugged chunks of rock, with small craters blasted by collisions with smaller space-particles. The biggest asteroid is called Ceres, and is about 930 km across.

Where is the biggest meteorite crater on Earth?

The biggest hole made by a meteorite is Meteor Crater in Arizona, USA – it is more than 1,700 m across and nearly 200 m deep. Occasionally meteors are big enough to hurtle through the atmosphere and smash into the ground. The charred rock that remains is a meteorite.

The biggest meteorites are massive chunks of rock, but few this big ever reach the ground.

Spot the comet

Comets and meteorites

Halley's Comet can be seen from Earth as it passes the Sun every 77 years, but there are other comets that can be seen more often. Comet Encke returns every three years, and Comet Grigg-Skjellerup every four years. Comet Hale Bopp was spotted by two astronomers on the same night in 1995, so it was named after both of them. Something very big, either a large meteorite or the fragments of a comet, hit the Earth's atmosphere in 1908.

It exploded before smashing into a remote region of Siberia, Russia. The explosion was heard hundreds of kilometres away and forest trees were flattened over a wide area. The Hoba meteorite, found in 1920, is big enough for an entire football team to sit on it. A smaller meteorite, weighing 44 kg, landed in Leicestershire, England, in 1965.

Meteors pass by the Earth often and a large one could collide with the Earth at any time. However, most are very small and burn up as they enter the atmosphere.

What are comets?

Comets are chunks of ice filled with dust and rock that orbit the Sun, just like planets. However, comets travel much farther out into distant space, often to the outer reaches of the Solar System, so comets can take up to thousands of years to make one orbit of the Sun. As a comet nears the Sun's heat, the ice core warms up and throws out a glowing tail that can be millions of kilometres long. It is a spectacular sight.

⊙ *Comets are Solar System wanderers, which return on schedule. This photograph of Halley's Comet was taken when it last came close to Earth in 1986. The comet comes back close to Earth, within visible range, roughly every 77 years (see panel below).*

⊙ *Small asteroids are burnt up by the Earth's atmosphere every day. The chances of a big one colliding with us and destroying the Earth, like in this illustration, are remote.*

What happened when an asteroid struck the Earth?

Many scientists believe that the effects of an asteroid collison about 65 million years ago may have been responsible for wiping out the dinosaurs (see page 100). An impact crater, called the Chixulub Basin in Mexico, lies partly beneath the sea and is 300 km across. It must have been made by a very large object, such as an asteroid, smashing into the Earth. Such a collision would have caused great climatic changes, and so altered conditions for life on Earth. Every 50 million years, an asteroid measuring more than 10 km across hits the Earth.

➥ *A comet that appeared in 1064 (probably Halley's) is shown in the Bayeux Tapestry, which tells the story of the Normandy Invasion of Britain in 1066.*

Halley's **Comet**

1682 British astronomer Edmund Halley saw it and worked out that the comet (now named after him) would return in 76–77 years.

1759 Great excitement: the comet returned as predicted.

1835 The comet was seen, but was not so bright.

1910 Despite scientific progress, some superstitious people still feared that the reappearance of the comet heralded the end of the world.

1986 Several spacecraft flew close to the comet.

2062 The next time Halley's Comet will return.

Large meteorites to hit **Earth**

Name	Where	Weight
Hoba	Namibia	54 tonnes
Campo del Cielo	Argentina	41 tonnes
Ahnighito	Greenland	31 tonnes

PLANET EARTH

There is no other planet like our Earth – so far as we know. The Earth is unique in the Solar System because it is the only planet with life. The Earth has a vast array of environments, from scorching deserts to misty rainforests, in which living things have thrived for millions of years. The Earth is still changing, reshaped by natural forces and, increasingly, by human activity.

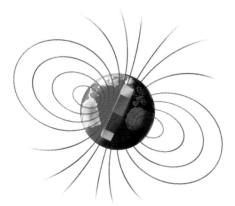

🔾 *The Earth's magnetic field stretches out invisibly into space.*

🔾 *The distance around the Earth at the Poles is slightly less than the distance around the Earth's middle, the Equator. Although the planet looks round, it has a bulge just south of the Equator.*

How big is the Earth?

The Earth is the fifth biggest of the Sun's planets, with a circumference of 40,075 km and weighing about 6,000 million million million tonnes. It is a ball of rock, mostly covered by water, wrapped in a thin, protective layer of gases – the air. Yet the Earth is tiny compared with the planet Jupiter, which is more than 300 times bigger.

When was the Earth formed?

The Sun and its nine planets formed at around the same time, about 4,600 million years ago. The Earth grew from a whirling cloud of gas and dust in space, which became squashed together by gravity. Most of the material in the cloud came together in the middle to make the Sun. The debris left over formed gas balls and rocky lumps: the planets. One of those lumps was the Earth.

🔾 *The young Earth was a violent planet, shaped by storms and volcanoes.*

How is the Earth like a magnet?

The Earth's magnetism is made by the Earth's electrical currents, generated by movements inside the planet. It has a magnetic field stretching far out into space. Like all magnets, the Earth has north and south poles where the magnetism is strongest.

Earth's vital **statistics**

Discovering Earth
The Earth was first measured in about 200 BC by a Greek mathematician named Erathosthenes. Using geometry, he measured the angle of the Sun's rays (shown by a shadow) at two places a known distance apart. Eratosthenes worked out that the Earth must be around 46,000 km in circumference – pretty close, compared to the modern figure of 40,075 km. Nowadays, the Earth can be measured by satellites using lasers.

In a year the Earth travels once around the Sun – a distance of over 938,886,000 km. This means that when astronomers look at the star through a telescope, they are actually looking back into the past – seeing the star as it was four years ago.

🔾 *The Earth spins as it travels in its year-long orbit around the Sun. Because it spins faster at the Equator than at the Poles, the Earth is not a perfect sphere. One rotation takes 24 hours, or one day.*

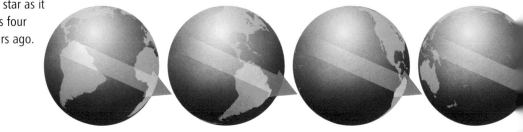

Seen from space, the Earth is a planet of oceans. Only about 29 per cent is land.

Why is the Earth a watery world?

Earth is a watery world because about 71 per cent of it is water. The water on the planet is in the oceans, as ice at the poles and on mountain tops, in lakes and rivers, and in water vapour in the atmosphere, which falls as rain. The rainiest places on Earth are near the Equator on the coast or on islands. In parts of West Africa and the Amazon region of Brazil it rains almost every day.

Pacific Ocean

Oceans contain 97 per cent of the Earth's water and the three biggest (Pacific, Atlantic and Indian) together cover an area of 350 million sq km.

Atlantic Ocean

Indian Ocean

How is the Earth moving?

The Earth moves in three ways: on its own axis, through space and as part of the Solar System. Firstly, it spins on its own axis – an imaginary line from pole to pole. Secondly, it races through space as it orbits the Sun, held in position by the Sun's gravity. Thirdly, it is part of the Solar System, and moves through space as the Milky Way galaxy, which contains the Earth, rotates at about 250 km/sec.

North Pole

Axis

Direction of spin

The Earth spins on its axis – an imaginary line between the Poles.

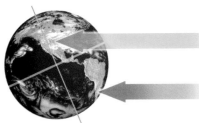

The Sun's rays provide the Earth with light and warmth. The planet is tilted at an angle, and as it spins in orbit around the Sun, different regions get varying amounts of sunlight. The part tilted away from the Sun has a cool winter season; the part tilted towards the Sun (here the Southern Hemisphere) is warmed up more and so has summer.

Earth's **vital statistics**

Equatorial circumference	40,075 km
Polar circumference	40,008 km
Surface area	509,700,000 sq km
Land area	29 per cent
Water area	71 per cent
Highest temperature	58°C in Libya, North Africa
Lowest temperature	−89.6°C in Antarctica
Most abundant chemicals	oxygen 47 per cent, silicon 28 per cent, aluminium 8 per cent, iron 5 per cent

The Earth is made of rocks. Geologists (scientists who study the Earth's rock history) can uncover the prehistory of the Earth by studying the rocks, which are laid down in layers rather like a gigantic sandwich. Rocks provide us with useful materials, such as coal for fuel and limestone to make cement. They also contain clues to life on Earth long ago, in the form of fossils – the hardened remains of long-dead animals and plants.

What is the Earth's crust?

The Earth's rocky skin is the crust, which is thickest (up to 40 km) beneath 'young' mountain ranges. The crust beneath the oceans is much thinner, between 5 and 11 km. The rocks of the continents are much older than the rocks under the oceans.

⬆ *The Giant's Causeway in Ireland is a formation of basalt, the most common volcanic rock in the Earth's crust.*

What is inside the Earth?

The Earth's crust rests on a layer of hot, partly molten rock called the mantle, which in turn surrounds the two cores. The core or centre of the Earth is a solid ball of very hot rock, about 6,400 km beneath the surface and under enormous pressure. The core is too hot and solid for us to drill down to. The deeper down, the hotter it gets – more than 4,000°C at the Earth's core.

Crust – between 6 and 40 km thick

Inner core – 1,300 km thick

Outer core – about 2,000 km thick

Mantle – about 2,900 km thick

How rocks are formed

Different rocks
The three main kinds of rocks are igneous, sedimentary and metamorphic rocks. Igneous rocks are made from molten rock called magma, deep inside the Earth. Magma is so hot, over 1,000°C, that it is molten. It is also crushed by enormous pressure. When magma gets pushed to the surface by volcanic action it cools to form igneous rocks.

Sedimentary rocks such as shale and sandstone are made by the action of wind and water, which grind other rocks into sand and mud, carried by rivers until they are deposited as sediments. Sediment piles up in layers, and is squeezed hard by the pressure of layers on top, until it becomes rock.

Metamorphosis means 'change' and metamorphic rocks are changed by chemical action, heat or pressure into another form of rock. This can happen when magma pushes through them or when the Earth's crust moves beneath mountain ranges. Limestone, for instance, becomes marble when subjected to these kinds of changes: a sedimentary rock becomes a metamorphic rock.

Igneous rock is formed when lava cools

As volcanoes erupt, hot magma is released from inside the Earth

What are fossils?

Fossils are the hardened remains of dead animals and plants. They are found in rocks that were once soft sand or mud, such as sandstone, often when ancient rocks are exposed by wind or rain weathering, or by quarrying and mining. Shells, bones and teeth are most likely to end up as fossils rather than soft parts, which decay. Sometimes scientists find a whole skeleton, which can be removed bone by bone and carefully reconstructed.

This fossil ammonite is a mollusc that swam in prehistoric seas. The soft body parts decayed millions of years ago but the impression of the animal's shell is preserved.

Fossil of a Tyrannosaurus rex *skull, a dinosaur that lived on Earth about 65–70 million years ago.*

This ancient trilobite, a shellfish, would have died millions of years ago. Over time only its bones and shell remain, buried by minerals in the seawater to become a fossil.

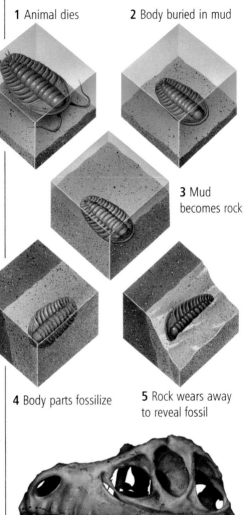

1 Animal dies

2 Body buried in mud

3 Mud becomes rock

4 Body parts fossilize

5 Rock wears away to reveal fossil

What are rocks made of?

Rocks are made of minerals. Most rocks are what geologists call aggregates – that is, combinations of several minerals. There are three kinds of rocks, made in different ways (see panel below). The most common kind are sedimentary rocks.

Chalk is a form of limestone, made from the shells of tiny single-celled sea animals called foraminiferans. Limestone is a type of sedimentary rock.

Which is the most common element?

The most common element in the Universe is hydrogen, but on Earth it's oxygen, which accounts for about 47 per cent of the planet's mass. Elements are substances that are made of only one kind of atom. All matter in the Universe is made of elements.

Rain and wind breaks down rocks

Rock fragments, broken by the weather, are washed down into the sea

Sedimentary rock forms on the seabed from rock debris

Rock materials are continually recycled to make new rocks.

Igneous rocks are made deep inside the Earth from cooled magma. Metamorphic rocks are made from other rocks, changed by heat and pressure, as in a volcano. Sedimentary rocks are formed from the worn and squashed fragments of other rocks and living things.

Scientists study the Earth's history to understand how it has changed, and is still changing, as natural forces reshape the landscape.

Continents are landmasses with water all around them, or almost all around them. The continents contain landscape – such as mountains, rivers, lakes, deserts, grassy plains, forests and cities. The continents are made of very old rocks, dating back some 3,800 million years. Yet, although they are so massive, they are not fixed in place but are drifting very slowly.

➡ *This is what Pangaea, the original super-continent, may have looked like. Scientists believe the present continents have reached their shape and position by a process of fracture and drift over millions of years.*

PANTHALASSA OCEAN

Pangaea

TETHYS SEA

Have the continents always looked the same?

No, all the continents once formed one huge landmass, which scientists call Pangaea. This was 280 million years ago. Over time, the super-continent broke up into two smaller but still huge continents – Laurasia and Gondwanaland. Laurasia included North America, Europe and part of Asia and Gondwanaland contained South America, Africa, Australia, Antarctica and India. Later, these fractured and the pieces drifted apart to form the continents as we know them today.

How many continents are there?

There are seven continents: Africa, Antarctica, Asia, Europe, Oceania, North America and South America. Each of the continents encompasses various countries and bodies of water. From the map (right), you can see how the outlines of South America and Africa look as if they might fit together – suggesting that they were once joined together.

➡ *The seven continents include Antarctica, which has land beneath its thick ice, but not the Arctic, which is mostly frozen ocean.*

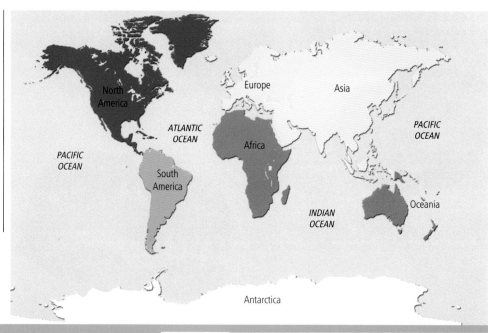

North America

Europe

Asia

ATLANTIC OCEAN

PACIFIC OCEAN

Africa

PACIFIC OCEAN

South America

INDIAN OCEAN

Oceania

Antarctica

Continental **facts**

Continental drift
Continental drift can be explained by the theory of sea-floor spreading. Hot molten rock is pushed up beneath the sea-floor, where the crust is thinnest, and forced into cracks in the mid-ocean ridges. As the molten rock cools, it hardens, pushing the ocean floor and the continents away from the ridges.

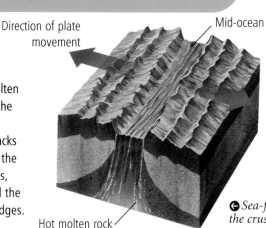

Direction of plate movement

Mid-ocean ridge

Hot molten rock

➡ *Sea-floor spreading helps to move the continents. Currents beneath the crust push molten rocks up to the mid-ocean ridges and into the ocean valleys. As the melted rock cools, it makes a new sea-floor.*

Amazing **facts**

• By 135 million years ago, South America was drifting away from Africa.

• By 100 million years ago, India, Australia and Antarctica were drifting away from Africa, too.

• And at the same time, North America was moving away from Europe.

• The plates are between 70 and 100 km thick.

Which is the biggest continent?

Asia (see pages 190–193) is by far the biggest continent. The land area of Asia is 44 million sq km, which is four times bigger than Europe and nearly twice as big as North America. Asia includes the biggest country by land area (Russia) and the two biggest by population (China and India).

How can continents move?

The Earth's crust is made of curved rocky plates, which float like pieces of gigantic jigsaw on the molten layer of hot rocks in the mantle. There are seven large plates and some 20 smaller ones, and they move very slowly (between 1 and 10 cm a year) on currents circulating within the mantle. Over millions of years, the continents that rest on top of these plates move, too.

Asia

PACIFIC OCEAN

INDIAN OCEAN

◑ *This view of the globe shows Asia, which extends into Europe and is the biggest of the continents.*

◑ *Ocean plates can be pushed down beneath other plates, producing unstable movements beneath continents. Rocks are folded by pressure and magma is forced up through volcanoes.*

Why do we have time zones?

Time is not the same all around the Earth because the Earth turns once on its axis in just under 24 hours. When one spot on the Earth is in sunlight and so has day, another place on the far side is in shadow and has night. The world has 24 different time zones, and the clock time in each zone differs by one hour from that in the next. The United States and Canada are such big countries that they encompass six time zones.

◑ *When the time is 12 noon in London, UK it is 7 a.m. in New York, USA (five hours earlier) and 11 p.m. in Wellington, New Zealand (11 hours later).*

11 p.m. in New Zealand

Noon in England

7 a.m. in the USA

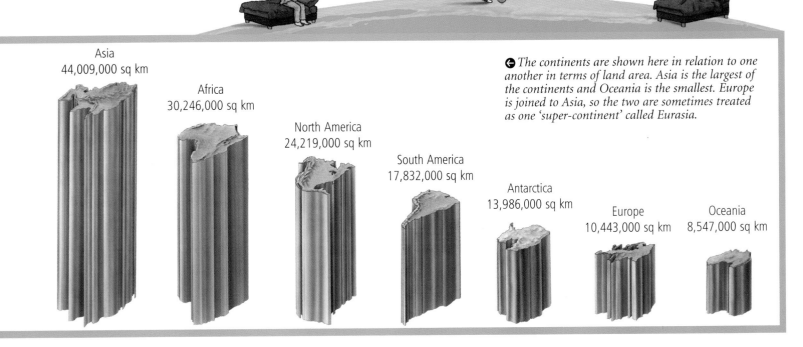

Asia
44,009,000 sq km

Africa
30,246,000 sq km

North America
24,219,000 sq km

South America
17,832,000 sq km

Antarctica
13,986,000 sq km

Europe
10,443,000 sq km

Oceania
8,547,000 sq km

◑ *The continents are shown here in relation to one another in terms of land area. Asia is the largest of the continents and Oceania is the smallest. Europe is joined to Asia, so the two are sometimes treated as one 'super-continent' called Eurasia.*

Geographers (scientists who study the Earth and its features) rely on maps. The word 'geography' comes from a Greek word meaning 'description of the Earth'. A map is a small picture of a large area, and is drawn to scale (for example 1 cm on the map might represent 1,000 km of land on the ground). Most maps are flat, but a globe is spherical, like the Earth. Modern maps are very accurate, made with the aid of computers and photographs that have been taken from aircraft and satellites in space.

● *The first reasonably accurate maps of the world were made in Europe in the 1500s. Lines of latitude and longitude are marked in degrees. On a map, 1° is one-360th of a circle.*

Who made the first maps?

About 5,000 years ago people in Egypt and Babylonia made drawings to show who owned which bit of land and where rivers were. The oldest map in existence is a clay tablet found in Iraq, which has what may be a river valley scratched on it. The first maps to show lines of latitude and longitude, to fix a position, were made by the ancient Greeks about 2,000 years ago.

Where are the tropics?

The tropics are the regions of the Earth that lie immediately north and south of the Equator, an imaginary line around the middle of the Earth. The northern region is the Tropic of Cancer, the southern region is the Tropic of Capricorn. Each tropic is about 2,600 km wide and here the Sun shines almost directly overhead at noon. The tropics are each approximately 2,570 km from the Equator. On a map, the tropics lie at a latitude of 23° north and south of the Equator.

● *The Equator is an imaginary line around the middle of the Earth, with the tropics north and south of it.*

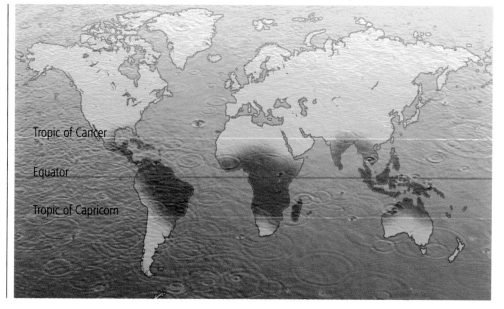

Tropic of Cancer

Equator

Tropic of Capricorn

Mapmaking

Projections

A flat map of a sphere like the Earth cannot be accurate unless certain adjustments are made. If you peel an orange carefully, you will discover that the peel won't lie flat on a table without breaking. Maps are drawn in a way that makes one feature (such as land area) accurate, but another feature (shape, for instance) less so. These different ways of mapmaking are known as projections. There are various kinds of map projection. One is named Mercator after a Flemish mapmaker named Gerardus Mercator (1512–94). This projection shows the correct direction between two points, because the lines of latitude and longitude are correct. It makes landmasses look wrong though – Greenland looks the same size as North America, which is actually really much larger.

● *A conic projection of a globe projects the lines of latitude and longitude into a cone shape, which can then be flattened to give a picture of the wide landmasses, such as the USA and Russia, as accurately as possible.*

What are latitude and longitude?

A network of lines across a map, forming a grid. Lines of longitude are drawn from north to south, while lines of latitude are drawn from east to west. The lines make it easier to locate any spot on the map. The Equator is the line of 0° latitude. The line of 0° longitude runs through Greenwich in London, England and is known as the prime meridian.

⊘ *Early navigators used a sextant to measure the height of the Sun above the horizon to help them work out latitude. Finding longitude become possible in the 1750s with the invention of accurate clocks for use at sea.*

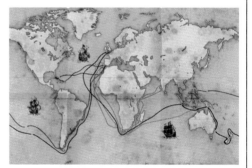

⬆ *Cook's voyage (shown in blue) and Magellan's voyage (shown in green) sailed around the Oceanic islands for the first time.*

Why do people need never get lost today?

Global positioning system (GPS) satellites in orbit around the Earth can inform travellers where they are, to within a few metres. The satellites send out radio signals that are picked up by a computer on an aeroplane, ship or car; three or more 'fixes' give a precise position. Satellite navigation began in 1960 with the US Transit satellite. The more advanced Global positioning system became operational in 1995.

Why is Australia not shown on early maps?

Because until the 1600s no one in the Northern Hemisphere knew it was there. Chinese and Indonesian sailors may have been the first outsiders to visit Australia, after the aboriginal people settled there some 40,000 years ago. European sailors discovered Australia by accident when straying off course on voyages to Asia. The discovery of the islands that make up the continent of Oceania was only made from the 1500s onwards when sailors such as Ferdinand Magellan and Captain James Cook sailed the Southern Hemisphere. However, the islands were already inhabited by this time by the Polynesians, Melanesians and Micronesians, who had settled there after arriving from Asia more than 1,000 years before.

⊙ *Navigation satellites now encircle the Earth, providing data for travellers to be able to find where they are at any given moment.*

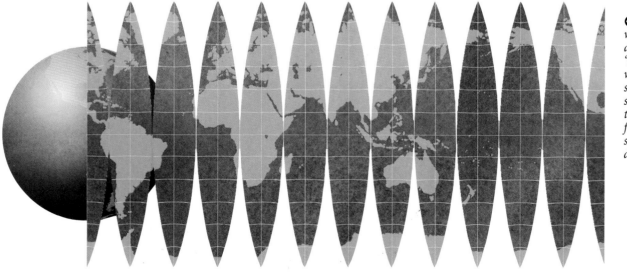

⬅ *If the Earth were an orange and could be 'unpeeled', this is what you would see. The curved surface cannot be transformed into a flat map unless some features are distorted.*

The surface of the Earth looks solid, but underground in some places there are holes or caves. Most were hollowed out of soft rock by water trickling down from the surface. Some are as big as soccer pitches! Others contain unusual mineral formations. People who explore caves are known as cavers, potholers or (in the USA) spelunkers.

Where are the world's longest caves?

The world's longest caves are the Mammoth Caves of Kentucky in the United States, first explored in 1799. This cave system has 560 km of caves and passages, with underground lakes and rivers.

○ *Some cave systems contain huge caverns, large enough for people to stand in. Others are cramped and narrow, and can only be crawled through by cave explorers.*

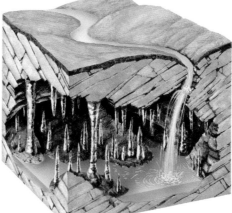

○ *Stalactites and stalagmites are made by the slow build-up of minerals in dripping water. They turn a cavern into a subterranean wonderland, full of interesting shapes.*

How can you tell a stalactite from a stalagmite?

Stalactites are mineral formations that look like giant icicles as they hang down from the roof of a cave. A stalactite more than 12 m long was measured in a cave in Brazil. Stalagmites grow up from the floor of a cave, as water drips down from the cave roof. A stalagmite more than 30 m high was measured inside a cave in Slovakia.

Which caves have the oldest paintings?

Prehistoric people lived in caves, for protection against the weather and wild animals. Some caves contain pictures of animals made by these cave-dwellers, and the best-known are those at Lascaux in France and Altamira in Spain. Similar paintings were found in 2003 at Creswell Crags in Nottinghamshire, England. A few large caves were home to many generations of prehistoric people.

○ *Stone Age people drew the cave paintings, such as this bison, at Lascaux in France more than 13,000 years ago.*

Going under

Underground

Caves are holes in the ground, usually hollowed out by water wearing away soft rock. But many 'potholes' are so narrow that explorers have to crawl on hands and knees, or even swim through flooded sections of cave, using flashlights to penetrate the gloom.

The biggest cave chamber is called the Sarawak Chamber, in a cave system in Sarawak, Malaysia. It is 700 m long, has an average width of 300 m and is about 70 m above the cave floor.

○ *An explorer inside a cave that has been made from lava from a volcano.*

Deep caves of the world

Krubera, Georgia, Asia	1,710 m
Reseu Jean Bernard, France	1,602 m
Shakta Pantujhina, Georgia	1,508 m
Sistema Huautla, Mexico	1,475 m
Sistema del Trava, Spain	1,441 m
Vercors, southeast France	1,271 m
Gunung Mulu, Borneo	470 m
Carlsbad Cavern, USA	316 m

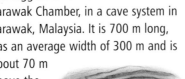
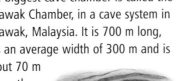

Stream flows underground

Underground waterfall

Stalactites

Stalagmites

Water emerges into a lake

Limestone rock worn away to form cavern

↑ *Limestone caverns and cave systems are eroded (worn away) by chemical weathering.*

What caves are made by chemistry?

The soft rock in limestone caves is worn away by 'chemical weathering'. Calcium carbonate in the limestone reacts with rainwater to form a weak acid, which gradually dissolves the rock. Water seeping down the rock forms cracks and potholes, which open up into caverns. The chemical 'drips' can create growths, and formations of stalactites and stalagmites. Underground waterfalls, rivers and lakes form, and water often flows into an open-air lake or river.

Do any animals live in caves?

Caves provide shelter for a number of animals, including bats and birds, such as cave swiftlets of Asia and Caribbean oilbirds. These animals roost in the cave by day (bats) or at night (birds) and come out to hunt for food. Cave swiftlets are hunted by the racer snakes who also inhabit the caves. Many insects also live in caves, and underground lakes are home to various species of fish. Many cave species are blind and so rely on smell, touch or echolocation (using echoes from sound to judge distances and obstacles) to find their way around in the darkness.

↑ *Birds such as swifts build their nests in caves.*

↓ *Rocks inside caves may contain impressions of fossil plants that grew millions of years ago.*

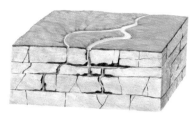

1 Streams enter from the surface and water trickles down through cracks in the stone

2 As the water dissolves the limestone, it hollows out tunnels and caverns

↑ ➔ *These diagrams show how limestone caves are formed by the action of water.*

3 In time, part of the cavern roof may collapse, and the stream becomes a subterranean river

In parts of the world violent upheavals shake the ground and send fire and smoke into the sky, causing terrible damage and loss of life. These are volcanoes and earthquakes, and they often occur in the same regions. Volcanoes belch smoke, fire, ash and molten rock. Earthquakes shake the ground with an energy many times greater than that of an atomic bomb.

⬆ *Erupting volcanoes throw smoke, ash and rocks into the sky.*

What makes a volcano erupt?

A volcano erupts when molten rock (called magma) is pushed up from deep inside the Earth and is forced out through the mouth of the volcano. When the magma reaches the air it becomes lava, flowing down the sides of the volcano. Some volcanoes explode violently, hurling rocks, lava and ash into the air.

What made the loudest ever bang?

The biggest volcanic explosion was in 1883, when Krakatoa Island in Indonesia blew up. The noise was heard four hours later almost 5,000 km away! The tidal wave Krakatoa produced killed 36,000 people. However, after the Tambora volcano (which struck Indonesia in 1815) 90,000 people were killed by the volcano, the tidal wave or the famine that occurred afterwards.

Why are some volcanoes not dangerous?

Not all volcanoes erupt. Extinct volcanoes can no longer erupt. Dormant volcanoes do so only occasionally. Some just 'grumble', trickling out lava and steam. However, active volcanoes erupt often. The most famous is Mount Vesuvius, above the Italian city of Naples. It destroyed the Roman city of Pompeii in AD 79, and will almost certainly erupt in the 21st century.

⬇ *Vulcanologists (volcano experts) keep a close watch on volcanoes they know are active and likely to erupt violently.*

Earth in **upheaval**

Famous volcanoes
Some volcanoes are particularly famous, either due to their size, or as a result of having erupted with devastating consequences.

The extinct volcano Aconcagua in Argentina is the highest volcano in the western hemisphere.

Mount Etna in Sicily, Italy, erupted in 1669, killing 20,000 people.

Mount Vesuvius in Naples, Italy, destroyed Pompeii and Herculaneum when it erupted in AD 79.

➡ *When a volcano erupts, molten magma explodes from the main vent. Ash and lava pour out and flow down the side of the volcano. Gas, dust and rock 'bombs' are thrown into the sky.*

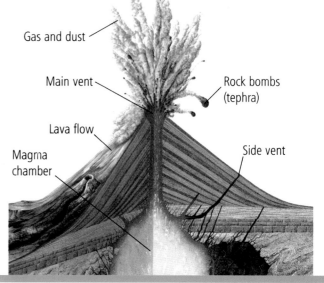

Gas and dust

Main vent

Rock bombs (tephra)

Lava flow

Side vent

Magma chamber

⬆ *During an earthquake, the rocks shift along a fault line in the crust. Here, part of a road has fallen away during a quake.*

➡ *Tsunamis are large and potentially devastating waves that are caused by undersea earthquakes.*

⬇ *During an earthquake, pressure waves ripple out from the epicentre. Earthquakes are caused as two blocks of rock crust move along a fault line (shown by the arrows) in opposite directions.*

What sets off an earthquake?

Like volcanoes, earthquakes occur where the rocks of the Earth's crust are put under tremendous pressure by movements of the plates on which the continents rest. Seismologists (scientists who study earthquakes) measure the strength of the shock waves with a seismometer. The earthquake is then graded using the Richter scale, which starts at 1 (slight tremor) and rises above 9 (devastating quake). The world's worst earthquake of modern times was in 1976, when a quake in China measuring 8.2 on the Richter scale led to the deaths of at least 250,000 people.

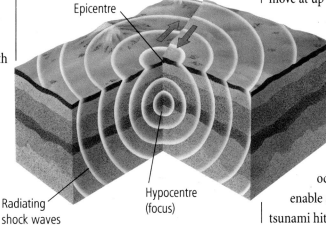

Epicentre

Radiating shock waves

Hypocentre (focus)

What is a tsunami?

Undersea earthquakes can produce huge waves, called tsunamis. These waves move at up to 800 km/h but may not be noticed in the open sea. In shallow waters however, the wave builds into a colossal wall of water up to 30 m high, which rushes inland drowning everything in its path. A warning system was developed in 1948 in the Pacific Basin, where most tsunamis occur. Several hours warning can enable areas to be evacuated before the tsunami hits, to minimize casualties.

Amazing **volcano facts**

• The biggest volcano is Mauna Loa in Hawaii, with a crater 10 km wide and 180 m deep. More than 80 per cent of this volcano is beneath the ocean.

• The highest active volcano is Ojos del Salado in South America at 6,887 m.

• The most restless volcano is Kilauea in Hawaii, which has been in constant eruption since 1983. Its lava flows have covered more than 100 sq km.

• There are more than 800 active volcanoes in the world. The country with the most is Indonesia, which has about 200.

• Tambora in Indonesia erupted in 1815, killing approximately 90,000 people.

Earthquakes of the **20th century**

Place	Date	Richter scale
San Francisco, USA	1906	8.3
Gansu, China	1920	8.6
Kanto Plain, Japan	1923	8.3
Assam, India	1950	8.6
Aleutian Islands	1957	9.1
Tangshan, China	1976	8.2

Mountains are made by movements of the Earth's rocky crust. The highest mountains are the youngest and are still growing, pushed up by enormous pressure deep inside the Earth. For example, the Himalayas have been built-up over the last 40 million years, whereas the Adirondacks in New York, which are over one billion years old, have been worn flat, or reduced to mere hills.

What is the highest mountain on land?

Mount Everest, which rises to 8,863 m in the Himalayan range of Asia. The Himalayan range has the world's 20 highest mountains, all more than 8,000 m high. An even higher peak, Mauna Kea in Hawaii, rises out of the Pacific Ocean. It rises 10,203 m from the ocean floor to its summit, but only 4,205 m of this is above water.

How do rivers shape the land?

Over thousands of years a river carves out a course through the rocks and soil, as it flows towards the sea or into lakes. These river courses create valleys and canyons, and where they wind slowly through flat country, they move in snaky curves called meanders. They wear away the bank on one side and pile up silt on the other.

⬆ *Rivers meander through the landscape to flow into open water, such as lakes, seas or oceans, shaping the land as they run.*

⬇ *The highest mountains in each continent.*

Jayakusuma
Oceania
5,030 m

Elbrus
Europe
5,642 m

Kilimanjaro
Africa
5,895 m

McKinley
North America
6,194 m

Aconcagua
South America
6,960 m

Everest
Asia
8,863 m

How **mountains are made**

Forming mountains
Mountains can be made in three different ways. Volcanic mountains are pushed up by volcanoes. Fold mountains are made when layers of rock fold like wrinkles on a blanket. Fault block mountains are made when a section of rock tilts or is pushed up during an earth tremor. This happens along faults or breaks in the Earth's crust.

Volcanic
mountain

Fold
mountain

Fault block
mountain

↑ *The biggest canyon on Earth is the Grand Canyon in the USA – in places it is 1.6 km deep.*

How can weather change a landscape?

The Earth's landscape is changing all the time because of erosion, which is the wearing away of rocks and soil by 'scouring' forces such as wind, water, ice and frost. In winter, water trapped in cracks in rock freezes, expands and causes chunks of rock to split off. Heavy rain can quickly wash soil down a slope, especially if there are no trees on the slope to 'bind' the soil with their roots.

➡ *The landscape is shaped by the weather often into formations like this rock arch.*

What is the world's biggest canyon?

The Grand Canyon is a huge gorge in the Earth's surface, which has been cut by the Colorado River in Arizona, USA. The process of cutting the canyon, 350 km long and in places more than 20 km across, has taken millions of years. In some parts of the canyon, rocks of up to two billion years old have been uncovered.

What starts an avalanche?

Avalanches can be started by strong winds, melting snow, loud noises or even by people skiing on loose snow. An avalanche is an enormous mass of snow that slips down a mountainside. Millions of tonnes of snow fall at speeds of up to 400 km/h. The biggest avalanches occur in the world's highest mountain range – the Himalayas.

↑ *The fastest avalanches are masses of dry snow. Wet snow moves at a more sluggish pace.*

Highest **mountains**

The five highest peaks in the world are all in the Himalayan range in Asia:

Everest	8,863 m
K2	8,610 m
Kanchenjunga	8,598 m
Lhotse	8,511 m
Makalu	8,481 m

Other **famous peaks**

Cotopaxi (Mexico)	5,897 m
Ararat (Turkey)	5,185 m
Mont Blanc (France/ Italy/ Switzerland)	4,807 m
Jungfrau (Switzerland)	4,518 m
Matterhorn (Switzerland/Italy)	4,478 m
Fuji (Japan)	3,776 m
Olympus (Greece)	2,917 m

➡ *Mount Everest was first climbed in 1953 by Sherpa Tenzing Norgay and New Zealander Edmund Hillary, supported by a British Commonwealth team of climbers.*

Water from the oceans is drawn up into the air as water vapour by the warmth of the Sun. It is blown over land by winds, cools to become water droplets and falls as rain. Rainwater fills up lakes and rivers, and eventually finds its way back to the oceans. All the water on Earth is recycled, over and over again.

4 Rivers flow into ocean

3 Water vapour falls as rain and snow

2 Moisture from ground evaporates

1 Ocean water evaporates

In the water cycle, water is drawn up from the oceans by evaporation and later falls as rain over the land. This is known as precipitation. The rainwater then flows back to the ocean in rivers.

Which is the deepest lake?

Baikal in Siberia, Russia, is 1,637 m deep, roughly four times deeper than Lake Superior in North America. Baikal is a very ancient lake, about 25 million years old, and is unique in being home to the world's only freshwater seal. Lake Tanganyika in Africa is the next deepest lake but is only two million years old.

Why are the Great Lakes so named?

Canada and the United States share the five Great Lakes, so named because they are the biggest group of freshwater lakes in the world. They are: Lake Superior (the world's biggest freshwater lake), Lake Huron (the 5th largest lake in the world), Lake Michigan (the 6th largest lake), Lake Erie and Lake Ontario. Canada has the most fresh water (by area) – twice as much as any other country.

Which river has the largest volume of water?

The Amazon River carries more water than any other. It pours 770 billion l of water into the Atlantic Ocean every hour. The Amazon also has the most tributaries (rivers that flow into it). Second to the Amazon in volume of water-flow is China's Huang He, which is the muddiest river. Another name for Huang He is the Yellow River, so-called because of the colour of the silt washed into it.

The Amazon River winds in and out of lush rainforest that grows on either side.

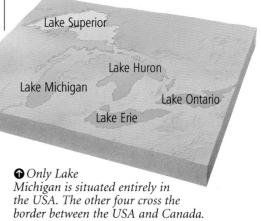

Lake Superior

Lake Huron

Lake Michigan

Lake Ontario

Lake Erie

Only Lake Michigan is situated entirely in the USA. The other four cross the border between the USA and Canada.

River **facts**

Mississippi-Missouri, North America – 6,020 km
Volga, Europe – 3,531 km
Murray-Darling, Oceania – 2,520 km
Chang Jiang (Yangtze), Asia – 6,300 km
Amazon, South America – 6,750 km
Nile, Africa – 6,673 km

This diagram shows the comparative lengths of the longest rivers in each continent.

World's longest **rivers**

Name	Continent	Length (km)
Amazon	South America	6,750*
Nile	Africa	6,673*
Chang Jiang (Yangtze)	Asia	6,300
Mississippi-Missouri	North America	6,020
Huang He (Yellow)	Asia	5,460
Congo (Zaire)	Africa	4,667

*The Amazon and the Nile can both be measured from various points, making their official lengths vary.

Where would you find a delta?

Where rivers meet the sea, they can form v-shaped deltas. The river flows slowly and piles up silt into sandbanks, through which the river flows into the sea. The biggest delta is in Bangladesh, where the Ganges and Brahmaputra rivers create a delta almost as big as England. The Mississippi River delta in the United States extends over 300 km into the Gulf of Mexico.

➲ *The River Nile empties its waters into the Mediterranean sea through a great delta.*

Can a river flow backwards?

An incoming push of seawater, as the tide flows in, can make a wave that rushes upstream – so making a river flow backwards. This wave is called a tidal bore, and there is a famous one on the Severn River in England, which moves upstream at about 20 km an hour. A bore more than 7 m high rushes up the Qiantang River in China. Normally, rivers flow from their source (often on a mountain) downhill to the sea, drawn by the pull of gravity.

➲ *The highest falls are the Angel Falls in Venezuela, South America, with one drop of 807 m, and a total drop of 979 m, more than twice as high as the Empire State Building! This diagram compares the largest waterfalls in each continent.*

➲ *Victoria Falls (see page 195) are on the Zambezi River, on the border between Zambia and Zimbabwe in central Africa. Waterfalls with such immense flows of water produce huge clouds of spray and a thunderous noise.*

What makes a waterfall?

Waterfalls occur when a river flows over a band of hard rock, and then over softer rock which is more quickly worn away by the water. The hard rock forms a step over which the river pours, creating a waterfall. Famous waterfalls include Niagara in North America, Angel Falls in South America and Victoria Falls in Africa.

Angel Falls
South America
979 m

Giessbach Falls
Europe
604 m

Sutherland Falls
Oceania
579 m

Ribbon Falls
North America
491 m

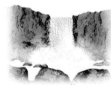
Jog Falls
Asia
253 m

Victoria Falls
Africa
108 m

Largest **lakes**

Name	Location	Area (sq km)
Caspian Sea	Asia	371,000
Lake Superior	North America	82,350
Victoria Nyanza	Africa	69,500
Aral Sea	Asia	66,500
Huron	North America	59,600
Michigan	North America	58,000
Tanganyika	Africa	32,900

Longest **lakes**

Name	Length (km)
Caspian Sea	1,201
Tanganyika	676
Baikal	636
Nyasa/Malawi	580
Superior	563

➲ *Glacier lakes are created by glacial erosion, which deepens the valley floor. Water fills these valleys and moraine debris falls from the glacier to form a dam to keep the water in.*

Viewed from space, the Earth looks like a planet of blue ocean – more than 70 per cent is water. About 97 per cent of all the Earth's water is in the oceans, which cover more than 360 million sq km of the planet. The oceans can be more than 10 km deep in places.

What causes tides?

Tides rise and fall twice every 24 hours, as the gravity of the Sun and Moon pull on the waters of the Earth – drawing the ocean towards them. The oceans move in different ways. Currents are streams of warm and cool water, some pushed by winds, others by the tides. The land is pulled too, but water moves more easily, causing a vast wave, which moves around the globe and forms the tides.

Spring tides (high)

As the tide rises, the sea flows upwards and inland

Neap tides (low)

As the tide drops, the sea ebbs, retreating from the shore

How many oceans are there?

There are five oceans, which all connect to make one vast body of water. The three biggest oceans are the Pacific, Atlantic and Indian Oceans. They meet around Antarctica, in the Southern or Antarctic Ocean. The Pacific and the Atlantic also meet in the smaller Arctic Ocean. Seas, such as the Baltic Sea are smaller areas of saltwater, but most seas are joined to an ocean, such as the Mediterranean Sea, which is linked to the Red Sea by the Suez Canal, and to the Atlantic Ocean at the Strait of Gibraltar.

There are two high and two low tides every 24 hours. The very high spring tides occur when the gravity from the Sun and the Moon combines to tug at the oceans.

Which is the biggest ocean?

The Pacific Ocean is the biggest of the Earth's oceans. About 45 per cent of all the seawater on the Earth is in the Pacific Ocean. It has a surface area of 181 million sq km, which is equivalent to one-third of the Earth. The Pacific Ocean is larger than the second and third biggest oceans (Atlantic Ocean at 94 million sq km, and Indian Ocean at 74 million sq km) combined.

Some maps name the North and South Pacific, and the North and South Atlantic separately, but the Pacific and the Atlantic are each one ocean.

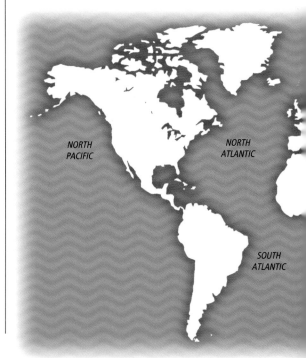

NORTH PACIFIC

NORTH ATLANTIC

SOUTH ATLANTIC

Seas and **oceans**

Seas, tides and waves

Seas are named parts of oceans, often partly enclosed by land. The biggest sea is the South China Sea, which covers 2,974,000 sq km.

Waves are blown along by winds. The highest wave ever seen was in 1933 when, during a Pacific hurricane, a US Navy ship survived a wave estimated to be 34 m high.

The highest tides (more than 14 m) rise and fall in the Bay of Fundy, on the Atlantic coast of North America.

Ocean **depths**

Ocean	Deepest point
Pacific	10,911 m
Atlantic	9,219 m
Indian	7,455 m
Caribbean	6,946 m
South China	5,016 m

The Pacific has the five deepest trenches in the oceans. In 1961, the US Navy bathyscaphe Trieste *dived to the bottom of the Marianas Trench, the deepest point.*

What is it like on the ocean floor?

The ocean floor is a varied seascape of mountain ranges, deep trenches, hot springs and mud oozing for hundreds of metres. At the coast, the land slopes gradually to a depth of about 180 m – this is the continental shelf. At the edge of the shelf, the ocean floor drops away in the continental slope, leading to the deepest part of the ocean floor, the cold and sunless abyss. On the ocean floor, hot springs reach temperatures above boiling point (100°C) in places.

🌀 The ocean floor has features, just like dry land, with ridges, canyons and mountains.

Continental shelf

Continental slope

Ocean trench

Why is the Dead Sea so salty?

The saltiest sea is the Dead Sea, which is enclosed by hot desert where the fierce heat evaporates so much water that what is left becomes very salty. Seawater tastes salty because it contains minerals washed into the oceans by rivers. The most common mineral in seawater is common salt (sodium chloride).

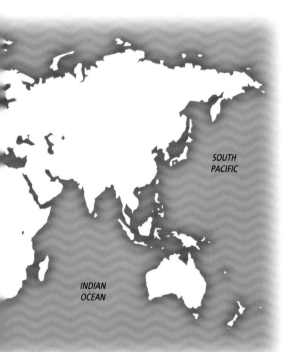

SOUTH PACIFIC

INDIAN OCEAN

🔵 The water of the Dead Sea is so salty that it is more buoyant than ordinary seawater.

Could you drink a melted iceberg?

Yes, because although icebergs drift on the ocean, they are made of fresh water. Icebergs break off the ends of glaciers – slow-moving rivers of ice – that move down mountain slopes in the polar regions. Icebergs also break off from the edges of ice sheets.

🔵 Only about 11 per cent of a tall iceberg shows above water; the rest is submerged.

Ocean trenches

The longest and deepest ocean trenches are:

Name	Length (km)	Depth (m)
Peru-Atacama	3,540	9,064
Aleutian	3,200	8,100
Tonga-Kermadec	2,575	10,882
Marianas Trench	2,250	10,911
Philippine	1,325	10,497

➔ Many islands in the Pacific Ocean, including those of Japan and Hawaii, were formed by volcanoes, which pushed up islands in 'chains'.

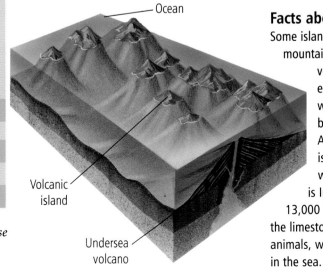

Ocean

Volcanic island

Undersea volcano

Facts about islands

Some islands are the tops of undersea mountains or are pushed up by volcanoes. Other islands (for example, the British Isles) were once part of continents but became cut off by water. A chain or group of islands is called an archipelago. The world's biggest archipelago is Indonesia with more than 13,000 islands. Reefs are made of the limestone bodies of tiny coral animals, which form rings and walls in the sea.

Dry desert, where the land gets less than 250 mm of rainfall in a year, covers almost one-eighth of the Earth's surface. The driest place on Earth is the Atacama Desert in Chile, South America, where many years pass without a single drop of rain. Not all deserts are hot though. The hottest ones are near the Equator, but even there it can be chilly at night.

⬤ *People and animals have adapted to desert life. Arabian camels are still used as baggage carriers by desert nomads, who traditionally travelled from oasis to oasis, living in tents that provided shade by day and warmth by night (when it gets cold in the desert).*

Which is the biggest desert?

The biggest desert is the Sahara (see page 188) in North Africa, which is 5,000 km across, bigger than Australia. It has the world's largest sand dunes, some of them more than 400 m high. Cave paintings found near the region, drawn by ancient people, depict grassland animals. This shows that thousands of years ago the Sahara was actually wetter, with lakes and plains.

⬤ *Dry deserts occur in warm areas where cool air sinks, warms up and then absorbs moisture from the land. The map shows the world's biggest deserts.*

Deserts and **desertification**

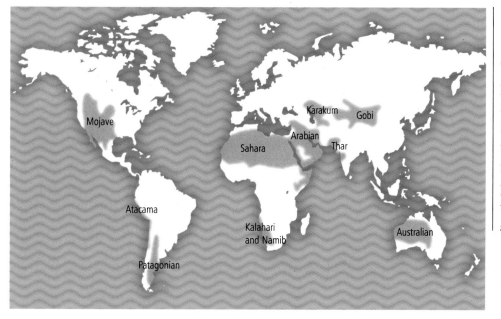

1 Sahara Desert

Desert environment
People on the edges of deserts are living in a very delicately balanced environment. Water is precious, and so are the trees and other plants that bind the thin soil and help hold back the desert sands. Careless farming, or too many people trying to scratch a living from the desert fringes, can turn half-desert into full-desert. This is called desertification. Farmers who keep too many sheep and goats, or cut too many trees for fuel-wood, find that the desert is encroaching onto once fairly fertile pastures and fields. Climate change can also cause deserts to expand. Deserts seem to ebb and flow, like the oceans. Satellite photos of the Sahara, for example, show that it spreads southwards for some years, then shrinks. About 450 million years ago, the Sahara was covered in ice. In the Sahara are huge seas of sand, called ergs. The biggest erg, between Algeria and Tunisia, covers an area as big as Spain.

Are all deserts sandy?

Only about 20 per cent of the Earth's deserts are sandy. The rest are rocky, stony, covered by scrub and bush, or ice-covered. In the Arabian Desert is the world's biggest area of sand dunes – the Rub' al-Khali, which means 'Empty Quarter' in Arabic.

⬆ *Underground water allows people to cultivate palms and vegetables in a desert oasis. Some oases support small towns.*

⬆ *Sand dunes can travel across the desert, like waves across an ocean.*

Can sand dunes move?

Loose sand is blown by the wind and piles up in wave-shaped formations called dunes. Sand is made up of tiny mineral grains, less than 2 mm across. Like waves of water, sand is blown up, rolls over the crest of the wave and down the steeper far side. Dunes rolls across the desert in this way.

What is an oasis?

An oasis is a green 'island' in the desert, a haven for thirsty travellers. Plants can grow there by tapping water from a well or underground spring. Even beneath the Sahara Desert a lot of water is trapped deep in the rock strata (layers).

⬇ *Many desert creatures, such as insects, scorpions, lizards and snakes feed at night, when it is cooler.*

How do desert animals and plants survive?

Desert animals are able to go for days without water, getting most of the moisture they need from their food. These animals include mammals such as antelope, camels, foxes and rodents, as well as birds and insects. Other animals, such as desert frogs, go into a state of suspended animation in burrows until the next rain.

⬇ *The largest desert in the world is the Sahara, followed by the Australian desert. Asia has more deserts than any other continent. They include the Gobi, Karakum, Taklimakan and Thar deserts.*

2 Australian Desert

3 Arabian Desert

4 Gobi Desert

5 Kalahari Desert

Biggest **deserts**

Name	Location	Area (sq km)
Sahara	North Africa	9 million
Australian	Australia	3.8 million
Arabian	Southwest Asia	1.3 million
Gobi	Central Asia	1 million
Kalahari	Southern Africa	520,000

➡ *This tree in the Namib Desert of southwestern Africa manages to survive, even in such a hostile, dry environment.*

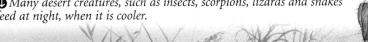

Many trees covering an area of land create a forest. A wood is a smaller area of trees. Some forests in cooler regions of the Earth have only two or three species of trees growing in them, but other forests have a tremendous variety of trees and other plants. The first forests grew in prehistoric swamps over 350 million years ago, but these were forests of tall ferns and moss-like plants, not trees.

Are there different types of forest?

There are different types of forest around the world, depending on the climate in the world's vegetation zones. In the warm tropics there are rainforests and seasonal forests (where trees lose their leaves during the dry season) and savanna (warm grassland) forests. Rainforests also grow in cooler zones, where there is a lot of rainfall. In cooler zones, there are forests of mixed deciduous trees (which shed their leaves before winter), and of evergreen conifers, such as fir and pine. Boreal forest or taiga is found in cold sub-polar lands.

Which is the world's biggest rainforest?

The Amazon rainforest of South America, which stretches from the foothills of the Andes Mountains in the west to the Atlantic Ocean in the east.

↑ *About 40 per cent of the the world's plants are found in rainforests.*

There are other rainforests in west Africa, Southeast Asia and northeastern Australia. Rainforests are abundant with wildlife. There are more species of animals and plants in the Amazon than anywhere else on Earth.

What starts a forest fire?

Forest fires can begin naturally, when the vegetation is very dry after months without any rain. Often humans are responsible for starting the fires by carelessly lighting campfires or sometimes even by deliberate arson. Many forest trees and other plants regenerate quickly after a fire, but wildlife can be seriously affected.

⊙ *Forest fires can spread rapidly. Firefighters often cut trees to create a strip of open ground, called a firebreak, to stop the flames spreading.*

Forest **facts**

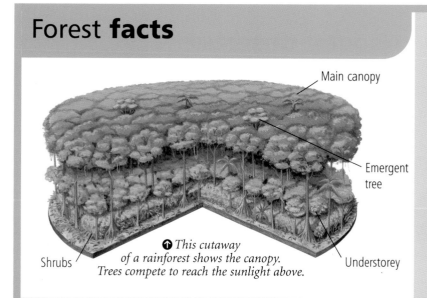

Main canopy

Emergent tree

Understorey

Shrubs

↑ *This cutaway of a rainforest shows the canopy. Trees compete to reach the sunlight above.*

Amazing **forest facts**

- Many forest trees grow to great ages if they are left undisturbed by people. Oaks of 500 years old are not uncommon in ancient forests.

- Just 1 ha of rainforest can contain 180 tree species.

- A rainforest has different levels, like floors in a building. The thickest part is the main canopy, about 30 m high, where most animals live. Taller trees emerge from the canopy.

- Tropical forests grow densely because the trees get sunlight and rainfall almost every day. It is a year-long growing season, so plants grow very fast.

⬆ *There are 450 different species of oak trees, most of which belong to the* Quercus *group, which grow mostly in the northern parts of the world. Oak trees can live for more than 1,000 years and some of the oldest trees in Europe are oaks. Wood from the oak tree is very strong and has been used in the building of houses and ships over the past centuries.*

Why do some forest trees shed their leaves?

Trees in a deciduous forest shed their leaves to save water, because their roots cannot soak up water very well from cold soil.

Deciduous forests grow in countries with warm summers and cool winters. The trees in these forests include oak, beech, maple, ash and chestnut, and as summer gives way to autumn, the leaves of the trees change colour and begin to fall.

What is meant by a sustainable forest?

Forests provide people with many products, including timber, foods, cosmetics and drugs. Coniferous forests of pine, spruce and fir are felled for timber or newspaper pulp. In a well-managed sustainable forest, new trees are planted to replace those that are felled. Sadly, many tropical rainforests are being destroyed not just for timber, but also to clear the land for farming and ranching. Felled trees are not replaced, leaving a stump-littered wasteland.

Natural forest

Trees are burnt

Farm crops

Rain washes away topsoil

Soil becomes useless

⬆ *Widespread deforestation can have devastating effects on the landscape. Tropical soil rapidly loses fertility. Rain washes off the topsoil, and once-lush forest becomes scrubland or desert.*

- Tropical rainforests grow luxuriantly because the rainfall is heavy and regular – often more than 2,000 mm of rain in a year.

- South American and Indonesian rainforests are most in danger from exploitation. Every year the Amazon rainforest loses about 80,000 sq km of trees.

- Some of the world's tallest trees grow in Australia's eucalyptus forests. Karri, mountain ash and blue gum trees grow to more than 40 m high.

- Some trees, such as the Douglas fir, are tough enough to survive even on cold and windy mountains. Conifers withstand the cold better than deciduous trees, but the higher a mountain is, the more difficult it is for trees to survive. Above the tree line is bare mountainside.

⬇ *Managed forestry means replacing trees that are cut by loggers (left) with new saplings (young trees) that will grow and ensure the forest survives.*

The atmosphere is the layer of gases that surround the Earth. It is held in place by the Earth's gravity, which keeps most of the gases in the atmosphere close to the ground. Most of the atmospheric gases are packed into the lowest layer of the atmosphere, starting at ground level, which is called the troposphere.

Exosphere 500–800 km

Thermosphere 80–500 km

Mesosphere 50–80 km

Stratosphere 10–50 km

Ozone layer

Troposphere 0–10 km

◐ *We live in the lowest layer of the atmosphere. Planes cruise in the layer called the stratosphere. Phenomena such as the auroras – Borealis of the Northern Hemisphere and Australis in the Southern Hemisphere – occur in the thermosphere. Above that lies space.*

How many layers are there in the atmosphere?

There are five main layers in the atmosphere. The lowest is the troposphere, up to 10 km high. Next is the stratosphere, about 50 km high, and above that is the mesosphere, to about 80 km. The upper layer is called the thermosphere. The higher you go, the thinner the atmosphere, and above 800 km there is no atmosphere left and the exosphere (a very thin fifth layer) gives way to the airless near-emptiness of space.

How does the atmosphere protect us?

In the upper levels of the atmosphere is a layer of ozone (a form of oxygen), which forms a protective layer blocking out harmful ultraviolet rays from the Sun. On the fringes of the atmosphere are two doughnut-shaped radiation belts, known as the Van Allen Belts, which shield us from cosmic rays coming from space.

◑ *The atmosphere is a protective belt, burning up meteorites and shielding life on Earth from harmful cosmic radiation.*

Atmospheric **information**

In the atmosphere
The atmosphere contains oxygen, nitrogen and tiny amounts of other gases – argon, carbon dioxide, carbon monoxide, hydrogen, ozone, methane, helium, neon, krypton and xenon. The most important gas in the atmosphere is oxygen, because people and animals need to breathe it. When we breathe, we take in oxygen and breathe out carbon dioxide. Green plants, such as trees, take in carbon dioxide and give off oxygen during their food-making process (photosynthesis).

At sea level, one cubic metre of air weighs less than 1,200 g. Imagine the weight of air pressing down on top of your head – it comes to almost a tonne. Luckily we do not feel crushed, because the pressure is balanced by the air pressing in all around us. At sea-level pressure is about 1 kg per sq cm. The pressure drops with altitude, so at 15,000 m the pressure is only one-tenth of a kg per sq m. The higher you go, the colder it gets, too. At a height of 9,000 m the air temperature is –50°C.

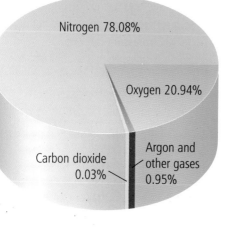

Nitrogen 78.08%

Oxygen 20.94%

Argon and other gases 0.95%

Carbon dioxide 0.03%

◐ *Nitrogen and oxygen together make up about 99 per cent of the Earth's atmosphere.*

Why does the sky look blue?

Light from the Sun passes through the atmosphere and is scattered by tiny particles of dust and moisture in the air. This has the effect of breaking up the white sunlight into its rainbow colours, just like a spectrum does. The blue rays scatter most, and reach our eyes from all angles. The result is that we see blue more than the other colours in sunlight, so the sky looks blue.

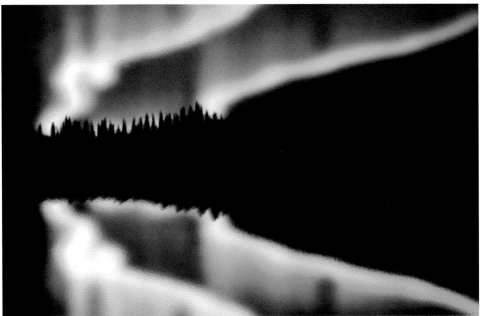

⊕ *The Northern Lights, or Aurora Borealis, makes the sky glow and streak in a beautiful display of colours ranging from purple to golden-green.*

⊕ *Clouds change shape all the time. Some are big billowing masses, others are feathery traces. The wind changes the shape of clouds, which often obscure the blue sky above.*

What causes the Northern and Southern Lights?

The Northern and Southern Lights are caused by the solar wind (radiation from the Sun) hitting the atmosphere. Most of the incoming energized particles are absorbed by the Van Allen Belts (see page 60), but at the poles, where the belts are thinnest, the particles impact on the atmosphere, producing a spectacular light show in the sky. The Aurora Borealis (Northern Lights) makes the night sky glow green, gold, red or purple. The aurora seen in the Southern Hemisphere is the Aurora Australis (Southern Lights).

Where is the air coldest?

Anyone who climbs a mountain soon realizes that it gets colder the higher you climb. The temperature falls by about 5°C for every 100 m altitude. However, in the atmosphere high above ground level, it is a different story. The outer layer of the atmosphere can be warmer than the layers closer to the surface. Within the layer called the troposphere it gets coldest when the air rises highest, which is over the Equator. It is actually warmer over the North Pole, where the air does not rise as high.

Air-pressure systems

Two main air-pressure systems control our weather. High pressure (anticyclones) form when cold air sinks. High pressure usually means fine, dry weather – warm in summer, cold in winter. Low pressure (cyclones or depressions) occur when warm air rises, bringing rainclouds and unsettled weather. Winds blow from high pressure zones into low pressure zones. The strength of the wind depends upon how great the difference in pressure is. If there is a big difference, then the wind is strong.

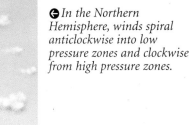

◑ *In the Northern Hemisphere, winds spiral anticlockwise into low pressure zones and clockwise from high pressure zones.*

◑ *In the Southern Hemisphere, winds spiral in the opposite direction to those in the Northern Hemisphere. spiralling clockwise into low pressure zones.*

Regular weather charts have been kept for only about the last 250 years, and accurate temperature readings date from the 1800s. But people have always been interested in the weather. Historic Chinese weather records show that 903 BC was a very bad winter in China, and the Romans recorded that the weather was poor when they landed in Britain in 55 BC.

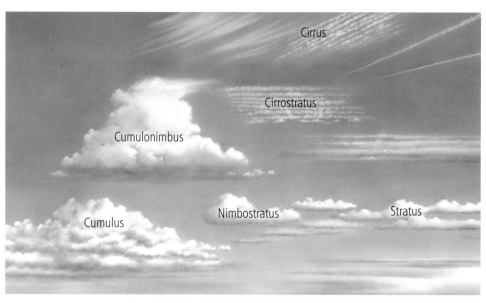

The different types of cloud in the sky form at different heights. Clouds are made of tiny droplets of water or ice.

What are the highest clouds in the sky?

The highest clouds are the rare 'mother of pearl' nacreous clouds, which can be found at 24,000 m. Cumulonimbus clouds can tower as high in the sky as 19,000 m. The more common cirrus clouds form at around 8,000 m. The lowest clouds are stratus clouds, from 1,100 m to ground level.

How deep can snow be?

The most snow to fall in 24 hours was 1.93 m – enough to cover a tall man. This snowfall buried Silver Lake in Colorado, USA between 14 and 15 April 1921. The deepest snow ever measured was 11.46 m in California in 1911 – enough snow to cover a small house to the roof (see page 189).

Snowfall tends to be heaviest in mountainous regions, such as the Rocky Mountains and Sierra Nevada ranges of North America. People who live in these regions have learned to cope with blizzards (heavy snowfall) that half-bury cars and houses.

Snowflakes are made up of snow crystals, that can be seen under a microscope. Each has six sides but every snowflake is different.

Weather **facts**

 Occluded front – where a cold front (blue triangle) meets a warm front (red semicircle)

Strength of the wind – the circle shows how much cloud cover there is

07 Very strong winds – evident from the three lines on the tail of the symbol

 10 Temperature at sea

× 1026 Air pressure

09 Cloud cover shown by circle

08 × 965 Centre of low air pressure

Meteorologists (scientists who study the weather) use an international set of symbols to represent different aspects of the weather.

Stormy **weather**

• In the USA, tornadoes are called 'twisters' and roar across the Midwest at speeds of 50 km/h.

• Britain's worst storm of modern times was the hurricane of 1987, which blew down about 15 million trees in southern England.

• Windspeeds are measured on a scale invented in 1806 by an English admiral, Sir Francis Beaufort. The scale goes from 0 (calm) to 12 (hurricane). Any winds stronger than force 8 can cause damage.

Cirrus

Cirrostratus

Cumulonimbus

Cumulus

Nimbostratus

Stratus

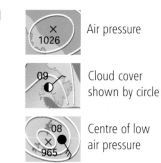

Where is the thickest ice?

The ice covering Greenland is about 1.5 km thick, but the ice in Antarctica is three times thicker, up to 4.8 km thick! Antarctic icebergs are flatter than Arctic ones. The biggest iceberg was spotted in the Antarctic in 1956. It was 335 km long and 97 km across. A country the size of Belgium would have fitted on top of it.

↑ Lightning flashes between clouds, or from cloud to ground, heating the air around it to more than 33,000°C. This is five times hotter than the surface of the Sun.

What is a hurricane?

The most destructive storms are hurricanes, known as cyclones in the Indian Ocean and typhoons in the Pacific Ocean. In a hurricane, winds spiral at speeds of more than 400 km/h, yet at the centre is a calm area, known as the 'eye' of the hurricane. A hurricane does most damage when it hits the land.

What causes lightning?

A lightning flash is a giant electric spark, caused by electrical charges that build up inside clouds and on the ground. Lightning is incredibly hot and so can seriously injure and even kill people. An American park ranger named Roy Sullivan was struck by lightning seven times (and survived) between 1942 and 1977.

← Hurricanes can be photographed from high above, in space. The 'eye' can be seen quite clearly on the photographs. Satellites in space track hurricanes over the ocean.

→ Each colour in the white sunlight is bent to a different extent. The light is split into the spectrum colours: red, orange, yellow, green, blue, indigo and violet, to form the rainbow.

When might you see a rainbow?

You might see a rainbow – an arc of up to seven colours in the sky – during a rainfall. A rainbow is caused by light being refracted (bent) by the raindrops. To see a rainbow, the Sun must be behind you. If the Sun is high in the sky, no rainbow will appear.

Extreme weather

Most thunder – Tororo in Uganda, Africa, has an average of 250 thundery days every year.
Worst hailstorm – A hailstorm in 1888 killed 246 people in India.
Biggest hailstone – Bigger and heavier than a tennis ball, at 44.5 cm around and weighing 1 kg, it fell in Kansas, in 1970.
Highest waterspout – A waterspout reported to be 1,500 m high was seen off the coast of New South Wales, Australia, in 1888.
Worst cyclone – In 1991, 138,000 people were killed when a cyclone and tidal wave hit Bangladesh.
Hottest place – In Death Valley in California, USA, the thermometer stayed above 49°C for 43 days in 1917.

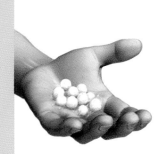

↑ Hailstones measuring up to 5 cm can fall during a hailstorm. A hailstone with a diameter of 17.8 cm was recorded in the USA.

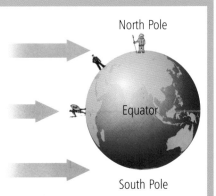

North Pole

Equator

South Pole

↑ The Poles are colder than the Equator because they receive less direct sunlight. At the Poles, the Sun's rays have more atmosphere to penetrate, and so lose some of their warmth.

The Earth has many natural resources, which sustain life. The planet has air, water, forests, minerals and a range of environments that living things can use. Some of these resources, such as the Sun's energy, are limitless. Others are renewable, such as plants, which means that they can be regrown. But some, like coal and oil, are non-renewable resources. Once used, they are gone for ever.

⊕ *Diamond is the hardest known substance.*

◐ *Oil is an extremely valuable natural resource that we use in our homes and for transport. It is found deep in the ground or below the seabed, pumped out by oil rigs that float in the sea, anchored to the seabed.*

How is water used to make electricity?

Water is stored in a vast dam, and runs through pipes at great speed to drive turbines that generate electricity. An electricity generator works by turning motion (one form of energy) into electricity (another form of energy). This motion may come from a turbine that is driven by steam or water.

Why is a diamond like a lump of coal?

Diamond and coal are both forms of carbon. About 95 per cent of all compounds (substances made of two or more elements) contain carbon, which is the key element in substance-building because it has atoms that form chains, rings and other structures, making them stronger and more durable.

◐ *A hydro-electric power station uses water to drive its turbines.*

What are raw materials?

They are the Earth's resources that make our lives more comfortable. We cut trees for timber to make homes and furniture. We mine minerals, such as copper, to make the electrical wire in our buildings. We mine coal to burn as a fuel. All of these materials are non-renewable, which means we cannot make more of them.

Clean energy **and recycling**

Energy
Wind power is one method of generating electricity without using up precious resources. The wind is a renewable resource because in many parts of the world it seldom stops blowing. Wind turbines with spinning blades are grouped in wind farms, which supply electricity to the grid system.

Other forms of renewable clean energy are wave and tidal power, which harness the motion of waves; and solar power, which turns the energy from the Sun into electricity.

In future, people will rely on a mix of these energy sources, but it is very important today to save energy and to recycle the things we use. Much of our 'rubbish' can be recycled – used again – in a variety of ways. Materials, such as glass, paper and metals can be treated and processed in a factory, to be reused in the same form.

◐ *Wind farms are usually in remote areas or offshore, where the noise of the turbine blades causes less disturbance to people.*

What is coal?

Coal was formed over 250 million years ago, from dead and decaying plants in prehistoric swamp-forests. Over that vast length of time, the plant matter got squashed so tightly that it changed and became a soft black-brown rock. Coal is found in seams or layers, with other rocks on top and beneath. It is extracted either by digging deep mine shafts and tunnels, or by 'stripping' coal seams near the surface, known as opencast mining.

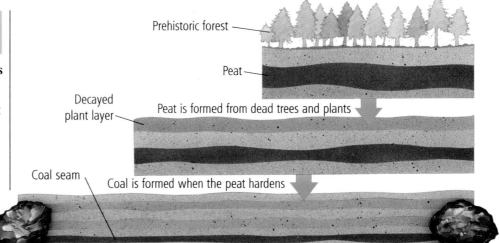

Prehistoric forest

Peat

Peat is formed from dead trees and plants

Decayed plant layer

Coal seam

Coal is formed when the peat hardens

Where is the world's richest gold-field?

The mines of the Witwatersrand in South Africa yield about 50 per cent of the world's annual gold production, making them the richest gold-mines in the world. Several times in history gold-miners have rushed to find gold in various parts of the world. The most famous gold-rush was in California in 1849. There was another in South Africa in the 1880s.

What is the 'greenhouse' effect?

Gases, such as carbon dioxide, act like the glass in a greenhouse, letting through the Sun's rays, but trapping some heat that would otherwise filter back into space. Since the 1800s, human activity (especially factories, vehicles and power stations) has caused an increase in the amount of carbon dioxide and other gases in the atmosphere. The trapped warmth that is created raises the Earth's temperature and many scientists believe this is bringing about climate change.

⊙ Few gold-rush prospectors ever made the fortune they dreamed about, by finding nuggets of gold.

⊙ This diagram shows how coal seams are formed over millions of years. Much of the coal lies deep beneath rock layers, called strata. The pressure of the topmost layer squeezes the layers below, turning sand and mud into hard rock, and plant remains from peat into coal.

⊙ Gases that have risen into the atmosphere trap the heat from the Sun, causing what scientists call the 'greenhouse' effect.

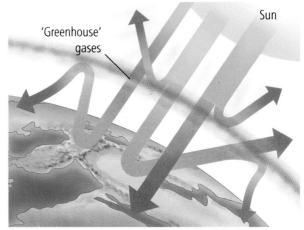

Sun

'Greenhouse' gases

Recycling **tips**

Cardboard boxes – can be recycled to make packaging.
Newspapers – can be recycled to make more paper.
Glass – can be melted down and reformed.
Metal cans – and other metal scrap can be melted down.
Some plastics – can be shredded and reused.

Many local town councils now operate recycling schemes for household rubbish.

⊙ Recycling saves precious resources and helps keep our environment 'healthy', avoiding an accumulation of household rubbish, which pollutes the environment.

Save **energy**

• Buy products with the least packaging.

• Turn off electric lights and appliances after use.

• Keep car use to a sensible minimum, to save fuel and air pollution.

• Recycle household waste, such as metal, paper, plastic and glass.

• Do not leave water taps running.

• Turn central heating down or off when the weather is mild.

Human beings are related to primates (monkeys and apes), and our earliest ancestors, some four million years ago, were ape-like creatures that walked upright on two legs. As these human-apes evolved, they became less like apes and more like humans. Scientists have found evidence of this from studying bones and simple stone tools that have been found. Modern humans, our direct ancestors, appeared about 100,000 years ago.

When was the earliest type of human discovered?

In 1974, the almost-complete skeleton of an *Australopithecus* female was found in Ethiopia. Scientists called the ape-like human 'Lucy'. She was no taller than a ten-year-old girl, though she was about 40 when she died three million years ago. Preserved footprints found by Mary Leakey in Tanzania proved that *Australopithecus* walked upright, like modern humans.

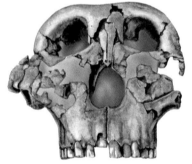

⬆ *Skull of* Australopithecus, *the human-like ape that walked on two legs, leaving its hands free to hold sticks or stones.*

When did people first make tools?

More than two million years ago. Remains of prehistoric people found in East Africa are accompanied by pebbles and rocks that had been flaked to make sharp cutting edges. The first tool-users have been named

Homo habilis, which is Latin for 'handy man'. These early humans used stone tools to kill animals and to chop up meat and skins.

⬆ *Stones were flaked by chipping away the edges and were made into cutting, scraping and chopping tools.*

➡ *Stone Age people lived in caves. They used fire for warmth and cooking. The flames also gave light for artists who painted animals on the cave walls.*

How did fire change people's lives?

People began to use fire to scare away wild animals, to keep themselves warm and to cook meat. The first people to use fire were *Homo erectus*, more than 500,000 years ago. They were skilful tool-makers. They learned how to rub sticks or strike sparks from a stone to start a fire, and then how to keep the fire burning. Without fire, people could not have survived in cold lands during the ice ages.

Steps towards **civilization**

Key **dates**
years ago

4 million	*Australopithecus.*
2 million	*Homo habilis*; stone tools.
1.5 million	*Homo erectus.*
500,000	Making fire.
120,000	Neanderthal people
100,000	*Homo sapiens.*
40,000	Painting and carving. *Homo sapiens sapiens*; widespread.
33,000	Neanderthals die out.

13,000	Making clay pottery.
11,000	Becoming farmers.
10,000	Farming begins; many tools are used.
7,000	First copper tools.
5,000	First bronze tools.
3,500	First iron tools.

➡ *Prehistoric flint mines were the best places for finding flint to make stone tools. Stone Age miners burrowed into the ground to gather the flint.*

⬆ *Hunters used fire to frighten mammoths, driving them into a pit-trap, then killing them with wooden spears tipped with stone points.*

How did people hunt mammoths?

Prehistoric people worked together to hunt animals as big as mammoths, huge relatives of the modern elephant. Groups of hunters drove the mammoths towards boggy ground, cliffs or into pits dug by the hunters, making it easier for the hunters to kill them. A mammoth provided not only meat, but also fat, skin, ivory and bones. The skins were used as clothing to keep people warm. The ivory and bones were used to make tools and framework for huts. Other animals, such as reindeer, were also hunted for their hides, bones and antlers.

What are barrows?

Barrows are ancient burial places, usually an underground chamber made of wood or stone, covered with soil and turf. The word 'barrow' comes from an old English word meaning mound or hill. Other names you might see on a map are 'tumulus', 'tump' or 'how' – these are barrows too. There are as many as 40,000 barrows in England. Most barrows are sausage-shaped, with one end higher than the other, and date from Stone Age times. The largest are over 100 m long. Later Bronze Age and Iron Age barrows were often round or cone-shaped. Barrows were made by people who believed that the dead would need their possessions with them in an afterlife. At Sutton Hoo in Suffolk, England, a king of East Anglia was buried in a wooden ship beneath a barrow mound in AD 600s. This barrow was excavated by archaeologists in 1939.

⬇ *Inside a barrow was a chamber in which the body of the dead person was placed, along with some of his belongings, such as weapons, clothing and jewellery.*

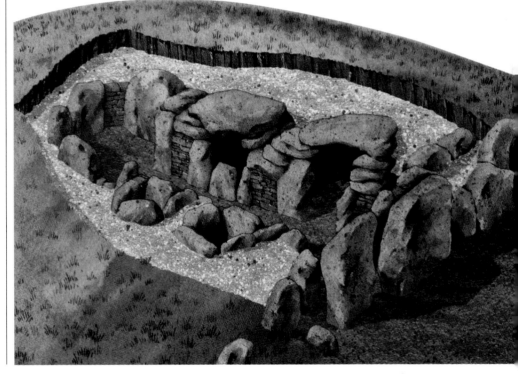

⬇ *Discoveries of bones have enabled scientists to name the stages of human evolution, from* Homo habilis *to* Homo sapiens, *with smaller evolutionary changes in between each stage.*

⬅ Homo habilis *means handy man. This era of humankind was so named because of the ability to wield tools at this time.*

Homo habilis   Homo erectus   Neanderthal man   Homo sapiens

Otzi the Iceman – murder victim?

In 1991, a frozen corpse was found in the mountains between Austria and Italy. Investigating scientists discovered that the corpse, named 'Otzi the Iceman', died some 5,300 years ago. He was between 25 and 40 years old, and it is believed that he was warmly dressed in animal skins padded with grass. He carried a bow and arrows, a copper axe, a backpack, a bag of charcoal, flints and dried fungus (to light a fire). He may have died of cold or exhaustion, but an arrow wound suggests he might have been the victim of a murder.

Once people started to farm and live in villages, the population in certain areas began to grow. Villages grew into towns, and towns into cities. Leaders of hunting bands became chiefs of villages and towns; the strongest chiefs became kings, ruling not just their own towns but also other settlements. These rulers created the world's first empires.

Who made the first laws?

The world's first law-making king was Hammurabi, sixth ruler of Babylon, who lived about 3,500 years ago. He drew up a set of laws to govern his citizens – for example regulating trade and taxes. Hammurabi's laws were introduced to protect the weak from being oppressed by the strong. The rulers of later empires, such as Assyria, followed his example.

Ashurbanipal was king of Assyria from 668 to 627 BC. He was a cruel soldier, but a lover of the arts, who built a grand palace at Nineveh.

Who used chariots?

Chariots were used by the first armies. A chariot was a wheeled vehicle, pulled by one or two horses. It was made of wood, with two big wheels, and was very fast. The Egyptians and the Hittites from Anatolia (present-day Turkey) fought one another on chariots. Chariots were also used by nobles for dashing around the countryside and hunting wild animals, such as antelope.

Where was Babylon?

Babylon was a great city between the rivers Tigris and Euphrates, in what is now Iraq. Civilization developed close to rivers, in fertile regions where farmers could trade with their neighbours. Two of the greatest kings of Babylon were the

Egyptian war chariots were drawn by a pair of horses. One man drove the chariot, the other fired a bow and arrow or hurled spears at the enemy.

Nebuchadnezzar II added new buildings to Babylon, including the Ishtar Gate, decorated with blue tiles and named in honour of the goddess Ishtar.

law-maker Hammurabi and the conqueror Nebuchadnezzar II, who built the Hanging Gardens of Babylon (see panel below) as a present for his wife, Amytis, to remind her of her mountain homeland. The gardens became one of the Seven Wonders of the World.

Wonders of the ancient world

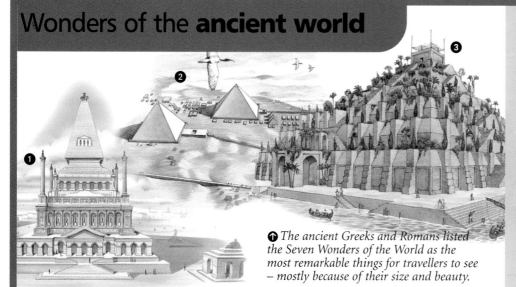

The ancient Greeks and Romans listed the Seven Wonders of the World as the most remarkable things for travellers to see – mostly because of their size and beauty.

The Seven Wonders of the World

❶ The Tomb of King Mausolus – at Halicarnassus.
❷ The Pyramids at Giza – in Egypt.
❸ The Hanging Gardens of Babylon.
❹ The Lighthouse – at Alexandria.
❺ The Statue of Zeus – at Olympia.
❻ The Colossus – at Rhodes.
❼ The Temple of Artemis – at Ephesus.

What were the first towns like?

The first towns were walled, and the houses were built of mud-brick. Two of the oldest towns we know about, because they were uncovered by archaeologists, are Jericho in Israel and Çatal Hüyük in southern Turkey. People lived in these towns over 10,000 years ago. All that remains of the towns now are ruins, but archaeologists have found pottery, textiles and fragments of walls, both plastered and painted.

Who made the first writing?

The earliest form of writing, dating from about 3,500 BC, comes from a region of Iraq, which in ancient times was called Sumeria. The Sumerians founded cities, such as Eridu, Uruk and Ur, all over Mesopotamia. They wrote on clay tablets with pointed tools, at first making picture-signs but then writing in symbols that represented sounds (see page 234).

◑ Sumerian writing tools made wedge-shaped marks. The writing is called cuneiform, from the Greek word meaning 'wedge'.

◐ The houses in Çatal Hüyük had no outside-facing doorways. People entered through holes in the roof – this security system kept out unwanted enemies.

Great **empires and rulers**

Egypt 3100 BC – united under King Menes (also known as Narmer).
Sumer (Mesopotamia) 4000–2000 BC – greatest ruler Sargon of Akkad.
Indus River Valley (Indian subcontinent) 2500–1500 BC – no rulers known.
Babylon 1800–500 BC – great kings Hammurabi and Nebuchadnezzar II.
China Shang kings from 1766 BC – first emperor Shih Huangdi 221 BC.
Ur (Mesopotamia) 2100 BC – at its strongest under King Ur-Nammu.
Minoan Crete 2000–1100 BC – named after legendary king Minos.
Mycenean (Greece and Turkey) 1600–1100 BC – greatest ruler Agamemnon.
Assyrian Empire about 800 BC – at its peak under the reign of the last great king Ashurbanipal in the 600s.
Persian Empire 521–486 BC – At its biggest under the Darius reign.

The ancient Egyptians lived beside the River Nile in Africa. In about 3100 BC, a king called Menes united two kingdoms, Upper and Lower Egypt, and established the first royal dynasty (ruling family). Later kings of Egypt were worshipped as gods. The Egyptians were great architects and artists, and developed an amazing system of picture-writing, known as hieroglyphics. Their empire lasted for almost 3,000 years.

⊕ *The gold funeral mask of Tutankhamun was one of the treasures found in his tomb, unseen for more than 3,000 years.*

Who was Tutankhamun?

Tutankhamun, pharaoh of Egypt, was only 18 when he died in 1351 BC. Later Egyptian kings were called pharaohs. His tomb, in the Valley of the Kings (not inside a pyramid) contained the most amazing treasures (because unlike other tombs it had not been robbed by thieves). Tutankhamun's tomb was opened by an archaeological team led by Howard Carter in 1922.

Why did the Egyptians build pyramids?

Pyramids were tombs built to guard the bodies of dead kings, along with their treasures. The first pyramid was built as a tomb for King Djoser of Egypt in the 2500s BC. This 'Step Pyramid', about 60 m high, was designed by Imhotep, the king's physician. Larger pyramids were built for later kings and some 80 pyramids still stand.

Royal burial chamber

Passages sealed after burial

Smooth facing stones

Entrance

Workers' escape passages

Mortuary temple

Life in **ancient Egypt**

The Egyptian soldier
Egyptian foot soldiers had to be very fit because they walked everywhere. Supplies were carried by donkeys. The soldiers fought with swords first made of copper, then bronze, and later (after about 1000 BC) iron. They also had daggers and wooden spears with metal points. Other favourite Egyptian weapons were clubs, axes, and bows and arrows. Many Egyptian boys learned to shoot bows while hunting ducks in the Nile marshes.

⊕ *An Egyptian soldier carried a long spear and shield.*

Key **dates**

before 5000 BC	First farm villages beside the Nile.
about 3000 BC	King Menes unites Upper and Lower Egypt.
2575–2130 BC	Old Kingdom – Great Pyramids.
1938–1600 BC	Middle Kingdom – wars with Nubians in south.
1539–1075 BC	New Kingdom – Egypt at its most powerful. Wars with Hittites and Sea Peoples. Ruled by Ramses II.
from 600 BC	Foreign rule – Egypt conquered by Persians, Greeks and Romans. Ruled by Queen Cleopatra.

What gods did the Egyptians worship?

The Egyptians had many gods. People worshipped local gods in their own city or region. The greatest local god was Amun, god of the air, who was later identified with the Sun god Ra or Re. Other gods included the cat-headed Bast, Thoth, god of learning, Osiris, god of farming and civilized life, Isis, the mother-goddess, her son Horus, god of heaven, and Anubis, god of the dead.

The Nile was Egypt's lifeline, a green strip of civilization next to desert on either bank. People used reed boats to sail up and down the busy river.

Two of the three Great Pyramids at Giza are over 130 m high. These amazing feats of engineering were built in the 2600s BC, by thousands of slaves hauling blocks of stone.

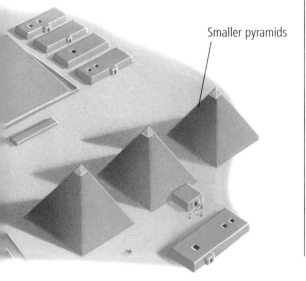

Smaller pyramids

Why was the Nile so important to the Egyptians?

The Nile is the longest river in Africa, and its waters made farming possible for the people of hot, dry Egypt. Every year the Nile floods, as snow melts in mountains to the south, raising the level of the water. As it floods, the river spreads fertile mud over the land, which enabled Egypt's farmers to grow plentiful crops. They dug irrigation ditches to carry the Nile water to their fields. The Egyptians also used some of the world's earliest boats, called 'feluccas' to sail up and down the Nile to travel between neighbouring farms and towns.

Ramses II was a great warrior-king, whose soldiers fought to defend and enlarge Egypt's empire.

Who was the greatest warrior-king of Egypt?

Ramses II who reigned 1289–24 BC. Ramses led the Egyptian army into battle against the warmongering Hittite people, and in 1275, fought a great battle with them at Kadesh for control of Syria. Ramses built a huge temple at Abu Simbel beside the Nile. Outside this rock temple were huge statues of the great king. His temple was moved in the 1960s when the Aswan Dam flooded its original site.

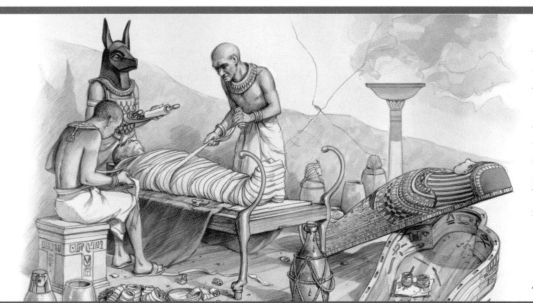

Making mummies

The word 'mummy' comes from the Persian word for 'tar', because the Persians wrongly thought the Egyptians preserved dead bodies in tar. In fact, the process took over a month and involved removing all the vital organs, except the heart, and drying the body in chemicals. The body was then stuffed with spices and linen, and wrapped in more linen. The aim was to preserve the body so that the spiritual parts of a person (known as ka and ba) would survive after death.

The priest in charge of the mummification wore a jackal mask to represent Anubis, god of the dead.

Civilizations, with towns, agriculture, laws and flourishing trade, developed in several parts of the world at roughly the same time. As well as the great cities of Egypt and Mesopotamia, other civilizations arose in the Indian subcontinent and in China. Like the earlier ones, these civilizations were first developed alongside rivers.

When did the Indus civilization flourish?

Between 2500 and 1500 BC. It emerged along the Indus River in what is now Pakistan. The Indus Valley civilization was larger than Sumer or ancient Egypt. Why this prosperous civilization came to an end is a mystery, but floods and foreign invaders may have helped bring about its downfall.

↑ The peoples of the Indus Valley lived as farmers and traders. Their two great cities were Harappa and Mohenjo-Daro.

↓ The houses in Mohenjo-Daro were built around a central courtyard. The walls were made using mud-bricks that had been baked in a kiln. The houses all had a flat roof. The streets were straight and crossings were at a right angle, creating a grid system similar to that found in many modern cities.

Where was Mohenjo-Daro?

This was one of the two great cities in the ancient Indus Valley. The name Mohenjo-Daro means 'Mound of the Dead'. The city was set out in a neat grid pattern with 40,000 people living in houses of mud-brick with bathrooms linked to the city drains, and a large bathhouse – which may have been used for public bathing during religious ceremonies. The other major city of the Indus region was Harappa.

Inventive **Chinese**

❶ The Chinese were very talented at devising water wheels turned by falling water and linked by other wheels and shafts to machinery.

↑ The 'Heaven-Rumbling Thunderclap Fierce Fire Erupter' was a gunpowder-fired device that shot out shells of poisonous gas.

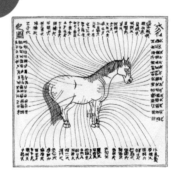

↑ Acupuncture is a treatment still used in medicine today. It involves sticking needles into special points – as indicated on this diagram – on the bodies of people or animals.

❶ The first earthquake detector worked using a metal ball, which fell from the dragon's mouth at the top of the jar, into the toad's mouth – when even a distant quake occurred.

⬆ *The Great Wall was built mainly during the Qin dynasty (221–206 BC). Its total length was more than 2,400 km.*

What are Chinese junks?

Chinese sailing ships, which had sails made of woven matting, which looked like 'venetian' window blinds and were simple to operate. Some junks had five or more masts and were bigger than any western ships. For steering, Chinese sailors used the stern rudder – long before it was known in Europe. Chinese ships sailed as far as Arabia, East Africa and Indonesia, and it is likely that Chinese explorers investigated the north coast of Australia. Such voyages increased trade and made the emperor feel more powerful, but the Chinese did not set up permanent trading posts in foreign countries, as European explorers did from the late 1400s. Fleets of junks were used by pirates to ambush merchant ships in the South China Sea and the Indian Ocean.

When did people first work with iron?

About 1500 BC, when the Hittites of the Near East began smelting iron ore (heating iron-bearing rock to extract the metal). People only had stone tools until around 7000 BC, when the Hittite people in Anatolia (present-day Turkey) started using copper. Later, people invented bronze (an alloy or mixture of copper and tin), but iron was harder, sharper and long-lasting.

➡ *The Zhou rulers, who ousted the last Shang king in 1122 BC, introduced iron tools and weapons to China.*

Why was the Great Wall of China built?

To protect the Chinese empire from foreign invaders. China had built a great civilization, beginning with the Shang rulers (about 1500–1027 BC). The first ruler to control all China was the emperor Shih Huang-di (221 BC). His greatest project was the Great Wall – not only did it keep out barbarians from the steppes of Central Asia. it also kept in the Chinese people.

⬇ *Chinese pirates such as Ching-Chi-Ling and Shap-'ng-tsai sailed in a fleet of junks. The South China Sea was perfect for pirates with its many small islands, swamps and narrow channels, in which ships could hide.*

⬇ *The Chinese invented mechanical clocks, such as this one – the 'Cosmic Engine' – built at Khaifeng in AD 1090.*

Important **inventions**

The Chinese produced an amazing array of inventions in science and technology.

Abacus – For doing sums.
Acupuncture – System of medical treatment.
Flame-throwers and gunpowder rockets – Weapons for use in war.
Horse harness – Breast strap that did not choke a horse when pulling a cart.
Magnetic compass – Using a naturally magnetic stone called a lodestone.
Paddleboat – For water travel.

Paper – Invented in AD 105, and kept from the rest of the world for centuries. The Chinese were also the first to print on paper.
Seismograph – For detecting the direction of earthquakes.
Stern rudder – For steering ships.
Umbrella – For use as a sunshade as well as for keeping off water.
Watertight compartments – In ships.
Waterwheels – For driving machinery.
Wheelbarrow – Some even had sails.

Greek civilization grew out of the earlier cultures of Minoan Cretians and the Myceneans – a race of people who lived in what became Greece. By about 800 BC, the ideas of Greek scholars started to spread throughout the ancient world. Ancient Greece was divided into small, self-governing city-states – the most powerful of which were Athens and Sparta.

What was the Trojan War?

The Trojan War was a ten-year war and the story is told by Greek poet Homer in his poem, the *Iliad*. Mainland Greece was dominated by warriors called the Mycenaeans from 1600–1100 BC. Homer's poem tells how the Myceneans destroyed Troy, a fortress-city in the region known as Asia Minor, about 1,200 years ago. The Greek army tricked their way into Troy, pretending to give up the siege and head home. Instead they hid soldiers inside a wooden horse, which the Trojans then took into their city. The Greeks clambered out at night and opened the gates to their army, winning the war.

↓ *Greek hoplites (foot soldiers) wore crested helmets and carried a long spear.*

Who were the greatest Greek philosophers?

Socrates, Plato and Aristotle – their ideas have influenced people over the last 2,400 years. First came Socrates (470–399 BC), who taught the importance of truth and virtue – he was forced to kill himself by his enemies. His friend and pupil Plato (427–347 BC), founded a school, the Academy in Athens. Aristotle (384–322 BC) was a student at the Academy and later also started a school, the Lyceum in Athens.

← *Aristotle came from northern Greece. He wrote about science, politics, art and religion.*

Why was Alexander so Great?

Alexander conquered a vast empire and became ruler of Macedonia, in northern Greece, in 336 BC. He founded cities such as Alexandria in Egypt. Alexander had ferocious energy: after defeating the Persians he set out to conquer India. He would have gone on marching across India had his exhausted soldiers not begged him to turn back. Alexander died in 323 BC, aged 32.

← *Alexander the Great on his favourite horse, Bucephalus. He led his soldiers from Greece to India, and created a vast empire in just nine years.*

The glorious Greeks

The ancient Greeks

While some ancient Greeks were scholars, writers, thinkers and scientists, most Greeks were farmers, fishermen or slaves. Greek colonists settled all around the Mediterranean lands and Greek philosophy, religion, art and science formed the bedrock of western culture.

→ *Greeks were excellent doctors, studying the human body closely to see how it worked. In the Roman world, almost all the best doctors were Greek.*

The Greeks loved going to the theatre. Plays were staged in open-air amphitheatres – bowl-shaped arenas located on hillsides.

→ *Plays were either comedies or tragedies, the two were never mixed. The actors wore masks to help the audience identify their characters.*

The sculpture of Athena was more than 12 m tall and made of gold and ivory

When was Crete the centre of a civilization?

Between about 3000 and 1100 BC. This period of Greek civilization is known as Minoan, after a legendary Cretian king named Minos. The remains of the royal Palace of Knossos in Crete show what a rich culture once existed there, until destroyed (perhaps by an earthquake) in the 1400s BC. The palace was rediscovered in 1899 by British archaeologist Arthur Evans in 1899.

↺ According to legend, the Greeks had to send seven girls and seven boys to Crete as sacrifices to a bull-headed monster called the Minotaur.

↑ The Parthenon was badly damaged in 1687 when in Turkish hands. The temple was once decorated with painted figures and friezes. Made from beautiful white marble, it is one of the best examples of Greek architecture.

What was the Parthenon?

The Parthenon was the most splendid temple in Athens, which was the leading city-state in ancient Greece. During the 400s BC, the Athenians built temples and shrines to the gods on a hill called the Acropolis. The Parthenon was more than 70 m long and about 18 m high, and was built to house a magnificient statue of Athena, goddess of wisdom and guardian of Athens.

Greek pottery and artists

Greek art was at its finest during the 'Classical' period, about 400 BC. The Greek artists loved to show human bodies naturally, in statues and in pictures on pottery. Everyday pots were used for storing oil, wine and foods, but the finest pots were precious ornaments.

↺ Pots were made in two main styles, with figures painted in red or black. They were often decorated with scenes from Greek mythology and history.

Key **dates**

500s BC	Greeks invent democracy.
490–431 BC	Greeks defeat Persians.
460–429 BC	Golden age of Athens under Pericles.
438 BC	Parthenon temple in Athens completed.
336 BC	Alexander becomes ruler of Macedonia.

↺ Coins were first used by the Lydians (who lived in what is now Turkey) some time before 600 BC. The Greeks quickly adopted the use of coins for shopping and business. This one shows the head of Alexander.

The Roman Empire was the greatest the world had so far seen. By the first century AD, Roman rule extended over much of Europe, North Africa and the Near East. The Romans took their way of life and government wherever they went. They used their skills of developing central heating and running water and introduced their food and their language (Latin) to each country they conquered.

How did the Romans come to power?

The Romans were originally farmers from central Italy who rose to power by fighting their neighbours. They developed the city of Rome, erecting grand buildings and temples and eventually ruling all Italy. After conquering Greece, the Romans adopted many Greek customs and gods. Originally a republic, Rome became an empire in 27 BC, under the rule of Augustus.

⬆ *Coin of the first Christian emperor of Rome – Constantine the Great (AD 275–337).*

When was Rome founded?

According to legend, Rome was founded by Romulus and Remus in 753 BC. The Romans enjoyed the story, but actually Rome grew up from a cluster of tribal villages on seven hills beside the River Tiber. It was first ruled by kings, but became a republic in 509 BC when the last king of Rome was driven out. Roman society was divided into citizens and non-citizens, or slaves, who did all the heaviest work.

⬅ *Slaves might have been servants, miners, farmworkers, artists or even teachers.*

Why was the Roman army so powerful?

The Roman army was well trained and better disciplined than the enemies it faced. The best Roman units were the legions of about 5,000 foot-soldiers, who went into battle throwing spears and then rushed in behind their shields using short, stabbing swords. Roman soldiers were trained to march all day, build roads and forts, and swim rivers. Roman officers were usually politicians.

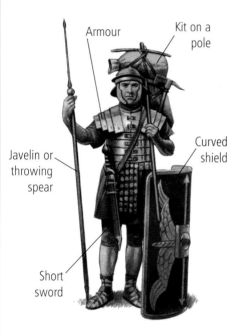

Armour · Kit on a pole · Curved shield · Javelin or throwing spear · Short sword

⬆ *A Roman soldier would march holding his javelin, sword and shield. His kit, tools and rations were tied to a pole over his shoulder.*

Rome wasn't built **in a day**

Key **dates**

c. 753 BC	Rome is founded.
509 BC	King Tarquin is driven out and Rome becomes a republic.
200s BC	Romans defeat Carthage (a rival state in North Africa).
146 BC	Romans take control of Greece, and adopt the Greek faith for their own.
49 BC	Julius Caesar rules as dictator in Rome.
27 BC	End of Roman Republic and start of Roman Empire.
AD 98–117	Roman Empire at its greatest under Emperor Trajan.
AD 286	Roman Empire divided into Eastern and Western empires.
AD 476	End of Western empire. Eastern empire continues as Byzantium.

⬆ *At its greatest, the Roman Empire ran from Britain in the west, as far as Africa in the south and Babylon in the east. The black lines on this diagram show the roads that the Romans built.*

What was a villa?

The Roman villa was a country house of a farm-estate, which produced grain, wine, meat, fruit and vegetables for the local people. Some villas were grand houses, with painted walls, baths and underfloor hot-air central heating. Rich Romans built themselves country and seaside villas as holiday homes.

⬆ *A Roman villa was a working farm. The family lived in the main house. The farm workers lived in smaller buildings on the farm.*

➔ *Soldiers did the digging and stone-laying. Most Roman roads were straight, paved with stones and cambered (sloped) so that rainwater drained off.*

⬆ *Gladiators would fight in an arena filled with thousands of spectators. The netman would try to entangle his opponent in the net.*

What was a netman?

A Roman gladiator, trained to fight in the arena. Roman rulers staged lavish and often bloodthirsty entertainments to keep the people amused. Gladiators fought one another or wild animals. There were various types of gladiator – the netman wore hardly any armour, and his weapons were a net and a trident (three-pointed spear).

Why did the Romans build roads?

Roman roads were built by the army to make sure that troops on foot and supplies in wagons pulled by oxen and horses could be moved quickly around the Empire. The Romans were excellent engineers and surveyed the route for a new road with great care, ensuring that the roads they built linked all parts of their vast empire to Rome. They also developed concrete, which was used in road building. Roman roads were built to last and many can still be seen today.

➔ *Wealthy Romans liked to feast. Often at banquets people would purposely make themselves sick, just so they could eat more!*

Caligula the crazy

The Roman emperor Caligula spent the family fortune in a year, banished or murdered almost all his relatives, and executed anyone he disliked. He even tried to make his favourite horse a consul (an important official).

➔ *When Caligula declared himself a god in AD 41, the army had him murdered.*

Most famous Romans

Julius Caesar (c. 100–44 BC) – General, almost became king but was murdered.

Augustus (63 BC–AD 14) – Winner of civil wars, first emperor, had a month named after him.

Mark Antony (c. 83–30 BC) – Soldier, fell in love with Cleopatra, Queen of Egypt.

Hadrian (AD 76–138) – Soldier and emperor, famous for his wall in north Britain.

Nero (AD 37–68) – During his reign the city of Rome burnt down.

The prehistory of Britain began when the British Isles were joined to the rest of Europe by land, and when the climate was very different. In warm spells, much of southern Britain enjoyed a near-tropical climate. Most of the land was covered by snow and ice during the Ice Age. As people arrived in waves, they settled and began altering the wild landscape.

⊙ *The first people to settle in the British Isles lived by hunting and fishing, and by gathering wild plants and fruits. They made tools from stone and bone.*

Who were the first Britons?

The first people to live in Britain were *Homo erectus* people, an early type of human, who reached Britain by walking across what is now the English Channel. After the Ice Age, a 'bridge' of dry land linked Britain to mainland Europe. People started to settle in Britain about 500,000 years ago. The first 'modern' people arrived about 30,000 years ago.

When was Stonehenge built?

Stonehenge, a group of ancient stones in Wiltshire, England, was built in three stages, beginning about 3100 BC. Some of the stones, called bluestones, were brought from Wales, a distance of 385 km. The last stages were completed about 1300 BC.

Stonehenge was almost certainly built for ceremonial reasons, where religious rituals could be held. People also used the circle of stones to help them fix dates by studying the Sun and stars.

⊙ *Building Stonehenge, using muscle power alone, was an immense undertaking. The stones form England's most famous ancient monument.*

Ancient, ancient Britain

⊙ *Smiths melted tin and copper to make bronze. The molten metal was poured into moulds to make items such as knives, swords and mirrors.*

Key dates

years ago

500,000	First people settle in Britain.
230,000	Neanderthal people in Britain. People make flint tools and weapons.
30,000	First modern humans reach Britain from mainland Europe.
15,000	Ice sheets cover much of Britain during the Ice Age.
6500 BC	Sea level rises, cutting off Britain from mainland Europe.

5000 BC	Hunters mark out tribal territories.
4000 BC	Farming people reach Britain in boats from Europe.
3100 BC	First stage of Stonehenge work.
2500 BC	'Beaker People' skilled in metalworking arrive from Europe.
750 BC	Iron Age begins in Britain.
500 BC	Celts begin settling in Britain.
55 BC	Julius Caesar makes first Roman expedition to Britain.
AD 43	Romans begin their invasion and conquest of Britain.

Round-houses were home to the Celts living in Bronze Age Britain. The Celts kept their cattle and sheep in pens beside the house. The biggest round-houses were up to 12 m high and 13 m wide, large enough for several families to occupy.

What was a Celtic home like?

The Celts were farmers and their homes were round-houses, as big as 10 m across, with room for several families. The roof was made of timber, covered with thatch. The walls were made of woven branches (wattle) plastered with mud and animal dung. On a central hearth burnt a fire over which people cooked food in large iron pots. It was dark and smoky inside because there were no windows and no chimney to let out smoke from the fire.

Why did ancient Britons build hillforts?

People built hilltop forts, with massive earth ramparts and wooden palisades to make it harder for enemies, such as the Celts, to attack. The Celts were people who moved across Europe westward, and reached Britain around 500 BC. They were warlike and quarrelsome, and often fought one another. However, hilltop forts were insufficient to protect people from the invading Romans in AD 43.

Maiden Castle in Dorset was a hillfort stronghold of the Celtic Britons, built during the Iron Age. It fell to the Roman army, but remains an impressive sight 2,000 years on.

How did the Celts go to war?

The Celts wore very little armour when they went to war. Some men even fought naked. Most Celtic warriors were taller than many Europeans, which helped intimidate the enemy. They dashed into battle in chariots, dismounting to fight. Warriors shouted and blew horns and trumpets as they went into battle. Afterwards, the survivors would boast of their bravery in songs and poems.

A Celtic warrior, with spiky hair and colourful trousers, armed with sword and shield was a fearsome enemy to go into battle against.

Amazing **facts**

- Most of ancient Britain was covered with thick forest. People cut down trees to use the wood for fuel and building. Most of the ancient woodland was destroyed.

- As many as 50 people could be buried in one Stone Age tomb, called a barrow.

- A henge was a circle of posts, made from stone or wood.

- The Celts took pride in their appearance. They had tattoos, spiky hair and enjoyed wearing jewellery.

Polished metal mirrors, such as this bronze one were used before glass became widely available. Celts favoured this swirling style of decoration.

Metal bracelets and neck ornaments, called torcs, were worn by both men and women.

The people of ancient Britain made pots from clay, incised (cut into) with decorative patterns.

The Romans brought peace and prosperity to Britain. However, Britain was always on the fringe of the Roman Empire, and when the Romans withdrew their troops to help defend Rome itself, Britain was defenceless against attacks from across the sea. Waves of new invaders, such as Saxons and Vikings, arrived and over the years settled to become the English.

➜ *When the Roman army withdrew, many Saxons landed in Britain, seeking land to farm as well as plunder, because their own lands had become overcrowded.*

Which queen fought the Romans?

Boudicca (sometimes called Boadicea), who was queen of a tribe called the Iceni. She and her people lived in what is now East Anglia. When the Romans invaded Britain in AD 43, they quickly conquered the south of the country. In AD 60–61, however, the Iceni rose in revolt against the Romans. The Iceni destroyed London, Colchester and St. Albans, but then were defeated by the Romans. More than 80,000 Britons were killed. Rather than be captured and taken to Rome, Boudicca killed herself.

⬇ *Boudicca led a revolt following ill-treatment by Roman officials.*

What were the forts of the Saxon Shore?

The 'forts of the Saxon Shore' were built to guard the southern coast of Britain and keep out invaders. Until the early 400s when the Roman empire started to crumble, the Romans ruled Britain as far north as Hadrian's Wall. When Britain was raided by Saxons and other Germanic peoples, from mostly Denmark and northern Germany, the forts were not enough to keep out the invaders. By AD 410, the Roman army had left the Britons to defend themselves.

Early British **History**

The legend of King Arthur
When the Saxons and other invaders moved into Roman Britain, a British leader fought back. He became known in legend as King Arthur. Nothing is known of him for certain; all we have are stories about him. He may have led the Britons in a battle at a place called Mount Badon. The legends tell of a noble king, possessor of a magical sword Excalibur, who lived in a palace called Camelot, and gathered around him a group of knights – the Knights of the Round Table. As well as fighting evil enemies, the knights pursue the quest for the Holy Grail, the cup used by Christ at the Last Supper.

⬇ *Vikings founded settlements in northern and eastern England, and in Ireland.*

◀ *The dying King Arthur ordered his sword to be thrown into the lake – and from the water, a mysterious hand caught it.*

How did Christianity reach Britain?

The Romans brought Christianity to Britain. Celtic monks founded monasteries and took Christianity to Scotland and northern England. When Roman rule collapsed, Christian Britons in the south fled to escape the pagan (those who believed in many gods) Saxons. In AD 597, the Pope in Rome sent Augustine to teach the Saxons (the 'English') about Christianity. Augustine converted King Ethelbert of Kent, and founded a church at Canterbury.

⬆ *This mosaic of Jesus from a Roman villa in Dorset was made in the AD 300s. It shows that the people who lived there were Christians.*

Where was the Battle of Clontarf?

This was a battle fought in Ireland in 1014, between the Irish high king Brian Boru and the Vikings. Viking raiders had made Dublin one of their key bases in the British Isles. In the battle, the Irish king was killed but his army won and ended Viking power in Ireland.

Which English king led the fight against the Vikings?

Alfred, king of Wessex. Viking attacks on England began in AD 789 and by the AD 870s the raiders from Scandinavia controlled much of eastern England. Alfred won a victory at Edington in Wiltshire in AD 878, after which the Vikings made peace and agreed to stay within an area that became known as the Danelaw. Alfred was a wise ruler, and well deserved his title: Alfred the Great.

⬆ *The Vikings were explorers and traders, as well as fighters and looters. They travelled in 25-m longships, which held up to 60 men.*

Why were the Vikings so feared?

The Vikings were fierce fighters who arrived suddenly from the sea to raid towns and monasteries. They stole valuables but burnt books, for which they had no use. These bold sailors crossed the North Sea from Scandinavia to raid Britain, landing on beaches or rowing up rivers in their longships. Later, armies of Vikings ravaged the country. However, not all Vikings were bloodthirsty looters. Many brought their families to settle on farmland, or trade in towns such as Dublin and Jorvik (York).

◀ *Irish and Viking warriors fought hand to hand at Clontarf.*

Characters in the legend include...

Guinevere	Arthur's queen
Merlin	A wizard and Arthur's counsellor
Lancelot of the Lake	The bravest of Arthur's knights
Sir Galahad	The 'perfect knight'
Sir Perceval	Knight who seeks the Holy Grail
Sir Mordred	Evil enemy of Arthur
Morgan le Fay	Arthur's half-sister
Uther Pendragon	Arthur's father
Ygerna	Arthur's mother

Key dates

407–410	Last Roman troops leave Britain. Saxons move in.
476	End of the Western Roman Empire.
503	Possible date of King Arthur's victory at Mount Badon.
582	Kingdom of Mercia founded in England.
597	Augustine arrives to preach Christianity to the English.
613	Northumbrians defeat Welsh Britons at Chester.
787	Vikings first land in England.
796	Death of Offa, great king of Mercia.
871	Alfred the Great becomes king of Wessex.
901	Edward the Elder recognized as King of all the English.
937	Athelstan is king of all Britain.
1016	Canute becomes king of England; he also rules Denmark and Norway.

The Middle Ages are the years between the ancient world (which ends with the collapse of the Roman Empire in the AD 400s) and the start of the modern world (roughly 1500). The early centuries of the millennium were years of war and conquest across much of Europe and Asia. Only the strong countries felt safe.

⬆ *The name of Mongol leader Genghis Khan (c. 1162–1227) struck terror into those who feared his army might sweep down on them.*

Who was Genghis Khan?

Of all the conquerors in history, few were more feared than 13th-century Mongol leader Genghis Khan, whose name means 'lord of all'. His horsemen conquered a vast empire stretching across Asia from China as far west as the Danube river in Europe. He destroyed cities and massacred thousands, yet under his rule trade prospered and all beliefs were tolerated.

What were the Crusades?

Wars for control of Jerusalem in the Holy Land, sacred to followers of three religions: Jews, Christians and Muslims. When the Turks prevented Christian pilgrims from visiting Jerusalem, the Pope called the First Crusade in 1096. Kings, soldiers, even children from all over Europe went on Crusade. There were eight Crusades in all, but the Crusaders failed to regain control of the Holy Land.

➡ *Muslim and Christian soldiers fought in the Holy Land. It was not all fighting – each side learned more about the other's way of life.*

What was feudalism?

Feudalism was a social system based on land. The king owned most of the land, though the Church was also powerful. The king let out some land (called a fief) to a lord or baron, in return for soldiers when he needed them. The barons in turn let out land to lesser lords called knights – again in exchange for service. Peasants and serfs (poor people) only lived on the land in return for the work they did for their lord.

Medieval **mayhem**

Key **dates**

1001–02	Viking Leif Ericsson sails to North America.
1066	Normans conquer England.
1096	First Crusade.
1206	Mongol chief, Temujin, is proclaimed Genghis Khan.
1249	Britain's first university at Oxford opens.
1265	First real parliament (De Montfort's) in England.
1270	Last Crusade.
1271	Marco Polo of Italy visits China.
1300s	First use of gunpowder and cannon in war.
1338	Hundred Years War between England and France begins (ends in 1453).
1368	Ming Dynasty begins in China.
1348	Black Death reaches England; Europe is hit with the disease.

➊ *The Bayeux Tapestry tells the story of the Norman Conquest of England in woven pictures. This section shows Norman knights on horseback and English foot-soldiers around the fatally wounded King Harold, struck in the eye by an arrow.*

↑ *Medieval peasants prepared the land for the next crop. In return for their work, they were protected by their lord.*

Why did the Normans invade England?

Duke William of Normandy led his army to England in 1066 after King Edward the Confessor died, believing that Edward had promised him the throne. The English, however, had chosen Harold Godwinson, a soldier, to be their king. The two rivals met in battle near Hastings in 1066. William won, and so became king: 'William the Conqueror'. The Normans, who spoke French, took over lands held by English nobles, and built stone castles to defend their conquest and prevent any rebellions.

↓ *Norman soldiers landed at Pevensey in Sussex in 1066. Knights on horseback played a key part in the Battle of Hastings.*

Who signed Magna Carta?

England's King John. Magna Carta (the Great Charter) was a list of rights requested by angry barons, who felt that John was ruling badly. In 1215, they forced the king to put his seal to (sign) the Charter and promise to obey the rules within. Ever since, Magna Carta has been seen as a landmark in the development of modern government.

← *King John signed Magna Carta at Runnymede, beside the River Thames.*

↑ *Domesday Book was a survey of land-holding in England, drawn up in 1086 on the orders of William the Conqueror. No other record like it exists.*

Amazing **facts**

Mongol feats...

Genghis Khan led an army of 250,000 men and more than one million horses.

Heavy catapults for sieges were carried in sections on ox carts and put together.

Mongol soldiers lived on a diet of smoked sheepmeat and dried milk.

Soldiers were armed with bows, swords, axes and lances (long spears) with hooks for unseating enemy riders.

...and Norman knights

The 75-m long Bayeux Tapestry was probably made in England, not in France.

The Normans were descendants of Vikings who had settled in northern France.

Harold fought two battles in three weeks in 1066. He defeated a Norwegian army at Stamford Bridge, Yorkshire, on 25 September. Then on 14 October, Harold was defeated and killed by the invading Normans at Hastings.

The Norman knights charged into battle on horseback with long lances. The English fought on foot, with weapons such as axes.

People first reached North America 15,000–20,000 years ago, crossing a land bridge from Asia and travelling on foot and by boat. They gradually spread across the continent. The great civilizations of the Americas were in Central America (around Mexico) and in South America (in Peru), where people built large cities. Much of this culture was destroyed by Europeans in the 1500s.

⬆ *The people of Ancient Mexico built temples like this one at Teotihuacan, a city at its height in about AD 500, when about 200,000 people lived there.*

Who built pyramids in America?

Ancient peoples of Central America, such as the people of Teotihuacan and the Maya. The Maya were at their most powerful from about AD 200 to 900. They built cities such as Tikal (Guatemala) and huge pyramid-temples. A Maya city contained a tall pyramid-shaped temple in the centre, with special courts surrounding the temple, including ball courts for games. The Maya studied the Moon, Sun and stars, invented the first writing in America, and had a number system based on 20.

➡ *Machu Picchu was the Incas' last mountain stronghold in Peru. It was unknown to outsiders until rediscovered by an American archaeologist in 1911.*

When did 180 men conquer an empire?

When Francisco Pizarro of Spain led his men to conquer the Incas of Peru in 1532. The Spaniards found the Incas fighting a civil war. They captured the Inca ruler Atahualpa, and demanded a huge ransom in gold and silver. They then murdered Atahualpa and soon made themselves masters of the Inca empire, which stretched along most of the coast of the Pacific Ocean. The last Incas held out in the mountains in fortress towns.

Astonishing Aztecs

About the Aztecs

The Aztecs ruled their empire in Mexico from their capital city, Tenochtitlan, founded on an island in a lake in the 1300s

Religion was so important to the Aztecs that they went to war to capture prisoners to be sacrificed to the gods.

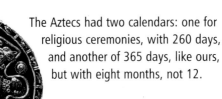

The Aztecs had two calendars: one for religious ceremonies, with 260 days, and another of 365 days, like ours, but with eight months, not 12.

The Aztecs did not use animals to carry loads or pull carts. They carried heavy loads on their backs or in canoes.

⬆ *This carving represents the Aztec view of creation – that the world had already been created and destroyed four times before the time of the Mayan era.*

The Aztecs' favourite war weapon was a wooden club studded with sharp pieces of obsidian (volcanic glass). The club was hard enough to knock an enemy out (to be taken prisoner) but not kill him.

⬇ *The serpent was one of 20 creatures that gave its name to a day on the Aztec farmers' calendar.*

Why did some Native Americans make human sacrifices?

Aztecs and some other peoples of Central America killed human victims to seek the favour of their gods. The Aztecs worshipped the Sun as the giver of life, and believed that unless they offered human victims to the Sun god their crops would fail. They thought that the hearts and blood of the victims served as food for the gods.

⬆ *A sacrificial stone knife used by Aztec priests to cut out the hearts of victims.*

What was the Aztecs' favourite game?

The Aztecs played a ball game rather like basketball. So did the Maya. The game was played in a walled court, which could be as large as 60 m long and was often next to a temple. Some historians believe the winners, not the losers, ended up being sacrificed to the gods – because they were the best!

➲ *The object of the game was to send a ball through a stone ring in the wall. Play was very fast and players were often injured during the match.*

⬆ *The Aztec warriors' clubs and spears were no match for Spanish steel, horses and muskets.*

Who was thought of as a god by the people he attacked?

Hernán Cortés, a Spanish soldier and explorer, who landed in Mexico in 1519. The Aztecs who lived there believed that the bearded Cortés was their god Quetzalcoatl, returned to them. Their calendar told them it was a special year and so they welcomed Cortés and his small army, though they were terrified of the Spaniards' guns and horses. Within two years, Cortés had conquered Mexico.

Key **dates**

1472 Aztecs at height of their power, after Tenochtitlan people conquer the rival city of Tlatelolco.

1502 Montezuma II became emperor.

1519 Cortés landed in Mexico from Cuba; Native Americans under Aztec rule rose against Montezuma and joined Cortés, who took Montezuma prisoner.

1520 Aztecs revolted against the Spanish; Montezuma was killed in the fighting.

1521 Spanish troops attacked Tenochtitlan and the new Aztec ruler Cuauhetmoc surrendered.

After 1521 Spanish conquerors destroyed Tenochtitlan and built a new city, now Mexico City.

➲ *Aztec musicians played music on drums, conch shells and rattles while crowds would dance around them.*

➲ *Women made tortillas by hand and cooked them on a hot stone over a fire. The Aztecs called these cornmeal pancakes tlaxcalli.*

This was an age of Renaissance – new ideas, discoveries, art and religious beliefs. European explorers set sail across the oceans, landing in America and also sailing around Africa to India and China. Art and science were changing, and so was people's approach to religion. The new ideas of the age changed the way people saw themselves and the world.

Columbus had three ships – the Santa Maria, Nina *and* Pinta. *Columbus persuaded King Ferdinand and Queen Isabella of Spain to pay for his voyage.*

Who won the Battle of Agincourt?

England's King Henry V won this battle in 1415 and claimed he was the rightful King of France. Henry led his army across the English channel and defeated a larger French army at Agincourt. The French king allowed Henry to marry his daughter and made him his heir. But Henry died in 1422, and never became king of both England and France. After his death, the English lost most of their gains in France.

Why was Columbus confused?

In 1492, Italian sailor Christopher Columbus believed he had reached Japan or China, when he had in fact discovered the 'New World'. Columbus had persuaded the King and Queen of Spain to finance a voyage to Asia, and his plan was to sail not east but west. Unfortunately, the map he had showed a very narrow sea, rather than the wide Atlantic Ocean, and it made no mention of America, which was unknown to geographers in Europe.

French knights rode towards the small English army at Agincourt, only to be assailed by arrows from Henry V's archers.

Who was the Virgin Queen?

Elizabeth I, who became England's ruler in 1558. She was the daughter of King Henry VIII and his second wife, Anne Boleyn. Female rulers were expected to marry and many kings and princes stepped forward as potential husbands for Elizabeth. However, despite pressure from her ministers to marry and produce an heir to the throne, Elizabeth was reluctant to share her power and knew that marrying a foreign prince would make her unpopular. So she remained unmarried, and when she died in 1603, her Scottish nephew King James VI (1566–1605) became King James I of England.

Middle Age **miseries**

Disease, wars and punishments

The Middle Ages could be pretty grim. The Black Death killed about a quarter of Europe's population, and wars such as the Hundred Years War and the Crusades lasted on and off for hundreds of years. Argue with the Church or act like a witch, and you might be burnt at the stake. To see if someone was telling the truth, there were 'tests' – holding a red-hot iron bar or being thrown into a pond. No wonder outlaws took to the forest.

Rats carried fleas…

…and fleas carried the Black Death germ.

Key **dates**

1450	Johannes Gutenberg invents printing with movable type.
1453	Turks capture Constantinople.
1487–88	Bartolomeu Dias of Portugal sails to the southern tip of Africa.
1492	Christopher Columbus sails from Spain to the Caribbean.
1497	Vasco da Gama of Portugal sails around Africa and on to India.
1499	Amerigo Vespucci sails to America, which is named after him.
1521	Cortés arrives from Cuba to conquer Mexico.

Who sent the Armada to England?

King Philip of Spain, who ruled over the most powerful country in Europe in the 1500s. Catholic Philip wanted to make Protestant England Catholic, too. In 1588, he organized a huge invasion fleet, called the Armada, to overthrow England's queen, Elizabeth I. The Armada was supposed to land a Spanish army in England, but it was attacked by the English navy and then driven north by storms. The great Armada failed.

Elizabeth I (1533–1603) gave her name to the Elizabethan Age.

Many Armada ships were wrecked on the long voyage home around Scotland and Ireland.

Who destroyed England's monasteries?

King Henry VIII, who reigned from 1509–47. Henry argued with the Pope in Rome over the issue of his divorce from his first wife (he married six times). The Catholic Church was facing Protestant 'reformers' who called for 'Reformation' – changes in the Church. Henry remained Catholic, but in order to get his divorce he made himself head of the Church in England, closing down the Catholic monasteries in England. Church lands were given to the king's supporters. Even so, Henry kept his title: 'Defender of the Faith', given him earlier by the Pope.

King Henry VIII's men, sent in by the king's minister Thomas Cromwell, looted monasteries in the 1530s and seized their treasures.

1519–22	Sebastian del Cano and survivors of Magellan's expedition complete first round-the-world voyage.
1533	Pizarro conquers Peru.
1534	Jacques Cartier discovers the St Lawrence River in Canada.
1543	Nicolaus Copernicus proves that the Earth goes around the Sun.
1577–80	Francis Drake sails around the world.
1577	Akbar the Great unifies northern India.
1582	Most of Europe changes to the new Gregorian calendar.
1590	Japan is united under the rule of Hideyoshi.

Amazing **facts**

Five ways of being killed in a siege...

Shot by an arrow/spear/crossbow bolt.

Falling off an assault ladder.

Scalded to death by boiling water or oil.

Having rocks dropped on your head.

Catching germs from a diseased corpse flung over the walls by an enemy catapult.

...and five painful punishments

Being burnt at the stake.

Having your ears or hands cut off.

Being dragged around town.

Sitting in the stocks and having rubbish thrown at you.

Whipping or hanging. Nobles could choose beheading instead, as it was considered a more dignified way to die.

Scientists used new technology to explore the wider universe and their new ideas were spread by the invention of printing. From 1700, the world entered an age of revolution, and political and economic change. By 1800, France had deposed its king, the American colonies had become the United States and the Industrial Revolution had begun.

➜ *Cook took with him scientists and artists to study and record the plants, animals and people of the Pacific lands.*

What caused the English Civil War?

The civil war in England was caused by a quarrel between King Charles I and his Parliament over royal power, religion and taxation. The war was fought between 1642 and 1651. The Parliamentary Army defeated the Royalists, and Charles was executed for treason in 1649. His son tried to regain the throne but was defeated in 1651, though he was eventually restored as King Charles II in 1660.

Where did Cook voyage?

James Cook (1728–79) was an English navigator who made three epic voyages to the Pacific Ocean. He explored the coasts of Australia and New Zealand, and reached the edges of Antarctica (see page 209). Cook was killed by islanders in Hawaii.

When was London almost burnt down?

In 1666, when a fire in one of the city's old medieval buildings spread so rapidly that thousands of homes went up in flames. London had no proper firefighting service, so there was little people could do except run away, though attempts were made to blow-up houses to make a 'firebreak' so the fire would stop spreading.

➜ *In the Civil War battles, cavalry rode on horses, while foot-soldiers brandished long spear-like weapons called pikes.*

The age of **reason**

Key **dates**

1609 Galileo studies the Moon through his telescope.

1649 Charles I of England is executed, after a war with his own Parliament.

1667 Isaac Newton publishes the laws of gravity and motion.

1690 John Locke writes about democratic government.

1698 Thomas Savery invents the first steam-driven pump.

1768 James Cook sets out on the first of three Pacific voyages.

1701 Jethro Tull invents the first farming seed drill.

1709 Abraham Darby discovers how to produce iron cheaply.

1715 Louis XIV of France dies.

1776 American Declaration of Independence.

1782 James Watt makes the first efficient steam engine.

1783 American War of Independence ends.

1789 French Revolution begins.

Robert Winter

Christopher Wright

John Wright

Thomas Bates

Who was Clive of India?

Robert Clive commanded the British East India Company, which fought against French rivals in India during the 1700s. From 1600, English, Dutch and French merchants competed to control trade between Asia and Europe. As a result of Clive's victories during the conflict, the Mogul emperor of India lost much of his power to the East India Company, which ruled India until 1857.

English redcoats fought Highlanders at Culloden, the last battle of the 1745–46 Jacobite rebellion.

What was the Battle of Culloden?

Fought in April 1746, in Scotland, it was the last stand of Charles Edward Stuart or 'Bonnie Prince Charlie', to restore the Stuart monarchy in Britain. His Highland army attempted to overthrow King George II, but it was beaten by the English army, which had more men (9,000 against 5,000). Bonnie Prince Charlie fled into the hills before eventually escaping by ship to France. The Stuarts' hopes of regaining the throne had ended.

War elephants were ridden during the Battle of Plassey in 1757, won by Clive and the East India Company army.

Why did the Americans declare independence?

The American colonists were fed up with being taxed without having a say in the British Parliament. In 1775, Britain and its American colonists went to war. In 1776, during the war, the Americans declared themselves independent, creating the United States of America. With the help of the French, the Americans won the war in 1783, under the leadership of General George Washington, who was later elected President of the USA.

The Green Mountain Boys were American soldiers of the revolution, who captured the British fort on Lake Champlain.

The Gunpowder Plot of 1605 was a conspiracy by eight English Catholics to blow up the Houses of Parliament in London and kill King James I.

Thomas Percy   Guy Fawkes   Robert Catesby

Thomas Winter

Charles II (1630–85), who was restored to the throne in 1660, was known in Britain as the 'merry monarch'.

Louis XIV (1643–1715) of France built the Palace of Versailles to show off his wealth.

The Sun King's legacy

In the 1600s, kings expected to get their own way. Charles I lost his head as a result. Charles II managed to survive, but his brother James II was forced off the throne because of his religious views. By the 1700s, it was clear a king could no longer ignore the wishes of Parliament and its people. In France, Louis XIV reigned longer than any French king, but refused to share his power with anyone. He also spent money lavishly and persecuted Protestants. People hated having to pay heavy taxes, and this resentment was one of the causes of the French Revolution (1789).

The Industrial Revolution was just one of several great changes in the 1800s. This was an age of factories, railways, steamships and fast-expanding cities in Europe and North America. European powers 'scrambled' to seize colonies in Africa, and the fast-growing United States became the youthful giant on the world scene. There were amazing advances in technology too.

What was the Industrial Revolution?

The Industrial Revolution was a great change that began in Britain in the mid 1700s. People began moving to towns to work in factories, inside which were new machines driven by water and steam. By the 1830s, steam railways were carrying raw materials, coal and finished goods to the new iron steamships in the docks.

⬇ *During the Victorian era in Britain, many people moved from their rural homes to work in factories and live in houses close by.*

Who was Napoleon Bonaparte?

Napoleon (1769–1821) was an officer in the French army. Born on the island of Corsica, he was a supporter of the French Revolution and won many battles, though he failed to defeat the British with their strong navy. In 1799, he seized power in France, making himself emperor in 1804. He invaded Russia in 1812 but it was a disaster. Finally defeated in 1815, he died in exile six years later.

⬆ *Napoleon was an infamous general, leading his army to conquer much of Europe.*

Why did Napoleon fight at Waterloo?

Napolean's enemies joined forces to meet him at Waterloo (in Belgium) on 18 June 1815 after he had given up the French throne the year before. He had left France for the island of Elba, but he was soon back, rallying his veteran soldiers for one last campaign. He was defeated by the combined armies of the English Duke of Wellington and the Prussian Marshal Blücher. He was exiled to the island of St Helena, in the Atlantic Ocean.

19th century **inventions**

Key **dates**

1804–05	Lewis and Clark map the West, to open the USA for settlers.
1805	Trafalgar – British fleet beats French and Spanish.
1815	Battle of Waterloo.
1827	First photograph, by Joseph Niepce, France.
1830	First passenger steam train in Britain.
1840	First stick-on postage stamps (Britain).
1854–56	Livingstone crosses Africa and sees the Victoria Falls.
1863	Battle of Gettysburg: Union army beats Confederates in American Civil War.
1864	Louis Pasteur discovers how to kill germs (pasteurization).
1869	Suez Canal opened.
1876	Telephone invented by Alexander Graham Bell.
1879	Electric light bulb invented by Thomas Edison.
1885	Karl Benz builds the first car.
1895	Marconi demonstrates wireless; first cinema films shown in Paris.

⬆ *Alexander Graham Bell (1847–1922) pioneered the first telephone.*

Which war split the United States?

The American Civil War (1861–65), which was fought over the issue of slavery. The Northern states and President Abraham Lincoln, elected in 1860, opposed slavery. The Southern states wanted to keep black slaves to work on plantations and tried to break away, splitting the nation, and so began a bitter civil war. Five days after the war ended, Lincoln was assassinated.

◆ Union (Northern) soldiers were called 'Yankees', Confederate (Southern) soldiers were known as 'Rebs'.

◆ British troops fired on the advancing French during the Battle of Waterloo.

⬆ Custer and his men were outnumbered by the Native Americans, who won this battle. However, the Native Americans eventually lost the Indian Wars.

Where was Custer's last stand?

George Armstrong Custer (1839–76), made his last stand at the Battle of Little Bighorn in June 1876. From the 1840s, settlers headed west across America crossing the territories of the Plains Indians. The US Army was ordered to keep the peace and had to move tribes onto reservations. Some Native American leaders fought against this. General Custer, commander of the 7th Cavalry, split his force and led about 210 men against 2,000 Native Americans, mostly Sioux and Cheyenne, across Montana Territory. Custer and all his men were killed and the wars continued until the 1890s.

◆ Sailing ships like this clipper were replaced by steamships, which could keep to regular schedules.

⬆ People headed for the goldfields of California, Australia and the Yukon to pan for gold, which would make them rich. However, few people made money through gold-panning.

◆ British rule lasted in India until 1947. British officials and their families moved to India during the period, which is now referred to as the Raj.

Influential **people**

Charles Darwin (1809–1882) – His theory of evolution in the 1850s was an explanation of why and how animals had 'evolved'.

Thomas Edison (1847–1931) – Edison was the brains behind the electrical revolution – the first light bulb and the first power station.

Michael Faraday (1791–1867) – Faraday had little schooling, yet his research led to the development of the electric motor and generator.

Florence Nightingale (1820–1910) – Nurse during the Crimean War (1854–56), who demanded changes in the way wounded soldiers were cared for.

The 20th century saw two terrible world wars, an economic depression that brought unemployment to millions, and revolutions and fights for independence in countries ruled by colonial powers. It was the century of flight, of the cinema and television, of computers and traffic jams, of spaceflight and social change, equal rights and globalization – the spread of 'mass culture' to almost every country.

Why was the First World War the first modern war?

The First World War (1914–1918) was fought with new weapons that changed the nature of warfare. These weapons, such as artillery, machine guns, barbed wire, poison gas and aeroplanes meant that it was unlike any previous war. Millions of men got bogged down in trench warfare. In just one battle, the Somme (1916), more than one million soldiers were killed.

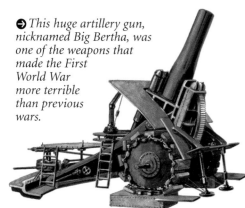
This huge artillery gun, nicknamed Big Bertha, was one of the weapons that made the First World War more terrible than previous wars.

Jobless men marched from Jarrow in north-east England to London, to protest at unemployment during the Depression.

What was the Great Depression?

The Great Depression was a financial crisis that struck the developed world in the 1930s. After the New York Stock Market 'crash' of 1929, banks and businesses closed and many people lost their savings. Panic spread to Europe, where factories laid off workers. The world's economies only started to recover from the late 1930s.

Why was the United Nations set up?

The United Nations was set up in 1942 as a measure to resolve the terrible global conflict of the Second World War (1939–45). In the 1930s, a body called the League of Nations had failed to stop Germany's Adolf Hitler, and war had started. In 1945, leaders and representatives from 50 countries drew up the United Nations Charter at a meeting in San Francisco, USA. The charter was based on proposals made by China, Britain, the USA and the Soviet Union.

Fifty countries signed the charter on 26 June 1945. Poland signed it shortly after, making the first 51 Member States of the UN.

A century of world wars

Warfare in the 20th century

The First World War (1914–18) was terrible but the Second World War (1939–45) was more costly. Few countries escaped the fighting between the Allies and the German–Japanese Axis forces. Aircraft dropped bombs on cities. There were new weapons, such as flying bombs and rockets, and finally the atomic bombs dropped on Japan in August 1945. Later in the 20th century, smaller wars were fought in Korea (1950–53), Vietnam (1957–75), the Middle East (1948, 1956, 1967, 1973) and the Gulf (1991, 2003).

The use of air power since the Second World War changed the way wars were fought and won.

During the Second World War, people in Britain were issued with ration books like this one, which limited what they could buy each week.

The German navy used submarines to sink supply ships travelling in convoys from the USA to Britain.

Whose little red book caused trouble?

Mao Zedong's, leader of Communist China from 1949 until he died in 1976. In 1966, he launched a 'cultural revolution'. His ideas were contained in a small red book, carried by young Red Guards who turned on those who opposed Chairman Mao, particularly the educated classes. The result was chaos – schools and factories closed, many people were forced out of their jobs or killed. After Mao died, China's new leaders got rid of the red books and order was restored.

⬆ *Chairman Mao's red book contained his communist philosophies.*

⬆ *Polish workers rallied behind the banner of their Solidarity trade union, which opposed the Communist government in the 1980s.*

What is Communism?

Communism is a social structure that, in theory, sets out to create a society of shared wealth and power. In 1917, a group of Communist rebels called the Bolsheviks turned imperial Russia into the Soviet Union. But by the late 1980s, Communism was failing. Factories were inefficient, people had little freedom and living standards were low. Many people wanted change, and across Eastern Europe Communist governments were removed. The Soviet Union broke up. Only China, Cuba and North Korea remain Communist.

What was the Cold War?

The Cold War was a time of suspicion between the USA and its allies, and the Soviet Union, China and other Communist countries. It began after the end of the Second World War in 1945. Each side distrusted the other, and each developed weapons of mass-destruction, such as hydrogen bombs. In the 1980s, more trade and the gradual collapse of Communism in most countries helped end the Cold War.

⬅ *During the Cold War, both sides held huge stocks of missiles and nuclear warheads, such as this US Minuteman missile.*

Key dates

1903	First flight in an aeroplane by the Wright brothers (USA).	**1940**	Italy joins on Germany's side. France falls; Battle of Britain.	**1968**	Soviet troops crush freedom movement in Czechoslovakia.
1909	Peary (USA) reaches the North Pole.	**1941**	Germany attacks Russia. Japan joins on Germany's side and attacks Pearl Harbor, Hawaii. USA joins war.	**1969**	US astronauts Neil Armstrong and Buzz Aldrin land on the Moon.
1911	Amundsen (Norway) reaches the South Pole.			**1975**	End of Vietnam War.
1914–18	The First World War is fought.	**1944**	D-Day invasion of France by the Allied armies.	**1989**	Collapse of the Berlin Wall in Germany, and end of Communism in Eastern Germany. Tiananmen Square demonstration in China.
1928	First antibiotic, penicillin, is discovered.	**1945**	Germany surrenders. USA drops two atomic bombs on Japan. Japan surrenders. UN charter signed.		
1929	Wall Street Crash in New York.	**1947**	Pakistan is independent from India.	**1991**	Break up of the Soviet Union, and the first Gulf War.
1930	Rise of Nazis in Germany.	**1953**	Hillary and Tenzing climb Everest.	**1994**	First free elections in South Africa.
1936	First TV broadcast in Britain.	**1957**	First space satellite, *Sputnik I* (USSR).	**2001**	September 11 tragedy in the USA.
1939	Germany invades Poland; The Second World War begins.	**1961**	Yuri Gagarin (Russian) circles the Earth in the *Vostok 1* spacecraft.	**2002**	War in Afghanistan.
				2003	The second Gulf War.

Life on Earth began over 3.5 billion years ago. How? Perhaps by chemical processes within the primeval 'soup' of elements; maybe by a haphazard collision of lifeless molecules; possibly by the impact of 'seeds' of life-bearing dust from outer space. Life began in the oceans and the oldest known forms of life are fossils of bacteria and algae. Today, there are at least two million species of living organisms on Earth.

How are living things unique?

Only living things can reproduce to make identical copies of themselves. The first living cell, bobbing in the ocean millions of years ago, was unlike anything else on the planet. It used chemical energy in seawater to feed and was able to reproduce.

⬆ *The gorilla is a primate, one of the most advanced of all animals. Yet it is made up of cells, just like the simplest forms of life.*

⬆ *The prehistory of the Earth is divided into very long periods of time called eras, and shorter ones called periods. This is a scene from the Jurassic Period, when plants and animals were very different from those today.*

What are the main groups of living things?

The two main groups of living things are animals and plants. There are five groups, or biological kingdoms. The other three groups are monera, protists (both microscopic one-celled organisms) and fungi. All living things are given names to identify them.

What are living things made of?

All living things are made of cells, which are like tiny chemical factories. Most cells can be seen only through a microscope. Our bodies, and those of every animal and plant, are made of many cells. The simplest plants and animals, such as diatoms, have just one cell, whilst plants, such as trees, or mammals, such as whales and humans, consist of many millions of cells.

⬇ *Diatoms are very simple life-forms, with just one cell. Most are less than 1 mm in size. They float in the oceans, trapping energy from sunlight by a process called photosynthesis (see page 114).*

◀ *An amoeba is a single-celled organism that reproduces by dividing, to create two new cells. There are many kinds of amoeba. Some live in water; others are parasites, living inside the bodies of animals.*

Evolution **facts**

Gradual change
Evolution is the process of slow change that takes place in animals and plants. Living things seldom stay the same. As habitats change, so do living things in order to survive. Over time, evolutionary changes may produce new species, that look different from their ancestors.

⬇ *Many mammal species died out by 10,000 years ago, at the end of the last Ice Age. But many survived, including horses. Modern horses have evolved from prehistoric ancestors that had long legs and more toes.*

DNA
Cells reproduce by dividing. Each new cell gets a copy of the genetic programme, the master plan controlling what that cell does. This programme is contained in a chemical structure called DNA (de-oxyribonucleic acid). It is DNA that determines what species of living thing is created.

What is an animal's most important activity?

For most animals, finding food is the most important activity. Unlike plants, which use energy in sunlight to make their food, animals have to seek out food to provide their bodies with the energy they need. Animals eat different types of food. Herbivores eat only plant food, carnivores eat other animals and omnivores eat both plants and meat.

⬇ *Male mandrills have colourful red and blue markings on their face as a display to attract females, whilst females have more muted coloured markings. The mandrill spends much of its time looking for food, such as fruits, seeds, eggs and small animals.*

⬆ *There are only three species of elephants alive today: the African elephant (left), the recently discovered African forest elephant, and the smaller Asian elephant (right). Other species of elephant existed in earlier times.*

What is a species?

A species is one kind of living thing. Male and female of the same species (two African elephants, for example) can breed. Individuals of different species (an African and an Asian elephant) cannot reproduce. Scientists use classification, in terms of species and genus, to group living things by appearance and relationship. So, for example, all red foxes belong to the same species and would be able to reproduce with one another. The red, grey, Arctic and all other foxes are then placed among the fox genus (with the Latin name *Vulpes*). The fox genus is then part of the larger dog family (*Canidae*).

Oldest **living things**

Species	Years old
Algae and bacteria	3.5 billion
Crustaceans	600 million
Molluscs	500 million
Fish	480 million
Non-flowering plants	400 million
Insects and spiders	370 million
Amphibians	350 million
Reptiles	290 million
Mammals	190 million
Flowering plants	140 million

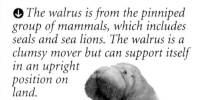

⬇ *The walrus is from the pinniped group of mammals, which includes seals and sea lions. The walrus is a clumsy mover but can support itself in an upright position on land.*

Animal **groups**

Number of species within these animal groups

Insects	1,000,000
Plants	375,000
Arachnids	110,000
Roundworms	100,000
Molluscs	50,000
Fish	27,000
Crustaceans	26,000
Birds	9,000
Reptiles	6,500
Mammals	4,500

For about 160 million years (from 225 million years ago to 65 million years ago) dinosaurs were the most successful animals on Earth. The giant dinosaurs were the biggest reptiles of all time, and were much bigger than elephants. Flying prehistoric reptiles were the biggest animals ever to take to the air. As well as land giants, there were also reptile monsters in the oceans.

⬆ *Fossil bones, such as this* Diplodocus *skull, remain as clues to tell scientists what the long-extinct dinosaurs were like.*

Why did the dinosaurs die out?

The most likely explanation for the extinction of the dinosaurs is that a comet, asteroid or meteorite hit the Earth. There have been other extinctions in Earth's history, but the disappearance of the dinosaurs around 65 million years ago was a cataclysmic event. Dust-clouds flung up by the impact caused climate change: plants died, eggs failed to hatch and mature animals died of starvation or cold.

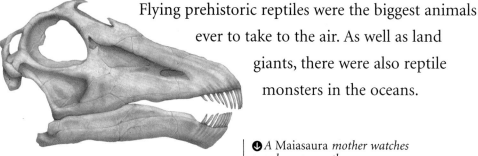

⬇ *A* Maiasaura *mother watches over her eggs as the young hatch.*

Which prehistoric animals could fly?

Insects and some reptiles. There were dragonflies as big as pigeons in prehistoric swamp-forests. Flying reptiles, called *Pterosaurs*, flew with bat-like wings of skin stretched between bony fingers. The flying reptile *Quetzalcoatlus* was as big as a small plane with a wingspan of 15 m. The bird-like reptile *Archaeopteryx* had feathers, but scientists believe that it would not have been able to fly very well.

⬆ Archaeopteryx *lived in the trees, hunting insects. It probably flew no more than a few metres between branches.*

What were baby dinosaurs like?

Like mini-versions of their parents. Being reptiles, dinosaurs laid eggs. Some dinosaurs, such as *Maiasaura*, were careful parents. They made nests, guarded their eggs against predators and stayed with the young until they were able to fend for themselves.

Dinosaur **data**

Dino defences
Plant-eating dinosaurs were preyed on by the fierce meat eaters, but they had effective defences in the form of armour plating, shields, spikes and club-tails. Neck frills and horns protected the slow-moving Ceratopsians or 'horn-faced' dinosaurs from predator's teeth.

⬅ Triceratops *was the largest of the ceratopsians.*

⬅ Styracosaurus *had frilled horns with bony centres that weighed heavily on the neck.*

Biggest **dinosaurs ever**

Seismosaurus	up to 50 m long, 50–80 tonnes
Antarctosaurus	30 m, 50–80 tonnes
Brachiosaurus	25 m, 50 tonnes
Diplodocus	23 m, 12 tonnes
Apatosaurus	20 m, 20–30 tonnes

⬅ Chasmosaurus *had large bumps called tubercules scattered among its scales.*

Which were the most awesome dinosaurs?

The most frightening dinosaurs that lived were the giant meat-eaters such as *Tyrannosaurus rex* and *Allosaurus* – up to 12 m long, weighing 6 tonnes, and with enormous jaws lined with sharp teeth. But just as awesome were smaller killers, such as the 'slashing claw' *Deinonychus*, the human-sized *Velociraptor* and the smaller *Stenonychosaurus*. These crafty carnivores were probably the most intelligent dinosaurs around.

Tyrannosaurus rex

⊕ *Tyrannosaurus rex preyed on weaker dinosaurs, and also ate carrion (dead animals), but some victims put up a fight – like this* Ankylosaurus.

Ankylosaurus

⊕ *Brachiosaurus had a very long tail and a long neck, which it probably used to reach treetop foliage to feed on. This dinosaur giant could grow up to 25 m long.*

What were the biggest land animals of all time?

Prehistoric reptilian sauropods, such as *Seismosaurus* and *Brachiosaurus.* These 50-tonne reptiles were as big as houses. They lived in herds, ate plants and had very long necks to reach up to nibble on treetops. Evidence from fossil footprints also suggests that they were able to run quite fast.

Mamenchisaurus, a herbivore (plant-eater) whose bones have been found in China, had a neck 15 m long. Some of these giants had tails even longer than their necks. The biggest land mammal was *Baluchitherium*, a kind of mega-rhinoceros weighing 30 tonnes. The largest land animal of today, the modern African elephant, weighs only 7 tonnes!

Shake those hips

Scientists divide dinosaurs into two groups, according to their skeletons. Saurischians had 'reptile-hipped' bones, while Ornithischians had hip bones shaped more like those of birds. It is probable that modern birds are descended from dinosaurs. Their scaly feet are similar to those of the dinosaurs.

Ornithischian hip bones

Saurischian hip bones

Amazing **facts**

- *Ankylosaurus* was 10 m long, and had a club-like tail.

- *Spinosaurus* measured up to 12 m long and weighed as much as 5 tonnes.

- *Stegosaurus* was about 7 m long, with a spiky tail and plates on its back.

- *Triceratops* was about 9 m long, with a bony neck frill and three horns: it had the biggest skull of any animal.

Mammals are not the biggest group of animals. But they are amazingly adaptable, and live in a wide range of habitats – on land, in the ocean and in the air – and in all sorts of climates. They have bigger brains (in relation to their body size) than other animals. The biggest sea and land animals are mammals – whales in the ocean and elephants on dry land.

→ *The platypus lives in rivers in western Australia. It has webbed feet and a paddle-tail for swimming.*

Which mammals lay eggs?

The only egg-laying mammals are the duckbilled platypus and the five species of spiny anteaters, or echidnas. These curious animals live only in Australia. The female platypus lays two eggs in a burrow, and suckles the young when they hatch. The female echidna lays one egg into a pouch on her body and the baby grows inside, sucking milk from her fur.

Do pouched animals live only in Australia?

No, some live in New Guinea and the Solomon Islands of the Pacific Ocean, and two kinds (opossums and rat opossums) live in the Americas. Mammals with pouches for rearing their young are called marsupials. Australia has the largest variety of marsupial animals, which includes kangaroos, koalas, wallabies, possums, wombats and bandicoots.

→ *A baby kangaroo (a joey) grows inside its mother's pouch. It climbs back inside for safety, until it grows too big for the pouch.*

What are carnivores?

Carnivores are flesh-eating hunting animals. Some of the best known hunters are the big cats – lions, tigers, leopards, jaguars, cheetahs – and many smaller cats. Most cats hunt alone, using stealth. Other families of carnivores include the dogs (wolves, jackals and foxes) and the weasels (otters, badgers, mink). Many marine animals such as sharks and dolphins are carnivores, hunting and feeding on fish and other living things in the water.

→ *A leopard usually hunts at night, and after a kill drags its meal into a tree out of reach of scavengers such as hyenas.*

Marvellous mammals

Mammal giants
There are about 4,500 mammal species, ranging in size from whales to tiny shrews and bats. Biggest of all is the gigantic blue whale, which can grow to 33.5 m long and weigh more than 130 tonnes.

Biggest hoofed animals

Name	Height	Weight
White rhinoceros	1.8 m	3,000 kg
Hippopotamus	1.5 m	1,400 kg
Giraffe	5.5 m	1,200 kg

Intelligent mammals

The most intelligent animals (not including humans):
1. Chimpanzee
2. Gorilla
3. Orang-utan
4. Baboon
5. Dolphin

↑ *Scientists assess a dolphin's reaction to various sights, sounds and situations in order to gauge their intelligence.*

Which mammals live in the sea?

Seals, dolphins and whales are sea mammals, whose ancestors lived on land millions of years ago. Their front legs have become flippers or paddles for swimming, and instead of back legs whales have horizontal tail fins, or flukes. Seals and sea lions can still move on land, but whales and dolphins are now entirely water animals.

🔽 *Like dolphins and other whales, killer whales are intelligent animals.*

How do mammals give birth?

The placental mammals (the biggest mammal group) give birth to live young. Inside the female's body the developing young are nourished by an organ called the placenta. Most mammal babies are fairly well developed when born, though they still need parental care to begin with.

🔼 *This baby rhino is a miniature replica of its massive mother, but will need her protection during the early months of its life.*

Which is the biggest group of mammals?

Surprisingly, bats. There are 960 species of bats – the only mammals that truly fly. The largest bats are the fruit bats and flying foxes, which can have wings almost 2 m across, but most bats are small, about the size of a mouse. Many bats are nocturnal insect-eaters, but some also prey on small rodents, frogs and fish. Night-flying bats use echolocation to find their way in the dark and to locate prey. They send out high-pitched squeaks that are reflected as echoes from nearby objects.

🔽 *Many bats have extra-large ears to pick up echoes as 'sonic images'. The bat homes in on its target, such as a moth. Many bats roost together in colonies, sleeping upside-down, dangling from their foot claws.*

Longest **gestation periods**

It takes a long time for a mammal baby to develop: nine months for a human, but even longer for other large mammals.

Elephant	660 days
Whale	500 days
Walrus	480 days
Rhinoceros	450 days
Giraffe	430 days

Mammal **champions**

Record	Held by
Biggest rodent	Capybara (as big as a goat)
Biggest ungulate (one-toed or hooved mammal)	Hippopotamus
Longest hair	Yak (hair up to 90 cm)
Largest bear	Polar bear (500 kg)
Smelliest mammal	Skunk
Sleepiest mammal	Dormouse
Slowest-moving mammal	Sloth
Heaviest tree-dwelling mammal	Orang-utan (up to 90 kg)
Mammal most at home in mountains	Pika (up to 6,000 m altitude)
Most armoured mammal	Armadillos and pangolins

Birds are warm-blooded vertebrates (animals with backbones). Their feathers keep them warm and help them to fly. They walk on two back legs, while their front limbs have become wings. All birds lay eggs. And all birds' bodies are strong but light, ideal for flying – though not all birds fly.

↑ *The graceful albatross glides through the air over the vast southern oceans, seldom having to beat its wings.*

Which bird has the longest wingspan?

The wandering albatross of the southern oceans has the longest wingspan with long, thin wings that can measure more than 3 m from wingtip to wingtip. Its wings enable it to glide for enormous distances with little muscular effort. These majestic birds cannot take off very easily, so they launch themselves into 'upcurrents' of air from their clifftop nests. The marabou stork comes a close second with a wingspan of almost 3 m.

Are all birds able to fly?

No, some birds have wings that are useless for flying. Some run or creep about, whilst others have wings adapted for swimming. Flightless land birds live in Africa (ostrich), South America (rhea) and Australia and New Guinea (emu and cassowary). The small, flightless kiwi lives in the forests of New Zealand, which was once home to a much bigger, flightless bird, the giant moa (see page 112).

⬇ *The ostrich relies on fast running to escape enemies, but it can also give a vicious kick.*

Birds of **a feather**

Feathered friends

Feathers are made of a horn-like protein called keratin, the same stuff your hair and nails are made of, but feathers are very light and very strong. A swan has about 25,000 feathers. Hummingbirds, which look as if they have scales not feathers, have the fewest of any bird – less than 1,000.

➡ *A bird's skeleton is very light to help it glide through the air easily.*

Design secrets

Bird bones are hollow but reinforced with cross struts to withstand the twists and turns of flight. Birds have very efficient lungs and their digestive system works very fast because flying takes a lot of energy.

⬇ *In flight, a bird's flapping wings make circular and up-and-down movements – the wing tips pushing forward on the upstroke.*

Do polar bears like to eat penguins?

They never get the chance. Polar bears are the top land predator of the northern hemisphere polar lands (the Arctic), while penguins live in the southern seas, as far south as Antarctica. Penguins cannot fly but their wings have evolved into flippers for swimming. A penguin is streamlined to dart after fish – and escape hungry leopard seals and killer whales.

Why do songbirds sing?

Birds sing to tell other birds where they are, or to defend their territory – where it nests and finds food. Singing is the bird's way of telling other birds to 'keep out'. Singing also helps male birds to attract females during the breeding season. Early morning in spring is a good time to hear birdsong, but some birds sing at dusk, too.

⬆ *A chinstrap penguin chases fish, using its wings like oars to 'row' through the water.*

⬇ *Storks, such as this yellow-billed stork, use their long beaks to probe for food in shallow waters and marshes.*

Why do birds have beaks?

The bird jaw has become a beak, which has adapted to catch and eat all kinds of food. Reptiles and mammals have teeth, but birds do not. Birds of prey have hooked beaks, for tearing flesh. Fish-eaters such as herons have long spear beaks. There are specialized beaks designed for seed-eaters, nut-crackers, fruit-pickers and insect-snappers. Some birds also use their beaks as tools, to make nests or to bore holes.

➡ *The song thrush has one of the most melodious songs of all European birds.*

Oldest birds
In the wild, small birds have many predators. Many are killed in their first year. Bigger birds tend to live longer. Birds kept in captivity and wild birds ringed by scientists are studied to discover how long they can live. A Siberian white crane, a sulphur-crested cockatoo and a goose have been recorded to reach 80 years old.

Take off
Taking off for most birds involves flapping the wings to produce thrust and lift. Broad, rounded wings give the best lift and acceleration – useful for escaping a predator. Big birds, such as geese, run into the wind to generate enough lift to take off. Birds with long, narrow wings, such as swallows, can only take off from a high point – falling into the air and letting the air carry them.

Bird-brained or bright?
Ravens and pigeons can work out simple counting sums. Parrots, budgerigars and mynahs can mimic human speech (though that is not the same as talking), and some parrots can name and count objects. The Galapagos woodpecker finch uses a twig as a tool to winkle out grubs from tree bark.

Birds' eggs
The ostrich lays the biggest egg. An ostrich egg is 20 cm long, and would be big enough to make 24 omelettes. The smallest bird egg, at 1 cm long, is laid by the hummingbird.

Reptiles and amphibians are cold-blooded animals, which means they need sunshine to warm their bodies, and so are not found in really cold climates. In cool climates, these animals often hibernate during the winter. Many amphibians are water creatures, but reptiles are found in dry deserts, rainforests, swamps and even in saltwater oceans.

Crocodiles, such as this Indian gharial, hunt in the water, grabbing land animals and also preying on fish and water creatures.

How many reptiles are there?

More than 6,500 species. There are more lizards than any other reptiles – about 3,700 species. Next come the snakes (2,800). The biggest living reptile belongs to one of the smaller reptile families – the crocodiles – with only 25 species. There are about 3,000 species of amphibians, most of them frogs and toads. In general, amphibians are smaller than reptiles.

This picture shows some reptiles and amphibians. The poison arrow frog is small but deadly. The Komodo dragon (the biggest lizard) and Nile crocodile are giants by comparison and highly dangerous carnivores.

Eastern green mamba snake

Komodo dragon

Jackson's chameleon

Nile crocodile

Indian cobra

Desert tortoise

Golden arrow poison frog

Common frog

Spotted salamander

Frilled lizard

Shingleback lizard

Head to tail **facts**

Throwaway tails

Lizards have many enemies. Some run away at speed, others stay still and hide. Others try to make themselves look bigger and fiercer. Some lizards shed their tails when in danger so that the predator is distracted by the wriggling tail while the tail-less lizard escapes.

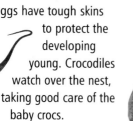

The frilled lizard raises a neck frill of skin to make itself look bigger to predators.

Eggs

Amphibian eggs have to be laid in water, otherwise they would dry out. Reptiles are better adapted to land life, because reptile eggs have tough skins to protect the developing young. Crocodiles watch over the nest, taking good care of the baby crocs.

Alligator egg

Python egg

Biggest crocs

The world's longest crocodile is the estuarine crocodile (7 m long), which lives in Southeast Asia and Australia, and sometimes swims far out to sea. The Indian gharial is 6 m long, the Nile crocodile and the American crocodile are 5 m long and the American alligator is 4 m.

How big can reptiles grow?

A large crocodile can weigh as much as 450 kg and live more than 100 years. As a reptile heavyweight, only a leatherback turtle outweighs a crocodile. The biggest lizard is the Komodo dragon, up to 3 m long. The longest reptiles are snakes. In 1912 a dead python was measured at 10 m long. The heaviest snake is the anaconda, at 200 kg.

⬆ *Snakes, such as this pit viper, have heat-sensing pits in its head, to track prey in the dark or underground.*

What are amphibians?

Amphibians include frogs, toads, newts and salamanders. They can live on land or in water, and most return to water to lay their eggs, even if they spend most of their life on dry land. The eggs hatch into tadpoles, which grow legs and become adult animals, able to live on land or water. Amphibians were the first animals to move onto dry land in prehistoric times.

➔ *Frogs mate in the water and lay clusters of eggs in a jellylike mass of spawn.*

How do snakes hunt?

Snakes have poor eyesight and hunt mainly by using smell, sounds and special heat-detecting organs on their heads. Some snakes, like grass snakes, simply grab prey with their sharp teeth. Others, such as boas and pythons, kill by constriction (crushing the prey until it cannot breathe). Many snakes kill by biting with curved fangs, which inject deadly poison. All snakes swallow their food whole.

How long do tortoises live?

As long as a hundred years. A tortoise given to the ruler of Tonga by Captain Cook some time before 1777 lived until 1965, so it was at least 188 years old. Tortoises move slowly – they have no need to dash around because they carry protective shells with them. This slow lifestyle means tortoises use only a small amount of energy, and so can live on very poor vegetation.

Which lizards can change colour?

Chameleons are tree lizards and can change colour (camouflage) to match their surroundings for protection. They also change colour when alarmed or angry. Chameleons catch insects by uncoiling very long, sticky tongues at high speed. They also have eyes that swivel independently to give them the best all-round vision of any reptile.

➔ *Chameleons move slowly, clinging onto branches with their claws.*

⬇ *Axolotls live in lakes and can spend their entire lives in water. If the lake dries up, the axolotls 'grow up' to become salamanders, able to move about on land.*

Amazing **reptile facts**

• Gecko lizards can crawl across ceilings because they have hairy feet and each hair tip contains thousands of microscopic 'stickers'.

• The tadpole of a frog of South America is three times bigger than the adult. In contrast to most living things, as it grows older, it gets smaller!

• The southern African rain frog lives underground and only comes to the surface when it rains. It cannot swim.

• You can usually tell whether a reptile is active by day or by night from its eyes. If the pupil (the black part in the centre of the eye) is a slit that closes almost completely in sunlight, the animal is nocturnal (active by night). A wide round pupil means a reptile is active by day.

Fish are the animals most perfectly adapted to living in water. They swim better than any other animal, and they can breathe by means of gills, rather than lungs. Fish can live in salty water (the ocean) or fresh water (rivers, lakes and pools). Some fish, such as eels and salmon, live in both. Sea fish tend to grow bigger than river and lake fish.

How many fish species are there?

Fish are the most numerous vertebrate animals (animals with backbones) and there are thought to be over 22,000 species. About a third of these species live in fresh water. There are three main groups of fish: jawless fish (such as hagfish); cartilaginous fish (sharks and rays); and bony fish – the biggest group.

⬇ *A shoal of yellow snapper. Swimming in shoals means a small fish stands a better chance of avoiding becoming a predator's next meal.*

⬆ *The dogfish is a small relative of the great white shark.*

Why does a dogfish have no bones?

A dogfish is a small shark and all sharks have a skeleton made of gristly material called cartilage. It is similar to bone, but more bendy and not so hard. Sharks have very rough skins, too, like sandpaper to the touch and, unlike bony fishes, they have no swimbladder to enable them to float without swimming.

Which river fish can strip meat from bones in minutes?

Many stories (mostly untrue) are told of fierce sharks, but the small piranha has razor-sharp teeth for chopping out flesh in chunks. This small fish lives in the rivers of South America. Unlike most predatory fish, piranhas hunt in shoals (groups). A shoal of piranhas can strip the flesh off a pig in less than a minute, leaving just the carcass.

➡ *The piranha is small, but ferocious when hungry.*

⬇ *The coelacanth has been around since the time of the dinosaurs.*

What is a coelacanth?

The coelacanth is a marine 'living fossil'. Scientists thought this primitive-looking fish died out 70 million years ago – until in 1938 a coelacanth was caught off East Africa. Since then, coelacanths have also been found living on the eastern side of the Indian Ocean, off the islands of Indonesia.

Fishy facts

➡ *The ocean sunfish is the heaviest bony fish. It lays an astonishing number of eggs – about 300 million. Most get eaten by other fish and sea animals.*

Sharks

The biggest fish is the whale shark. It can grow up to 18 m from the tip of its tail to its big, gaping mouth. But this 15-tonne monster is a gentle giant and eats only tiny plankton. Some of its relatives are among the most powerful predators in the natural world. They include the mako shark, which grows up to 3.5 m; the white shark (5 m); the tiger shark and the hammerhead (5 m). All of these sharks have been known to attack people in the water.

Whale shark

What do deep-sea fish look like?

Some look very strange. Their world is black and cold – no sunlight filters down below around 750 m. Food is scarce, so many deep-sea fish have wide gaping mouths, to make sure of catching whatever prey comes near. Some use 'fishing rods' to attract prey. Many deep-sea fish have special organs to make their own 'bio-light', to help identify one another in the darkness.

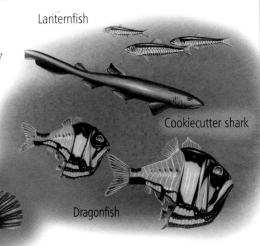

⬇ *Many deep-sea fish glow to confuse predators.*

Lanternfish

Cookiecutter shark

Dragonfish

⬅ *Anglerfish are dark-coloured for camouflage, but a glowing tip extends from its dorsal fin to attract prey.*

⬇ *The viperfish has a lure and huge jaws to grab the next meal, while lanternfish make their own light.*

What is a devil fish?

This is another name for the giant manta ray. The manta ray looks fearsome, with a 'wing' span of up to 7 m across. Sailors in the past told stories of mantas rising up out of the ocean to shroud a ship in their wings and drag it underwater. In fact, the manta is a harmless giant that will even allow divers to hitch a lift clinging on to its body. The manta has broad fins for swimming effortlessly through the water, using its 'horns' to guide plankton into its gaping mouth.

⬇ *The manta is the largest of the rays. Rays and skates are fish with flattened bodies, and are related to sharks.*

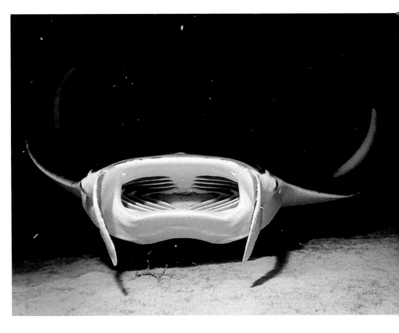

Fishy tails and scales

Fish swim using a side-to-side movement of their bodies. Muscles make up approximately 70 per cent of a fish's weight. A fish uses its fins for steering – the tail fin, for example, acts as a rudder. Like all animals, fish need oxygen – but they take in oxygen, which is dissolved in water, through their gills. The older a fish is, the bigger its scales – as the fish gets bigger, its scales get bigger, too.

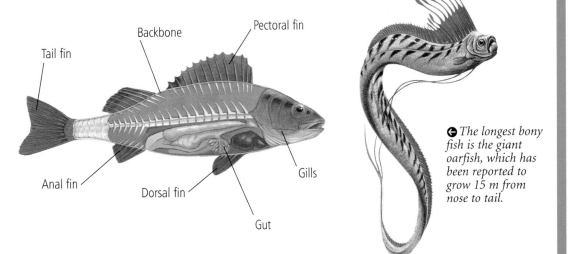

Tail fin

Backbone

Pectoral fin

Anal fin

Dorsal fin

Gut

Gills

⬅ *The longest bony fish is the giant oarfish, which has been reported to grow 15 m from nose to tail.*

There are two main groups of animals – animals with backbones (vertebrates) and animals without backbones (invertebrates). About 96 per cent of all animals are invertebrates – they include insects, spiders, crustaceans, molluscs, worms, starfish and corals. Insects can live almost anywhere and eat almost anything. It is just as well that their body design limits their size, so that giant insects exist only in horror films.

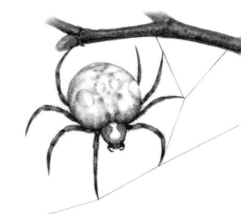

● *The bolas spider twirls its thread around to catch a moth, and then hauls in its meal.*

What makes an insect an insect?

Every insect has three pairs of legs and a body that is divided into three parts: head, thorax (middle) and abdomen. All insects have certain features in common. On the head are eyes, mouthparts and a pair of antennae or feelers. Most, though not all, insects have wings.

● *A bombardier beetle, like all insects, has six legs. This beetle has an unusual defensive weapon – it sprays a jet of hot gas at an enemy.*

Which animals have the biggest shells?

Giant clams of warm oceans have the biggest shells – over 1 m across. Insects have hard bodies, but many molluscs, such as snails and cone shells have elaborate, decorative shells. Crustaceans (crabs, lobsters and shrimps) also have shells. Like insects, crustaceans are arthropods (animals with jointed legs), and most of them live in the sea.

● *The hermit crab has a soft body, and so makes its home inside the empty shell of a mollusc.*

What do spiders eat?

All spiders are carnivores, and most feed on insects and other small creatures. Spiders catch their food in a variety of ways; some just chase their prey, but many spiders make silk web-traps to snare their victims. The bolas spider dangles a sticky ball from a silk thread. The sticky ball gives off a chemical smell similar to a female moth to attract male moths flying nearby. When the moth flies in, it gets stuck to the ball.

Intriguing **insects**

Metamorphosis
Many insects, such as butterflies and moths experience a complete metamorphosis when developing into an adult insect. All insects lay eggs. Butterflies and moths lay their eggs on plants, on which their young – the larvae or caterpillar – start to feed as soon as they hatch. The next stage in the process is when the caterpillar spins a cocoon around itself to becom a chrysalis. Inside, a transformation takes place and from the chrysalis an adult insect emerges, the form of a butterfly or moth.

Insect **numbers**

Insect	No. of known species
Beetles	400,000
Butterflies and moths	165,000
Ants, bees, wasps	140,000
Flies	120,000
Bugs	90,000

● *The caterpillar makes a cocoon and becomes a chrysalis. An adult butterfly emerges to start the cycle all over again.*

Thorax

Abdomen

Dragonfly can fly swiftly with a set of four wings

Head

⊕ *Dragonflies catch other insects in mid-air, using their front legs as a 'net'. They have eyes larger than any other insect to be able to spot prey.*

Which insects fly fastest?

The fastest fliers in the insect world are dragonflies, which can speed along at up to 90 km/h when in pursuit of their next meal. Second fastest are the bot flies, flying at around 50 km/h. The bumblebee flies at speeds of about 18 km/h.

⊕ *It takes 21 days for a bee to develop from an egg to an adult.*

What are social insects?

A few species of insects live in groups, or colonies, making them social insects. These insects include honeybees, some wasps, and all ants and termites. All the members work for the good of the colony, helping to build a nest and care for the young. Ants work together with the use of chemical pheromones, which send signals among the group. One beehive in summer will contain one queen, up to 60,000 worker bees, and a few hundred fertile males. Only one individual female, the queen, lays eggs.

⊕ *Honey bees build nests of wax sheets, called combs. Brood cells in the comb contain grubs that hatch from the eggs laid by the queen.*

Insect **record breakers**

Biggest insect	Birdwing butterfly and Atlas moth – 300 mm across
Heaviest insect	Goliath beetle – 100 g
Longest insect	Stick insect – 400 mm long
Fastest runner	Tropical cockroach – more than 5 km/h

Chomping jaws

Praying mantids are fussy eaters. Usually, they will only eat other insects that they have captured alive. They hold their spiny front legs together, as if praying – then grab the victim and start to chew.

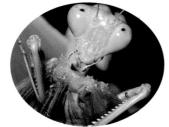

Amazing **insect facts**

• There are at least one million known insect species, and some scientists think there could be up to ten million species.

• Insects, such as ants, can drag objects many times heavier than themselves. They can construct enormous homes, such as the termites' mound.

• A flea can jump 130 times its own height, and a caterpillar has six times more muscles than a human.

• A rhinoceros beetle can carry up to 850 times its own weight!

⊕ *A green mantis from Malaysia settles down to a meal.*

Thousands of animals have died out naturally in the course of evolution. Several mass extinctions happened in prehistoric times – the biggest was 240 million years ago, when perhaps 96 per cent of living things vanished. Another, 65 million years ago, saw the disappearance of the dinosaurs. The rate of extinction has accelerated in the last 200 years and today more than 5,000 species are endangered.

Why is the koala at risk?

Because it is a specialized feeder. This Australian marsupial eats only eucalyptus tree leaves. Being dependent on one food source is dangerous, because if the forests are cut down, the koalas cannot find anywhere else to live, or anything else to eat. A similar threat faces the Chinese giant panda, whose diet is mainly bamboo shoots. A shortage of bamboo means starvation for pandas.

What is the greatest threat to wildlife?

Habitat loss is the most serious threat to endangered animals and plants. For example, when tropical rainforests are felled for timber or agriculture, most of the wildlife dependent on the rainforest cannot survive anywhere else. They cannot find food or breed, and so their numbers start to decline. Many lost species are insects and other

➊ *A snow leopard needs a large hunting territory. Human interference, hunting for the fur trade and loss of its natural prey make survival difficult for big predators.*

invertebrates never studied by scientists. Changes to farm methods, housebuilding, hotel developments along the beaches, and over-hunting all threaten wild species.

➜ *Koalas survived hunting in the early 20th century and are now a protected species.*

Endangered and **extinct**

Key **dates**

1870 North American bison almost wiped out by hunting.
1872 Yellowstone National Park (USA).
1935 White whales protected from hunting by whalers.
1961 World Wildlife Fund (now Worldwide Fund for Nature) founded.
1975 First international convention on banning trade in products from endangered animals.

1989 *Exxon Valdez* oil-spill in Alaska – not the first oil-spill but it raised public awareness.
1997 More than 5,000 species listed as endangered by the International Union for the Conservation of Nature and Natural Resources.

➜ *Marine turtles face threat from fishing nets at sea and tourists on their breeding beaches.*

➊ *The giant panda lives in China and feeds on a specialized diet of bamboo. Its numbers have never been large, and attempts to breed giant pandas in captivity have not been very successful.*

Which pigeons went missing for ever?

A flightless pigeon called the dodo lived undisturbed on the island of Mauritius in the Indian Ocean until European sailors arrived in the 1500s. Sailors killed the birds for food, rats and cats ate the eggs, and by 1680 the dodo was extinct. The most unexpected extinction was that of the passenger pigeon. Billions of these birds lived in North America until hunters began killing pigeons for food. Between 1850 and 1880 the vast flocks vanished and the last passenger pigeon died in a zoo in 1914.

⊙ The dodo was flightless and had no defence against humans or introduced predators.

⊙ Rhino horn is wrongly believed by some to possess magical properties, so the horns are used in medicine and in making weapons.

Why is oil in the water a killer to seabirds?

Seabirds that come into contact with the greasy surface of oily water cannot fly because their feathers become clogged with oil. This means that the birds cannot hunt to feed and soon die. Some birds are rescued by conservationists and cleaned up in order to be able to fly again, and eventually returned to the wild.

How can cutting off horns save some animals?

Removing the horns from rhinos living in game reserves does not hurt the animals, nor affect their lives seriously, but it makes them less of a target for poachers. Poachers in Africa kill rhinos for their horns, which are actually made of hair. The horns are used in traditional medicines in some countries, and in the making of ornamental weapons, such as knives. Poaching for rhino horn, elephant tusks and even elephants' feet is a serious problem in parts of Africa. By removing a rhino's horn, poachers have no need to hunt and kill them.

⊙ This seabird died as a result of having wings clogged with oil, which made it unable to fly and hunt for food.

Extinct **species**

- The great auk was called the 'penguin of the north'. It was hunted for its eggs and skins, and the last one was killed in 1844.

- Diatryma was a carnivorous flightless bird, 2 m tall and fierce enough to eat a pony!

- Megatherium was a ground sloth as big as an elephant.

- Glyptodon was an armadillo as big as a rhinoceros.

- Diprotodon was a giant Australian wombat, as big as a bear.

- Steller's sea cow was related to the manatee. It was 7 m long and weighed 10 tonnes. It was killed off in the 1700s by hunters.

Endangered **species**

African wild dogs – less than 5,500 left.
Californian condor – Numbers fell dramatically until the last pair in the wild were captured for breeding. Numbers have since risen again.
Lions – population in Africa fell from 230,000 in 1980 to under 23,000 in 2003.
Tigers in Asia – less than 10,000 left.
Turtles – declining worldwide.
Wolves and bears – very rare in Europe.

⊙ The giant moa was a huge, flightless bird from New Zealand that was wiped out by people who hunted it for its meat.

There are about 375,000 kinds of plants. The biggest plant family is the flowering plants, or angiosperms, with over 250,000 species. Plants make their own food, using sunlight (photosynthesis). Fungi used to be classed as plants, but as they cannot make their own food, they are now put in a class of their own, which includes about 100,000 species.

⬇ *Tropical cycads are primitive cone-bearing plants that look rather like palm trees.*

What are the most abundant plants?

The flowering plants – grasses, cacti, trees, peas and beans, vines, potatoes and many wild and garden flowers.
Flowers help plants to reproduce. The flower produces male and female cells (pollen and egg cells), and it also makes sure that seeds are spread – by attracting animals such as bees. The biggest groups of flowering plants are orchids,17,000 species; legumes (peas and beans) 16,000 species; and compositae (daisy-like flowers) 14,000 species.

Which plants have no flowers?

Mosses and ferns have no flowers.
Instead of seeds, they produce spores, which fall to the ground and develop into a structure called a prothallus – it is this structure that produces male and female cells to make a new plant. Conifers have no flowers either. They are 'gymnosperms', and have cones containing pollen and seeds. Male and female cones may be on the same plant, as in most conifers, or on separate plants, as in cycads.

⬇ *Flowering plants, non-flowering plants and fungi grow together in woodlands.*

Bracket fungus

Birch sapling

Fern

Mushroom

Fly agaric

Bluebell

Cuckoo-pint

Foxglove

Acorn

Surprising plant **facts**

Super seeds
Frozen seeds of the Arctic lupin thawed and started growing in 1966 after scientists reckoned they had been in deep-freeze conditions for 10,000 years.

➔ *A fern reproduces by spores, not by seeds. Ferns are among the oldest plants living on land.*

Photosynthesis
Photosynthesis is the process plants use to make food. The food-producing parts of a green plant contain chlorophyll. Using water and carbon dioxide gas as raw materials, and energy from sunlight (harnessed by the chlorophyll), the plants build up food sugar in their cells.

➔ *Chlorophyll in a plant's leaves makes photosynthesis work. Oxygen and water are given off as the plant makes its food.*

Carbon dioxide

Oxygen

Sunlight

Water

Water and minerals

How do fungi grow?

Fungi take food from other plants or feed as scavengers from dead, decaying matter, such as a fallen tree. Fungi contain no chlorophyll so they cannot make their own food, like green plants. Instead, they can grow on anything made of cellulose – such as food, clothes, wooden furniture, even old books – especially in damp places.

⬆ *Fungi, such as this cat-tail fungus, produce chemicals that feed on cellulose – the material of which green plant cells are made.*

⬆ *All we see of the water lily is its flower on the surface of the water, but underneath the surface, long stalks connect it to the roots on the river bed, like an anchor.*

How can plants live in water?

Over 90 per cent of a plant is water, so it is not surprising that plants manage to live in water perfectly well, so long as they can obtain sunlight. Some plants float on the surface, others root in the bottom of ponds or streams. Seaweeds growing in the oceans are very tough, to survive being pounded by waves or being dried and then soaked again as the tides come in and go out on the seashore.

➡ *Instead of a root, a seaweed has a 'holdfast' foot which sticks to a rock, to keep the plant in one place.*

⬇ *It is hard to imagine a lawn of bamboo, but lawn grass and bamboo are related plants.*

What is the tallest grass?

Bamboo looks like a tree but is actually a giant grass. It is the tallest grass (growing up to 25 m) and the fastest-growing plant, shooting up almost 1 m a day. Grasses have very small flowers, with no petals, and form the largest group of wind-pollinated plants. There are about 10,000 species.

Biggest and oldest **plants**

Biggest leaf	Raffia palm – 20 m
Biggest seed	Coco de mer palm – 20 kg
Longest seaweed	Giant kelp – 60 m
Oldest plant	Creosote plant and Antarctic lichen – 12,000 years

Amazing **facts**

- A single orchid can make more than 4.5 million seeds.

- A single fungus can produce up to 5 million spores.

- The most deadly fungus is the death cap, *Amanita phalloides*.

Plant **families**

Angiosperms – have enclosed seeds and easily seen flowers.
Gymnosperms – wind-pollinated, 'naked seeds' in cones.
Pteridophytes – simple plants, such as ferns, horsetails and clubmosses.
Bryophytes – liverworts and mosses, the simplest true land plants.
Algae – most live in water; they range from single-celled diatoms to giant seaweeds.

➡ *A few plants are carnivorous. Pitcher plants supplement their diet by catching insects, which fall into the plant's trap.*

Flowering plants are successful because they are good at spreading their seeds and are very adaptable. Flowering plants live in most of the Earth's environments, including hot deserts and high mountains. There are more than 250,000 species of flowering plants, including flowers, vegetables, grasses, trees and herbs, which are all divided into two main groups: monocotyledons, such as grasses and bulb-plants, and the bigger group – dicotyledons.

↑ *The huge flower of the rafflesia, which is also called the stinking corpse flower because of its pungent smell used to attract insects.*

Which are the biggest flowering plants?

The biggest flower belongs to the smelly rafflesia of Southeast Asia. Its metre-wide flower smells like rotting meat, to attract insects. Some flowering plants are enormous – a Chinese wisteria in California has branches 150 m long and produces 1.5 million flowers every year.

How do plants live in dry deserts?

Some desert plants have long roots to reach deep underground where the water supply can be found. Others store water in their thick stems and fleshy leaves. Desert plants may look dead until the rain comes when they burst into life, grow and flower – and the desert briefly blooms.

↓ *Cactus plants can grow in deserts, providing it rains occasionally.*

How plants **work**

Parts of a flower

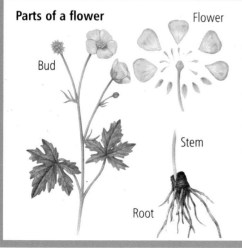

Flower

Bud

Stem

Root

Plants need light
A bulb can be kept in a dark cupboard while it is dormant or beginning to shoot, but if you keep the sprouting plant away from sunlight, it will die. Mushrooms on the other hand, which are fungi, can live in darkness because they get their nourishment from plants or dead matter.

➔ *Germination is when a seed starts to grow. It puts out a shoot first. Then the seed-leaves emerge, followed by the main stem and proper leaves.*

Thirsty plants
Without water, plants wilt and die. Plant cells cannot do their jobs without water, nor can photosynthesis take place to feed the plant. Water also helps keep plant cells rigid. Without enough water, the cells go limp and the plant wilts.

Why does a sprouting plant grow upwards?

Because its leaves must reach the sunlight. A plant starts life as a a bulb or seed in the soil. Even if planted upside down, the roots will start to push downwards, under the influence of gravity. The shoot, bearing the leaves, pushes upwards towards the sunlight, to start making food for the growing plant.

➡ *A tulip starts life as a bulb, which sends out roots and a shoot. The leaves emerge into the sunlight and then, finally, the flower.*

Why do flowers have bright colours?

To attract animals, which transfer pollen from one plant to another. This is called cross-pollination. The chief pollinators are insects, which are attracted to flowers by their colours and scents. Insects do not see the same colours as us. To a bee a red flower looks grey, while a white flower probably looks blue. Birds, bats, rodents and even marsupials pollinate flowers in some parts of the world.

⬆ *The dandelion produces the familiar fluffy seed-head. Blow it to 'tell the time', and you are helping the plant spread its seeds.*

Why do some plants have wings and parachutes?

To ensure the wind can carry a plant's seeds as far from the parent tree as possible. Dandelion seeds are so light that they blow about easily. The fruits of some other plants, such as maple trees, have winged seeds, which spin as they fall from the tree like the rotor blades of a helicopter.

⬅ *When bees and other insects feed on flowers, pollen sticks to them, which they carry to other flowers of the same species.*

How do plants survive on windy mountains?

Plants such as mosses, shrubs and some flowers can survive the high winds and winter cold of mountains by staying small – they cling close to the ground. They have long roots to hold tight to the soil and to reach down to find as much moisture and food as possible. The trees best suited to alpine heights are conifers.

⬇ *An alpine meadow in spring, with many flowers in bloom.*

Transpiration

Plants lose water through tiny pores (holes) called stomata in the undersides of leaves. This is called transpiration and helps keep the plant cool.

Upper leaf layer

Spongy cells

Stomata (leaf pores)

Roots

Roots draw up water from the soil. The flow of water up the plant stem brings with it minerals to feed the plant.

Waterproof wax coat

Leaf veins with tiny tubes

⬅ *Inside a leaf: carbon dioxide gas from the air passes through tiny holes called stomata into the leaf. The leaf gives off oxygen and water.*

Lower layer of leaf

Plant **defences**

- Hairy, stinging leaves (like a stinging nettle's) stop hungry animals nibbling them.

- Silica-toughened leaves are too hard for most animals to chew.

- Spines, thorns and prickles keep animals at a distance.

- Nasty-tasting or poisonous chemicals make sure the animal does not eat the same plant again.

There are two main groups of trees. Conifers, or cone-bearing trees, are known as softwoods and keep their leaves throughout the year. Broad-leaved trees are hardwoods, and those growing in cool climates lose their leaves in autumn. Trees play a vital role in maintaining life on Earth, because their leaves give off oxygen as part of the tree's food-making process.

How can you tell a bush from a shrub?

Shrubs are small, tree-like plants while bushes have more branches than shrubs, and are usually smaller. Shrubs have woody stems and several branches, spreading out near to the ground. Gardeners often grow bush roses, fruit bushes such as gooseberries, and ornamental shrubs such as fuchsias, azaleas and rhododendrons. Shrubs provide useful cover for wildlife, especially birds and small mammals.

⬇ Woodland with a mixture of trees and shrubs is a good habitat for animals.

Why do some trees lose their leaves?

⬆ Autumn leaves provide a brilliant colour show as the trees prepare for winter.

Losing their leaves in autumn helps trees save water as they 'shut down' their food-gathering system in winter. Food pipes inside the tree branches are sealed. Enough food has been stored within the tree to make buds grow in the spring. The leaf is cut off from its food supply and dies. The chlorophyll that keeps it green breaks down, and the leaves turn red, yellow and brown, before they fall to the ground.

Tree **facts**

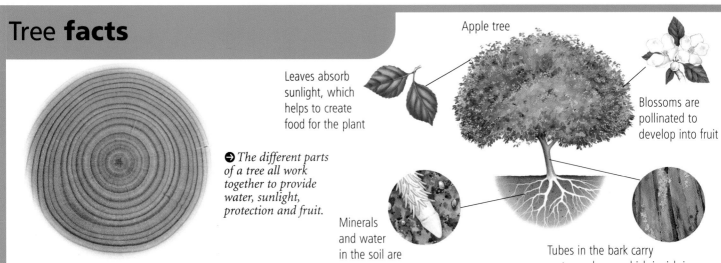

Leaves absorb sunlight, which helps to create food for the plant

Apple tree

Blossoms are pollinated to develop into fruit

➡ The different parts of a tree all work together to provide water, sunlight, protection and fruit.

Minerals and water in the soil are absorbed by the roots

Tubes in the bark carry water and sap, which is rich in energy, to all parts of the plant

⬆ Annual growth rings can be seen when a tree is cut. The tree adds a new ring every year.

Why do trees have bark?

Bark protects the living wood inside the tree. It keeps moisture in, so the tree does not dry out. It protects the tree from insects and parasites, and shields against extreme weather. The outer layer of bark is a tough, dead shell. The inner layer is soft and alive, and carries food through tiny tubes.

Where are the biggest forests?

The biggest forests are the tropical rainforest of Brazil and the cold boreal forest of Siberia. Many trees growing together make a forest. Once 60 per cent of the Earth was forested, but humans have cleared much of the ancient forest to build on. Forests are home to many plants and animals.

🔽 *Forest life exists in layers from the floor through the shrub and understorey to the canopy (the tallest trees).*

Why do conifer trees bear cones?

Male cones produce pollen, female cones produce eggs, which are sticky and attract the pollen. All conifer trees have cones. Seeds are made in the scales of the female cone, and spread by the wind. Most conifers are evergreen and grow best in cool climates. Typical conifers include spruce, pine and firs.

🔼 *Redwood trees have soft, spongy bark and are one of the tallest trees.*

🔽 *Conifers can grow in places where there is little water (or where the water is frozen in winter). Having thin leaves means they lose little moisture.*

Coast redwood

Silver fir

Norway spruce

Italian cypress

Cedar of Lebanon

Stone pine

Phoenician juniper

Amazing **tree facts**

- The heaviest tree is the giant sequoia 'General Sherman', growing in California, USA. Its weight is estimated at 2,500 tonnes.

- A Douglas fir cut down in British Columbia, Canada, in the 19th century was 128 m high.

- The oldest living trees are bristlecone pines found in the mountains of California. They are believed to live for 5,000 years.

- The oldest species of tree is the gingko or maidenhair. Fossil leaves of this tree dating from 160 million years ago have been found.

- Probably the weirdest-looking tree is the baobab. Its bottle-shaped trunk, used for storing water, can measure 50 m in diameter.

- The banyan tree of India grows aerial roots that hang down from the branches to the ground, forming a mini-forest 600 m wide.

➡ *The strange-looking baobab tree.*

People need plants, as sources of food, for raw materials, for fuel, and to maintain the natural balance of the planet. Many plants have been altered by people through selective breeding. This process began when people first became farmers, about 10,000 years ago. Today's farm crops look very different from their wild ancestors.

↑ The sunflower turns its head throughout the day, following the Sun's path across the sky.

Why are sunflowers useful as well as pretty?

Sunflowers produce useful foodstuffs, such as sunflower oil and sunflower seeds. Sunflowers have inspired artists, and children like to grow them to see how tall they become. A field full of sunflowers makes a brilliant sight, a mass of yellow blooms. So sunflowers are both a useful crop and a popular flower to grow.

What are tubers?

Tubers are food-stores, and probably the best-known tuberous plant is the potato. The tuber is the thick, swollen part of the stem, which grows underground. Potatoes were unknown in Europe until the first explorers brought them back from America in the 1500s. The eyes of a potato are tiny buds, which will sprout and grow into new plants if put into the soil.

→ Gardeners 'earth up' the plants to make sure the tubers are covered by soil in plants such as this potato plant.

↑ Vast areas of what was once prairie in North America is now planted with wheat, one of the most important world crops.

Which plants are staple foods?

Staple foods make up the largest part of a person's diet and include potatoes, wheat (made into bread and pasta) and rice. Potatoes and wheat are popular in western countries, while people in poorer parts of Africa and Asia rely almost entirely on plants such as rice, cassava and yams.

Fruit, vegetables and firewood

Working the land
In poorer countries, about half the population works on the land. Many are subsistence farmers – this means they grow just enough food to feed themselves and their families.

In richer countries, the number of people employed on farms is much less – under 10 per cent of the population on average. In the developing world, many people burn wood for fuel. About 90 per cent of the timber cut in India is burned for cooking on wood-stoves. Timber is used for construction, furniture and (as pulp) for making paper for newsprint. In well-managed forests new young trees are planted to replace the mature trees cut down. But many tropical forests are being felled thoughtlessly, for quick profits.

↑ Harvesting by machine means a farmer needs few workers.

➡ *Terraced ricefields are a common sight in many parts of Asia.*

Which parts of plants can we eat?

The roots, bulbs, flowering heads and leaves of some plants are edible.
Cauliflower and broccoli are the flowering heads of plants belonging to the cabbage family. Onions are bulbs. Carrots and parsnips are roots. We eat the leaves of lettuces, and the fruits of many plants, such as apples. Some plants are dangerous to eat – rhubarb leaves, for example, are poisonous, though the stems can be eaten. Mistletoe berries are poisonous, and so are yew and laburnum seeds.

➡ *Pineapples are grown in Central America, Asia, Australia and Africa. The bit we eat is the fruit, which is normally seedless.*

➡ *Rice is a cereal, like wheat, which needs warm, wet conditions in which to grow.*

How is rice cultivated?

Young rice plants are grown in flooded 'paddy' fields and the water is drained off before the rice is harvested. More than half the world's population eat rice as their main food. Once harvested, the rice grains are boiled and eaten, rather than ground into flour (like wheat grains).

Can we eat seaweed?

Seaweed is rich in vitamins and minerals, and many kinds are good to eat. In Wales, a red seaweed known as laver is boiled up into a jellylike mass, fried and eaten as 'laver bread'. The Japanese pioneered seaweed farming. Seaweed farmers drive rows of stakes into the shallow seabed to provide the plant with something to cling to. When the seaweed is harvested, it is used as an ingredient in various foods. If you see the names agar, algin or carrageenin on food packets, you will know those products contain seaweed.

➡ *A farmer harvesting seaweed, which is used in many food and cosmetic products. Ice cream is one of many foods that may contain seaweed.*

First-grown **vegetables**

Vegetable	Date first grown
Pea	9000 BC
Wheat	7000 BC
Rye	6500 BC
Runner bean	5000 BC
Barley	4500 BC
Lettuce	4500 BC
Radish	3000 BC
Rice	3000 BC

Radishes

Lettuce

World food **production**

Top rice producers: China, India, Indonesia
Top potato growers: Russia, Poland, China
Top sugar producers: Brazil, India, Russia
Top wine producers: Italy, France, Spain

Continent	Produces and exports
Asia	43 per cent
Europe (including Russia)	27 per cent
USA and Canada	11 per cent
Africa	7 per cent
Oceania (including Australia)	2 per cent

In order to find food, escape danger and to reproduce successfully, animals use a variety of natural strategies. For example, camouflage and protective colouration enable some animals to escape being seen or to appear so visibly that a predator is startled or scared away. The range of animal defences is amazing, from armadillo armour, porcupine's quills, mimicry and camouflage to lobster claws and the skunk's foul-smelling spray.

⬆ *Baby loggerhead turtles head for deep water. Many turtles are killed by waiting predators.*

Where do marine turtles lay their eggs?

Marine turtles lay their eggs on sandy beaches. The females dig a shallow hole, lay the eggs, cover them with sand, then crawl back to the water. When the babies hatch, they have to dig their way up to the light and air. They head straight for the water because waiting on the shore are a host of predators, such as seabirds, that seem to know just when the hatchlings will emerge.

⬇ *Woodland animals hibernate during the winter months, only emerging when the weather warms up.*

Why do some animals hibernate?

Hibernation is a strategy for surviving winter, when food is scarce. Bears fatten themselves up in autumn, then sleep in a cosy den. Badgers stay in their underground sets. Some animals, such as dormice, shut down their bodies so much that they appear to be dead. Hiberating animals live off the reserves of fat stored in their bodies until spring returns and warmer weather awakens them.

Survival **champions**

Safest when seen
Not all animals choose to hide from danger. Some make sure they can be seen.

Bees and wasps are boldly marked with black and yellow stripes to warn birds that if they peck they risk being stung.

Poisonous animals, such as the poison arrow frog and coral snakes, are often vividly coloured, too, to warn off predators.

Some animals with no real defences 'mimic' animals that are dangerous. There are flies that are harmless, but that look just like wasps and there are harmless milk snakes that look like poisonous coral snakes.

The bee orchid flower looks like a bee – to attract male bees eager to mate, making sure its pollen gets carried away.

⬇ *Some non-venomous snakes, such as this green snake, mimic poisonous snakes as a method of defence. Predators are warned off, thinking it to be dangerous.*

Why do some mammals live in groups?

Living together in a group is a good defensive strategy. An antelope has a better chance of escaping a lion if it stays in a herd – lots of eyes keeping watch are better than just one pair. Elephants have no real enemies (except some humans), but female elephants stay together to share the task of bringing up the young. Lions, unlike most cats, co-operate when hunting. So do wolves, wild dogs and hyenas who hunt in 'packs'.

A herd of elephants is usually led by an old female – the matriarch cow. The herd will look after an injured member and protect the young from predators such as lions.

Why do animals build homes?

Many animals have territories, but homes are usually only for rearing young. Females prepare a den or a nest for their young. Birds make the most ingenious homes, mostly in treetops or bushes. Fish, such as the male stickleback, guard their young fiercely. One of the most remarkable mammal homes is the beaver's underwater lodge. Built from mud and sticks, the lodge provides a dry, weatherproof home safe from land-predators.

North American beavers dam streams by cutting down small trees to make a pond. In the pond, they make their lodge with an underwater entrance.

What is migration?

Animals such as whales, fish, lobsters, caribou and butterflies all migrate – make seasonal journeys – to find reliable food supplies and the best breeding places.
The most remarkable migrants are birds, and many species migrate as the seasons change. Songbirds, seabirds, waterfowl and waders all migrate.

The Arctic tern is the most-travelled bird. It breeds in the Arctic during the northern summer, then flies south for summer in the Antarctic. The round trip covers more than 25,000 km.

Marine iguanas are the only reptiles to feed in the ocean. They dive into the sea to browse on seaweed, then crawl back onto the rocks to warm up in the sunshine.

The hornet's vivid markings are a warning to potential predators: "I sting".

Animal **hibernation**

Bats – find a dry cave to sleep in because in winter, there are few insects to feed on.

Frogs, toads, newts and snakes – hibernate in crevices in rocks or trees.

Hedgehogs – curl up inside piles of dead leaves, waking on milder days.

Squirrels – collect a store of nuts in autumn to last the winter. They do not hibernate completely, waking up on mild days.

Stoats – normally brown, turn white in winter – this camouflages them in the snow.

The record-breakers in the natural world come in all shapes and sizes. Many animals are unbelievably strong. Some insects and mammals have incredible appetites. The fastest animals can easily outrun a human sprinter. And no creature in the history of the Earth has been bigger than the majestic blue whale.

⬆ *The peregrine falcon reaches maximum speed in a dive to catch prey.*

What is the world's fastest animal?

The peregrine falcon, which in a dive or 'stoop' on its prey can reach a speed of more than 200 km/h. Ducks are probably the fastest fliers in level flight, reaching up to 100 km/h. The cheetah is the fastest land animal and the sailfish is the fastest fish, both clocking in at approximately 100 to 110 km/h. The cheetah cannot keep up its sprint for long, whereas the pronghorn antelope can sustain a speed of over 70 km/h for longer. In comparison, a top Olympic sprinter can reach about 43 km/h.

What is the world's biggest big cat?

The Siberian tiger is the biggest of the big cats. It is the most northern species of tiger, at home in the snow. It can measure 3.2 m from nose to tail and weigh up to 300 kg. Carnivores (meat eaters) include some of the most powerful predators in the animal world. The biggest land carnivores are bears and big cats.

What is the largest cactus?

Most cacti are fairly small, but the saguaro is an exception at a height of 18 m. It grows in the deserts of Arizona, California and Mexico. The saguaro has a column-like trunk from which sprout upturned branches. A big one can weigh up to 9 tonnes.

⬆ *The Saguaro cactus is as tall as a tree.*

◀ *The Siberian tiger is a magnificent animal. It is an endangered species (at risk of extinction) and needs protection from hunters.*

Remarkable **record-breakers**

⬆ *Bristlecone pines are the world's oldest trees, up to 5,000 years old.*

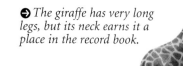

➔ *The giraffe has very long legs, but its neck earns it a place in the record book.*

◀ *The most fearsome jaws are those of the great white shark.*

Fastest **movers**

Peregrine falcon	200 km/h
Canvasback duck	110 km/h
Sailfish	109 km/h
Cheetah	100 km/h
Pronghorn antelope	70 km/h
Swift	95 km/h
Gazelle	80 km/h
Lion	80 km/h
Race horse	70 km/h
Jackrabbit	70 km/h

Which are the most deadly sea animals?

Perhaps the most deadly sea creature to humans is the sea wasp jellyfish with a sting that can kill a person in less than three minutes. The most feared hunters of the ocean are great white sharks and killer whales, which eat seals and sea lions, and will even attack larger whales. Sharks lurk off seal beaches during the breeding season, while killer whales pursue fleeing seals into shallow surf and grab them off the beach itself. However, more people are killed every year by jellyfish than either of these larger animals.

🠿 *Killer whales grab seals from shallow water and from along the shore's edge.*

🠿 *The sea wasp jellyfish.*

What are the smallest animals?

The smallest bird is the 5 cm-long bee hummingbird, the smallest reptile is the dwarf gecko at half that size, and the smallest amphibian, the short-headed frog is just 1 cm long. The smallest horse, the Falabella, is only the size of a dog. Small means safe sometimes, for a small animal can hide where no large predator can follow. However, there are weasels small enough to pursue mice down their holes. There are tiny flies that lay their eggs on the bodies of larger flies. There are a whole host of mini-beasts, some of which can be seen only under a microscope.

🠿 *The world's smallest gecko at 2.5 cm, and the world's smallest frog at just 1 cm, shown to scale on a human hand.*

Most massive **predators**

Name	Weight	Length
Killer whale	9,000 kg	9 m
Great white shark	3,300 kg	4.5 m
Elephant seal	2,300 kg	5 m

Animal **records**

Longest worm	North sea bootlace worm	55 m long
Biggest spider	Bird-eating spider	28 cm across
Biggest mollusc	Giant squid	17 m long
Biggest crab	Japanese spider crab	2 m across

Amazing **animal facts**

- The biggest land animal is the African elephant. A big bull (male) weighs more than 7 tonnes.

- The blue whale (heaviest recorded weight 190 tonnes), gives birth to the biggest baby. At birth, a whale calf is already 6–8 m long.

- The giraffe is the tallest mammal, with the longest neck – a giraffe can reach 6 m above the ground to reach juicy leaves.

- The Goliath beetle is the heaviest insect at 70–100 kg.

- The animals with most legs are centipedes and millipedes. Millipedes have the most, up to 370 pairs. But centipedes run faster.

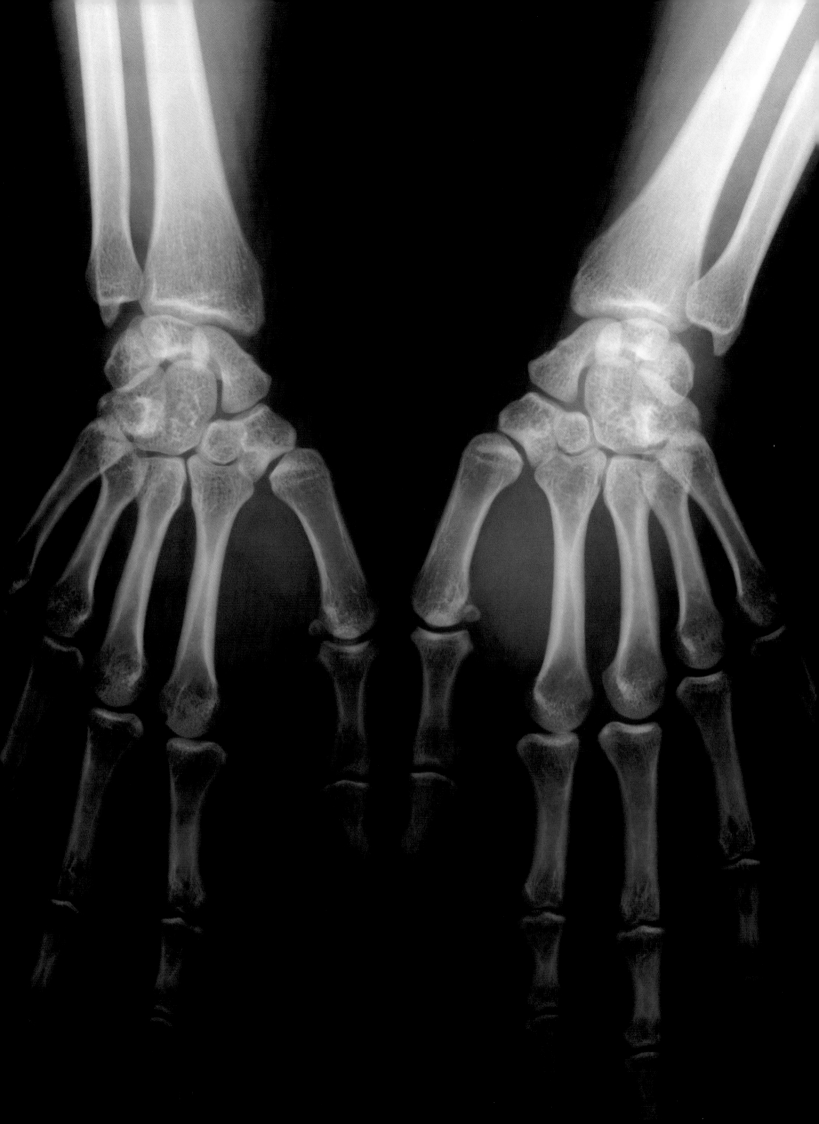

What do we know more about than anything else in the world? You! Perhaps not you as an individual, but the way you live, eat, drink, think, feel happy and sad, daydream and sleep – the human body. There are more than six billion human bodies in the world, and each and every one of those has unique characteristics but, inside, they are all made and work in much the same way.

What are body systems?

A body system is a group of parts that work together to carry out one job or particular task to help keep the body alive and working well. For example, the heart, blood vessels (tubes) and blood make up the circulatory system. This pumps or circulates blood all around the body, to supply every tiny part with essential substances such as oxygen and nutrients, and to collect wastes for removal.

Humerus
(upper arm bone)

Radial artery
and vein

Radius
(forearm bone)

Carpals
(wrist bone)

➲ *Inside the arm are many organs and tissues, including bones, blood vessels and nerves. Muscles and connective tissues link all these parts together.*

How can we learn about the body?

Modern medical science uses hundreds of complex machines and tests to find out more about the body every year. They include scanners, chemical tests, microscopes and electrical monitors. Scanners and X-ray machines see inside the body. Chemical tests on the blood and other parts show the substances they contain. Microscopes reveal the smallest cells and even genes. Electrical devices, such as heart (ECG) and brain (EEG) monitors, show readings as wavy lines on a paper sheet or screen for doctors to examine.

➲ *A typical body cell is far too small to see without a microscope. Yet it contains many even smaller parts, called organelles.*

What are organs?

Body organs include the heart, brain, stomach and kidneys and are the body's main parts or structures. The biggest organ within the body is the liver, while the largest organ of the whole body is the skin. Usually, several organs work together as a body system.

Cell membrane (outer covering)

Nucleus (control centre)

Internal membranes
(make cell products)

Mitochondria (energy centre)

Discovering **the body**

Key **dates**

160 Galen of ancient Rome starts to carry out some of the first studies of the human body, seeing its insides through the terrible wounds suffered by gladiators.

1543 Andreas Vesalius produces the first detailed book of body anatomy, *On the Fabric of the Human Body*.

1610 The newly invented microscope reveals cells and other tiny body parts.

1628 William Harvey discovers that blood is pumped around the body by the heart, rather than continually being made and used up.

1895 Wilhelm Röntgen discovers X-rays and how they pass through flesh but not bone.

1900 Karl Landsteiner works out the system of blood groups, making blood transfusions safer.

1970s Early CT and MR scanners show detailed pictures of inside the body.

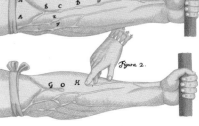

➲ *A diagram from William Harvey's book shows blood flow in veins in the arm.*

2000 The order of chemicals is worked out in the entire set of the body's genetic material, DNA, known as sequencing the human genome.

➲ *Some body parts, such as bones and joints, can be replaced by artificial versions made of tough plastics, stainless steel and titanium. Artificial or prosthetic joints are shown here coloured in white.*

Can body parts be replaced?

Some body parts can be successfully replaced to enable the person to move about easily again. For example, people who have trouble with one or both of their hips, knees, shoulders, elbows or any of their fingers can be given metal or plastic artificial joints in place of the damaged body parts. Broken bones can be held together with plates, strips and screws. Some blood vessels can be replaced by manufactured plastic tubes. Internal organs, such as the heart, lungs, liver or kidneys, can be replaced. The new organs often come from deceased people who donated them before their death.

What are tissues?

Tissues are groups or collections of microscopic cells that are all the same type and do the same job. Examples include muscle tissue, which can shorten or contract to cause movement, nerve tissue, which carries nerve signals, and connective tissue, which fills the gaps between other tissues. Most organs are made of several kinds of tissue.

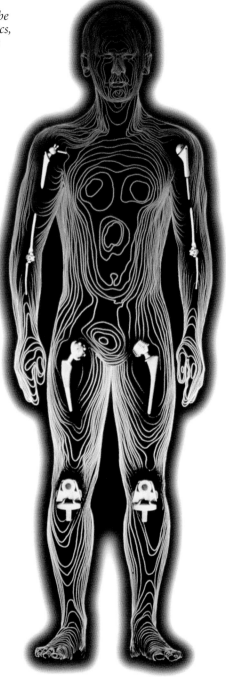

What are cells?

Cells are the smallest living parts of the body. They are like microscopic 'building blocks' in many shapes and sizes, which carry out different jobs. There are some 200 different kinds such as nerve cells, muscle cells and blood cells. On average, about 100 cells in a row would stretch across this 'o'. The whole body contains more than 50 billion billion cells.

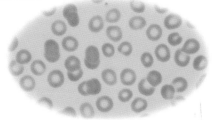

⬆ *Under a light microscope, magnified about 1,500 times, red blood cells appear as blobs with pale centres. This is due to their dished shape, rather like a doughnut.*

⬆ *Physiologists study how the body uses energy during strenuous activity such as swimming, when the heart beats faster, the lungs breathe more quickly and the muscles work harder.*

Body **imaging**

Ordinary X-rays – show the hardest, heaviest or densest body parts, such as bone, cartilage and teeth, as white or pale against a black background.
CT or CAT (computerized axial tomography) scans – use very weak X-rays to show bones and also softer parts such as blood vessels and nerves, in three dimensions.

MR or NMR (nuclear magnetic resonance) scans – use powerful magnetic fields and pulses of radio signals to show similar images to CT scans in even more detail.
Ultrasound scans – use the reflections or echoes of very high-pitched sound waves beamed into the body to build up an image such as an unborn baby in the womb.
Computers – all of these images can be given added colours by computers to make the details even clearer.

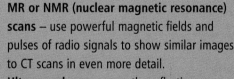

⬅ *An X-ray defines the bones in the hand – and a ring worn on the finger.*

⬆ *A head scan reveals the inside of the brain as if 'sliced' into layers. Carrying out many scans at different levels builds up a 3-D structure of the brain and head.*

When you look at a human body, most of what you see is dead. The surface layer of the skin, and the hair and nails, were once made of living cells. But these gradually die off and then get rubbed or worn away as we move about, change clothes or wash and rub dry with towels, as part of daily living. The only visible parts of the body that are truly alive are the eyes.

Hair shaft
Epidermis
Touch sensor
Sebum gland
Hair follicle
Pressure sensor

◄ *The epidermis, the tough outer layer of skin, is mostly dead. The dermis below contains hair follicles, sweat glands, tiny blood vessels, and micro-fibres of elastin for flexibility, and collagen for toughness.*

▲ *When undertaking hard physical work, the rubbing on the skin of the hands may be greater than normal. The epidermis (outer layer of skin) may develop calluses (rough patches of skin) against further damage.*

What is skin made of?

Like the rest of the body, skin is made of billions of microscopic cells. These cells form two layers, the epidermis on the outside and the dermis below it. The epidermis is tough and hard-wearing. The dermis is thicker and contains millions of microscopic sensors that detect different kinds of touch on the skin.

Why doesn't skin wear away?

It does – but it is always growing to replace the bits that wear away and are rubbed off. The tiny cells at the base of the epidermis continually multiply to make more cells. These gradually move upwards, filling with the tough substance keratin as they die, to form the hard-wearing surface. The whole skin surface is gradually worn away and replaced every four weeks.

How thin is skin?

Skin can be between 0.5 and 5 mm thick. The thinnest skin is found on the eyelids and other delicate, sensitive parts of the body. The thickest skin is on the soles of the feet. This can be 5 mm or more, and grows even thicker in people who often walk and run in bare feet. It grows thicker to adapt and protect the soles of the feet from damage.

◄ *An enlarged view of the skin shows surface flakes that are about to be rubbed off.*

Skin, nail and **hair facts**

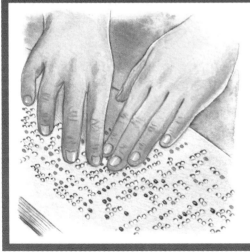

◄ *The sense of touch is vital to a person who is blind. Braille is a system of raised dots and patterns, which each symbolize different letters or words. Through the use of braille, a blind person can feel, and so read, the words on a page.*

Skin **sensations**

Touch may seem like one sense. However, it is much more complex:

• There are at least seven different kinds of microsensors in skin. In sensitive areas such as the lips and fingertips, hundreds of microsensors are packed into an area the size of this 'o'.

• The sensors work together to detect light touch, heavy pressure, movements and vibrations, heat and cold – and the pain that warns us that skin may be damaged.

How quickly does hair grow?

In most people, if a single head hair was left uncut, it would grow about 1 m long, over four to five years. Then the hair naturally falls out of its follicle, which is the tiny pit in the dermis where it grows. However, this does not mean a bald head, since the follicle soon starts to grow a new hair. Follicles over the scalp do this at different times, so there are always plenty of hairs – in most people.

⬇ A hair is alive and growing only at its root, down in the base of the follicle. The shaft that sticks out of the skin is dead, and is made of flattened cells stuck firmly together.

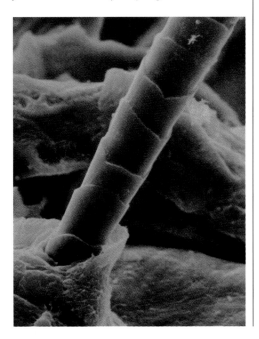

Why do we have fingernails?

To form a firm layer at the back of the fingertip. This stops the flexible fingertip from bending too much, so we can feel, press and pick up small items more easily and without damage. A nail grows at its root, which is under the skin at its base, and slides slowly along the finger.

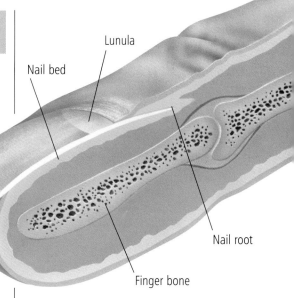

Lunula

Nail bed

Nail root

Finger bone

⬅ Black hair is coloured by lots of melanin.

⬅ Reddish hair has carotenoid colouring substances.

➡ A nail has its root under the skin and grows along the nail bed, which is the skin underneath it. The paler, crescent-like area is the lunula or 'little moon'.

Why do people have different coloured hair?

Hair colour depends on the genes inherited from parents. The colour of both hair and skin is due to natural pigments, mainly the very dark brown substance melanin, contained in cells known as melanocytes at the base of the epidermis. In some people the melanocytes are more active and make more melanin, and so the skin and usually the hair are darker.

➡ Light hair has less of the pigment melanin.

⬇ Eyelashes are among the thickest of hairs on the body, and are replaced quickly when they fall out.

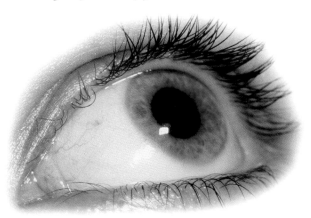

Amazing **facts**

- A typical head hair grows up to 3.5 mm each week.

- An average person has between 100,000 and 120,000 head hairs on the scalp.

- There are many other hairs, including tiny ones over most of the body – up to 20 million in total!

- Each eyelash lasts only one to two months before it falls out, then a new one grows from the same follicle.

- A typical nail gets longer by about half a millimetre each week.

- The fingernails on the favoured hand grow slightly faster. So if you are left-handed, the nails on that hand grow faster than those on your right hand.

- All kinds of nails grow faster in the summer than the winter.

- Fingernails grow slightly faster than toenails.

Bones provide the strong framework that supports the whole body and holds its parts together. Without bones you would flop down on the floor like a jellyfish! All of the bones together are called the skeleton, and this gives protection as well as support.

Neck bones (cervical vertebrae)

Breastbone

Ribs

Hip bone (pelvis)

Shin bone (tibia)

➡ The skeleton has a total of 206 bones, including 32 in each arm, 31 in each leg, 29 in the head, 26 in the spinal column and hips, and 25 in the chest.

What do bones do?

Bones form a framework inside the body, which holds it upright, makes limbs such as the arms and legs strong and protects many internal organs. Long bones in the arms and legs work as rigid levers, so when muscles pull on them, they can push, lift or make other movements. Some bones are protective. The skull forms a hard case around the delicate brain, and the backbone, ribs and breastbone make a strong cage around the heart and lungs.

➡ A typical bone has a hard outer layer, a spongy, honeycomb-like middle layer, and marrow at the centre, as well as tiny blood vessels and nerves.

Periosteum (covering)

Hard bone layer

Spongy layer

Marrow

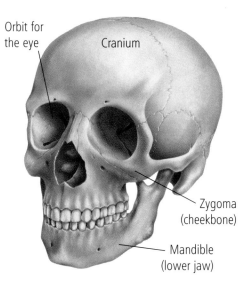

Orbit for the eye

Cranium

Zygoma (cheekbone)

Mandible (lower jaw)

➡ The skull consists of 22 bones (including the lower jaw) linked by joints called sutures, which fix the bones firmly like glue. The sutures show up as faint wiggly lines.

What is inside a bone?

A typical bone has three layers, which consist of collagen, minerals and bone marrow. On the outside is a 'shell' of compact or hard bone. This contains crystals of minerals such as calcium and phosphate for hardness, and fibres of collagen that allow the bone to bend slightly under stress. The middle layer is spongy or cancellous bone, with tiny spaces like a honeycomb. In the middle, the jelly-like bone marrow makes new cells for the blood.

Bone **facts**

Artificial joints

In some people, joints become stiff and painful due to disease, injury or stressful use over a long period of time. In many cases, these natural joints can be replaced with artificial ones – joint prostheses. These are usually made of supertough plastics and strong metals shaped like the original joint. An artificial hip allows some people to walk again without pain for 20 or more years.

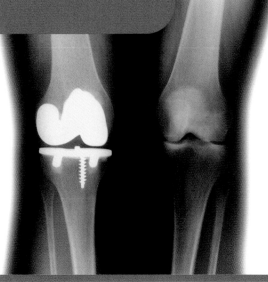

The spine (backbone)

The spine or spinal column is the body's central support. It is made of 26 block-like bones called vertebrae, one on top of the other, which hold up the skull and head while allowing the main body to flex and bend. The spinal column also protects the body's main nerve, the spinal cord, which links the brain to all body parts. The spinal cord is inside a tunnel formed by the lined-up gaps or holes within the vertebrae.

➡ This artificial knee joint has two rounded plastic 'knuckles' at the base of the thigh bone, and a metal plate on top of the shin bone.

What happens if a bone breaks?

It starts to mend itself straight away!
Bones are made of living tissues, and once the parts of the bone are put back into their natural positions, usually by a doctor, microscopic cells called osteoblasts begin to make new bone that fills the break or gap. After a few months the gap is joined and the bone is repaired.

Are there different kinds of joints?

Yes, there are several different kinds, such as synovial joints, which allow movement, and suture joints, which do not. Synovial joints are found throughout the body, especially in the shoulder, elbow, hip and knee. These allow various kinds of movements, depending on their design. The elbow and knee are hinge joints, which allow only a to-and-fro movement. The shoulder and hip are ball-and-socket joints, which enable more flexibility such as twisting.

Collarbone

Upper arm bone

➲ *In the shoulder the ball-shaped end of the upper arm bone fits into a cup-like socket formed by the shoulder blade and collarbone.*

What is inside a synovial joint?

In a synovial joint the ends of the bones have a covering of shiny, slippery cartilage. The joint also contains oil-like synovial fluid, which is made by a bag-like covering around the joint, the synovial capsule. This fluid moistens the cartilage, making movements smooth, with hardly any rubbing and wear. The bones are prevented from moving too far or coming apart by strap-like ligaments, which are strips of strong tissue holding the bones and joints together.

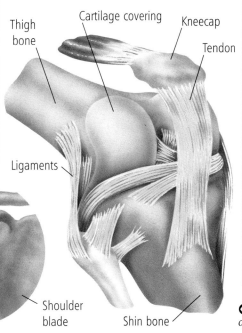

Thigh bone

Cartilage covering

Kneecap

Tendon

Ligaments

Shoulder blade

Shin bone

➲ *Regular exercise and movement help make joints flexible and supple to keep them healthy.*

Do bones change with age?

Yes, a baby's bones are softer and more flexible than an adult's. They tend to bend, rather than snap, under stress, which is helpful because young children tend to fall over or suffer bumps quite often. A baby's skeleton also contains more than 340 bones compared to 206 in the adult skeleton. This is because in early life some bones merge with others to form one bone. All bones are fully formed and at their strongest between about 20 and 45 years of age. In later life the bones become stiffer and more brittle, so they tend to crack rather than bend.

➲ *Strap-shaped ligaments criss-cross the outside of the knee joint to hold the bones in place.*

➲ *The spinal column has 26 bones called vertebrae. There are seven in the cervical or neck region, 12 in the chest (thorax), five in the lumbar or lower back region, and two at the base: the sacrum and the coccyx.*

Cervical vertebrae

Thoracic vertebrae

Lumbar vertebrae

Sacrum

Coccyx

Amazing **bone facts**

- Most of the body parts are about two-thirds water, but bones are only one-fifth water.

- The skull has 22 bones, including 14 in the face and eight in the domed brain case or cranium.

- The smallest bones are the three tiny ossicles inside each ear.

- The longest bone is the thigh bone or femur, making up about one-quarter of the body's total height.

- The broadest bone is the hip bone or pelvis.

- Most people have 12 pairs of ribs, but about one person in 500 has 13 or 11 pairs.

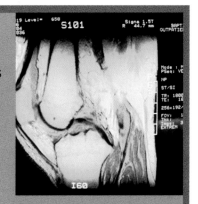

➲ *A scan through the knee joint shows the oval-shaped patella or knee cap on the left, the joint itself in the centre and the rear leg muscles to the right.*

Every movement, every breath, every mouthful you chew – all of these actions and more are carried out by the body's muscles. A single muscle can do only one task, which is to get shorter to pull on body parts. But working together in very precise and co-ordinated ways, the body's hundreds of muscles carry out thousands of different activities every day.

Occipitalis

Deltoid

The muscles just under the skin are called the superficial layer. Beneath them are the intermediate or middle layer of muscles, and then the deep layer muscles, which are next to the bones.

Latissimus

Gluteus

Vastus

Gastrocnemius

How many muscles are there in the body?

There are about 640 muscles in the body. The biggest ones are in the torso, hips, shoulders and thighs. As you move you can see them bulging under the skin. But some muscles are much smaller. Each eyeball has six small ribbon-shaped muscles behind it, so it can swivel to look around.

Inside a muscle are bundles of myofibres, each about as thick as a human hair. Every myofibre is made of even thinner myofibrils, which contain numerous strands of the substances actin and myosin. These slide past each other to make the muscle contract.

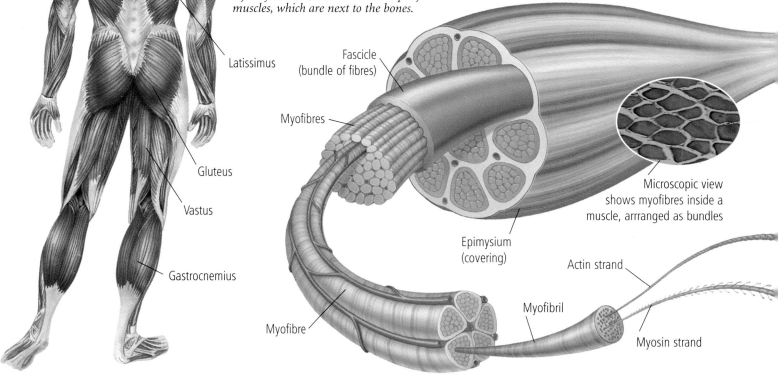

Fascicle
(bundle of fibres)

Myofibres

Epimysium
(covering)

Myofibre

Microscopic view shows myofibres inside a muscle, arrranged as bundles

Actin strand

Myofibril

Myosin strand

Reflexes – **look out!**

Reflex action
A reflex is a body movement that happens automatically, without any conscious control by the brain (without 'thinking'). Many reflexes help the body to avoid injury or damage, by making muscles contract to pull a part away from harm. For example, if an object comes fast towards the face, such as a ball in sport, the body has several reflexes for protection, all of which react within a fraction of a second:

- The eyelids close to guard the delicate surfaces of the eyes.
- The face 'screws up' as the facial muscles tense and harden.
- The neck and upper body muscles jerk the head out of the ball's path.
- The shoulder and arm muscles throw up the arms and hands to block the ball.

When the finger feels pain, a reflex quickly pulls the hand away.

Brain

Nerve signals into spinal cord

Nerve signals to muscle

Finger detects pain

Nerve signals

Can muscles push?

No, they can only pull, or contract. Most muscles are long and slim, and connected at each end to bones. As the muscle contracts it pulls on the bones and moves them, and so moves that body part. Then another muscle on the other side of the bone contracts, to pull it back again. Muscles work like this in pairs or teams to move body parts to-and-fro.

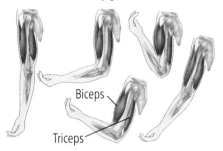

Biceps

Triceps

⬆ *Most muscles are arranged in opposing or antagonistic pairs to pull a bone one way and then the other, like the biceps and triceps in the upper arm.*

How fast can muscles work?

Very fast – as quick as the blink of an eye! But the speed depends on the type of muscle. 'Fast-twitch' muscles in the fingers, face and eyes can contract in less than one-twentieth of a second. They are speedy but soon tire. 'Slow-twitch' muscles, such as those in the back, take longer but can keep contracting for a greater period of time.

What controls muscles?

The brain controls muscles by sending nerve signals along nerves to the muscles, to tell them when to contract, by how much, and for how long. Luckily we learn many common movements such as walking, speaking and chewing early in life, so that we can do them almost without thinking. The brain is still in control, but it is the lower or 'automatic' part of the brain, which does not need our concentration or conscious awareness. Even standing requires muscle power, as the neck and back muscles tense to keep the body balanced and upright.

Why do muscles get tired?

Blood carries oxygen and energy to the muscles in order to keep them active, but the blood flow is sometimes too slow and so the muscles get tired. If the heart cannot pump blood fast enough to active muscles, the supplies run short and the muscles become tired or fatigued and can no longer work. Also, a busy muscle makes a waste product, lactic acid, which is taken away by blood. Again, if the blood supply is insufficient, lactic acid builds up in the muscle and may cause cramps.

Can the body make more muscles?

No, but the muscles it has can become larger, by undertaking exercise and activity. This helps the muscles stay healthier and the body become stronger, with added muscle power. Exercise also makes the heart pump faster and the lungs breathe harder, which has many benefits for the whole body. In fact the heart itself is mostly muscle, and the movements of breathing are muscle-powered, too. So any form of exercise helps to keep all muscles fit and healthy.

⬅ *As a tennis player serves, muscles are working not only in the arms, but in the neck, back and legs, to keep the body well-balanced and supple, in order to run forwards without causing injury.*

➡ *Exercise makes muscles larger and stronger. But practise, movement skills and muscle control techniques are also vital, especially in very physical actions, such as weighlifting. A good lifting technique helps to avoid strain and injury to the body.*

Amazing **facts**

• Muscles make up about two-fifths of the body's total weight.

• On average, men have a greater proportion of body weight as muscle, compared to women.

• The biggest muscle is the gluteus maximus in the buttock, used to push the leg back and body forwards when walking, running and jumping.

• The smallest muscle is the stapedius, deep in the ear, hardly thicker than this letter 'l'.

Stapedius muscle

Stirrup

⬆ *The tiny stapedius muscle pulls on the stirrup (stapes) bone inside the ear, during very loud noise to prevent damage to the ear's delicate inner parts.*

You might not think you are doing much at the moment – except reading, of course. But many parts of the body are busy. One of the vital processes that never stops is breathing, every few seconds during the day and all through the night, too. Along with the heartbeat, it is the body's most essential activity.

Nasal chamber

Throat

Voice-box (larynx)

Windpipe (trachea)

Left lung

Right lung

Diaphragm muscle

↰ The respiratory system includes the parts of the body specialized to take in oxygen from the air. Some parts have others uses too, such as smell in the nose, and speech in the voice-box (larynx).

Why do we need to breathe?

To get oxygen into the body. Oxygen is a gas which forms one-fifth of air. The body needs it for an inner chemical process that happens in every microscopic cell. It breaks down the high-energy substance glucose to release its energy for powering life processes. Oxygen is required for glucose breakdown. Since the body cannot store oxygen, it must always obtain new supplies.

Where does breathed-in air go?

Through the nose and down the throat, into the windpipe (trachea) in the neck, and then along air tubes called bronchi into the two lungs in the chest. All of these parts form the body's respiratory system. Breathing is sometimes called respiration or bodily respiration.

↓ Air flows to and from the lungs along the windpipe, which branches at its base into two bronchi, one to each lung. The heart fills the scoop-like space located between the lungs.

Windpipe

Left bronchus

Right bronchus

Upper lobe of left lung

Upper lobe of right lung

Space for heart

Lower lobe of right lung

Lower lobe of left lung

Breathing **facts**

Breathing muscles
Half a litre of air passes in and out of the lungs each time you breathe. Breathing uses the sheet-like diaphragm below the chest, and the strip-like intercostals between the ribs.

To breathe in, both muscle sets contract. The diaphragm changes from a domed shape, to a flatter shape, pulling down the bases of the lungs. The intercostal muscles force the ribs up and out pulling on the lungs. Both these actions stretch the spongy lungs to suck in air.

To breathe out, both muscle sets relax. The stretched lungs spring back to their smaller size, blowing out air.

➜ Breathing-in or inspiration (left) is powered by muscles and so uses energy. Breathing-out or expiration (right) is due to the stretched lungs becoming smaller, like an elastic band contracting, and so does not need muscle power.

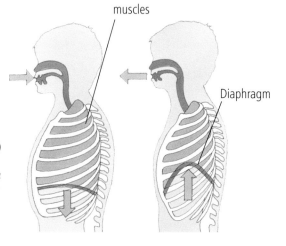

Intercostal muscles

Diaphragm

What are the lung's smallest parts?

Alveoli, which are shaped rather like miniature balloons. There are about 250 million alveoli in each lung! Each alveolus is wrapped in a network of even smaller blood vessels – capillaries. Oxygen from the air in the alveolus can seep easily into the blood in the capillaries, to be carried away around the body by the blood circulation.

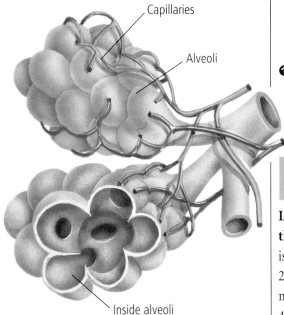

Capillaries

Alveoli

Inside alveoli

⬆ *The bubble-like alveoli are in groups or bunches at the ends of the narrowest air tubes, wrapped in blood capillaries. They make up about one-third of the total space taken up by the lungs.*

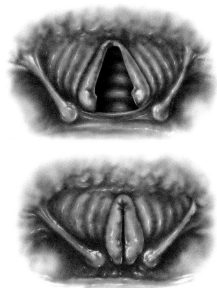

⬆ *The two vocal cords are in the voice-box in the neck. Each one sticks out from the side like a flexible flap. The cords have a triangular-shaped gap between them for normal breathing (top), and move almost together for speech (bottom).*

What is in breathed-out air?

Less oxygen but more carbon dioxide than is present in breathed-in air. There is about 16 per cent oxygen, compared to 21 per cent in breathed-in air. But there is much more carbon dioxide, more than 4 per cent compared to almost none in breathed-in air. Carbon dioxide is a waste product made by the breakdown of glucose for energy. If it builds up it will poison the body. So it is collected by the blood, passes into the air in the alveoli and is breathed out.

When is breathing out noisy?

When you talk, sing, hum, shout and scream. These sounds are made by the vocal cords inside the voice-box (larynx), at the top of the windpipe. As air passes up the windpipe, it blows through a narrow gap between the strip-like vocal cords and makes them vibrate to produce sounds. Breathing out harder makes the sounds louder, and stretching the cords longer makes the sounds higher-pitched.

⬇ *The basic sound of the voice comes from the vocal cords. But the shape and position of the air chambers in the throat, mouth, nose and sinuses (air-filled spaces in the skull bone) all affect the voice quality, so we all sound different.*

Yawning **facts**

- Yawning happens when the body has been still for a time, with shallow breathing, so more oxygen is needed. The body takes an extra-deep breath – the yawn.

- Yawning moves the jaw and face muscles and makes more blood flow to the brain, for greater alertness.

- Some people open their mouths to yawn so wide when they yawn forcefully that they dislocate or 'detach' their jaws and cannot close the mouth again.

Amazing **facts**

- As you rest or sleep, you breathe once every three or four seconds.

- After much exercise, you may breathe as fast as once each second.

- Deeper breathing moves 2–3 l of air each time.

- Restful breathing moves less than 10 l of air in and out of the lungs each minute, compared to more than 150 l during strenuous breathing.

- No matter how much you breathe out, about 0.5 l of air stays in your lungs.

- After holding your breath for a time, it is the amount of carbon dioxide in the body, dissolved in the blood, which causes gasping for air – not the lack of oxygen.

The body needs to breathe fresh air every few seconds to stay alive (see page 17). But it cannot live on fresh air alone. Its other main needs are food and drink. The body needs food which contain many substances, used to help the body grow and repair itself, as well as provide the energy to move about. Drink is needed to continually replenish the supply of water in the bloodstream.

Why do we need to eat?

To provide energy for life processes, and to obtain many kinds of nutrients for bodily growth, maintenance and general health. Taking in food and breaking it into tiny pieces, small enough to absorb into the body, is known as digestion. Ten or so main parts, called the digestive system, work together to carry out this task. As swallowed food is moved through the digestive system, nutrients are absorbed into the bloodstream.

➡ *The digestive system includes the mouth, teeth, tongue, throat, gullet, stomach, the small and large intestines, which together form a long tube, the digestive tract, the liver and pancreas.*

Mouth
Salivary glands
Teeth
Tongue
Throat
Gullet
Liver
Stomach
Small intestine
Large intestine
Appendix
Rectum
Anus
Pancreas (behind stomach)

How many teeth do we have?

The human body has 52 teeth – but not all at once! The first set of 20 grow from around the time of birth to three or four years of age. They are called milk or deciduous teeth. From about six or seven years old, they fall out naturally as the second set of 32 teeth grow. These are larger and stronger, and are called the adult or permanent teeth.

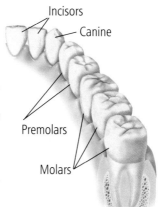

Incisors
Canine
Premolars
Molars

➡ *In each side of the jaw, the adult set of teeth includes two incisors at the front for biting, one taller canine for tearing, and two broad premolars, plus three wider molars for crushing and chewing.*

⬇ *In the centre of a tooth is a soft pulp of blood vessels and nerves. Around this is tough dentine. On the outside of the top part, the crown, is even harder enamel. The roots fix the tooth into the jawbone.*

Enamel
Dentine
Pulp
Jawbone
Nerves and blood vessels

The digestive system

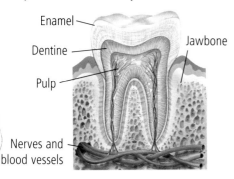

⬅ *To help doctors investigate problems within the digestive system, patients drink barium meal, a special substance that shows up as white on an X-ray. This helps doctors to diagnose exactly what and where the problem might be.*

Timeline of digestion

0 hour – food is chewed and swallowed.
1 hour – food is churned with acids and juices in the stomach.
2 hours – partially-digested food begins to flow into the small intestine for further digestion and absorption.
4 hours – most food has left the stomach and passed to the small intestine.
6 hours – leftover and undigested foods pass into the large intestine, which takes the water and returns it to the body.
10 hours – the leftovers begin to collect in the last part of the system, the rectum, as faeces.
16–24 hours – the faeces pass through the last part of the system, the anus, and out of the body.

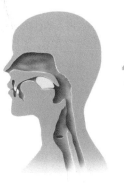

➜ *Swallowing involves a complicated series of muscle actions as the tongue pushes the lump of food (shown in yellow) into the throat, past the entrance to the windpipe and down the gullet.*

1 Tongue presses food to back of mouth

2 Food passes over the top of the windpipe

3 Food is pushed down the gullet

What happens before swallowing food?

The teeth bite off lumps of food, chew them and mix them with watery saliva (spit) to make the food soft and easy to swallow in small lumps. Food is swallowed into the gullet (oesophagus), a muscular tube that pushes it down through the neck into the stomach where it is churned around with gastric juices.

What does the stomach do?

The stomach breaks down food in two main ways. It is a muscular bag that can squeeze, mash and squash the food into a soft pulp. It also attacks the food by adding strong chemicals called acids and enzymes, which break down the food into a soup-like substance called chyme.

Which is the body's longest organ?

After the stomach, the semi-digested food flows into the body's longest part – the 6 m-long small intestine. This is coiled up in the middle of the lower body. It adds more enzymes and other chemicals to break the food into the smallest nutrients. These seep through the small intestine lining into the blood, and are carried away for use around the body.

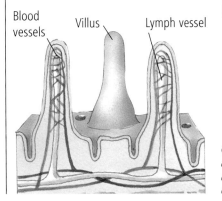

Blood vessels Villus Lymph vessel

Which is the biggest internal organ?

The liver, which is to the right of the stomach. It receives blood that is rich in nutrients, and processes or alters these nutrients so they can be stored or used around the body. To the left of the liver, under the stomach, is the pancreas. It makes powerful digestive juices that flow into the small intestine. The pancreas produces about 1.5 l of digestive juices each day.

⊙ *The liver is a large, wedge-shaped organ with a plentiful blood supply, carried by the portal vein, direct from the intestines. It makes a fluid, bile, which is stored in the gall bladder and then flows into the small intestine, where the bile helps to digest fatty foods.*

Main lobe of liver

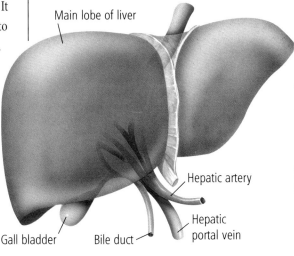

Hepatic artery

Hepatic portal vein

Gall bladder Bile duct

⊙ *The inner lining of the small intestine is covered with small, finger-like parts, villi, each about 1 mm long. These provide a huge surface area for absorbing nutrients into the blood.*

Main **food groups**

⊙ *Different kinds of food provide a varied selection of nutrients. The main food groups are shown in the panel on the right.*

The body needs a variety of substances in foods, called a balanced diet, to provide all the nutrients needed for good health:

Carbohydrates (sugars and starches) – used mainly for energy. They are found in bread, rice, potatoes, pasta, and various fruits and vegetables.

Fibre – not absorbed into the body, but keeps the digestive system working well. It is found in wholemeal bread, pasta and rice, fresh fruits and vegetables. Meat has little fibre.

Oils and fats – provide some energy and building materials for body parts. Healthiest are plant-based oils. Too many fats from animal sources, especially fatty meats, are less healthy.

Proteins – vital for growth, to maintain and repair body parts, and for strong muscles and bones. They occur in most meats and fish, dairy products and some vegetables.

Vitamins and minerals – needed for many body processes, such as calcium for strong bones and teeth, and iron for blood. They are plentiful in fresh fruits and vegetables.

The body is a busy place. Every second there are thousands of chemical processes inside every tiny cell, which use energy, nutrients and other raw materials, and produce unwanted wastes. The circulatory system is a complex network of blood vessels, such as arteries, veins and capillaries, specialized to bring these raw materials to every part of the body and take away the wastes – and it never stops.

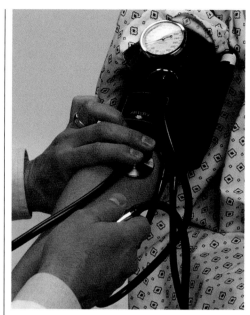

⊕ *Blood pressure can be measured by placing a cuff around the top of the arm and inflating it briefly. The reading then appears on a gauge that is connected to the cuff.*

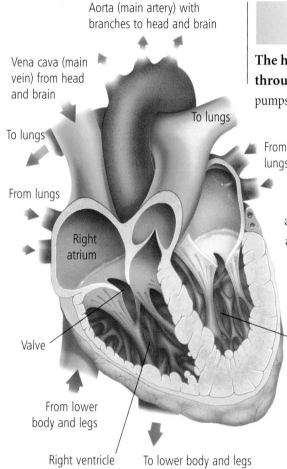

Aorta (main artery) with branches to head and brain

Vena cava (main vein) from head and brain

To lungs

To lungs

From lungs

Right atrium

Valve

From lower body and legs

Right ventricle

To lungs

From lungs

Left ventricle

To lower body and legs

← *Inside the heart are four chambers. On each side are an upper atrium, which receives blood from the veins, and the lower thick-walled ventricle, which pumps it out into the arteries. One-way valves make sure blood flows in the correct direction.*

Which part of the body never rests?

The heart does not stop beating throughout life. It is a muscular bag that pumps blood round and round the body. The heart is divided into two pumps, left and right. The right pump sends used or stale blood to the lungs to pick up oxygen. The blood comes back to the left side, is pumped all around the body to deliver the oxygen, and then returns to the right side to complete the circulation. It takes blood an average of one minute to complete the whole journey.

How fast can the heart beat?

At rest the heart pumps about 60–75 times each minute, but after plenty of exercise this rises to 130 times or more, before returning to the resting rate. The speed of the heartbeat varies according to the body's needs. With each beat blood is pushed under pressure into the vessels and makes them bulge. This bulge can be felt in the wrist as the pulse. Doctors measure the pressure during and between heartbeats to tell how healthy the heart is.

In the **blood**

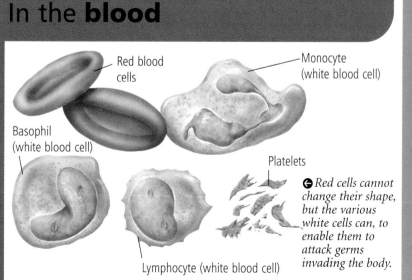

Red blood cells

Monocyte (white blood cell)

Basophil (white blood cell)

Platelets

Lymphocyte (white blood cell)

← *Red cells cannot change their shape, but the various white cells can, to enable them to attack germs invading the body.*

Blood **facts**

In a drop of blood as big as this 'o' there are:

• About 20 million red blood cells, also called erythrocytes. Each one contains the substance haemoglobin, which easily joins to and carries oxygen. A typical red blood cell lives for about three months.

• Around 20,000 white blood cells, known as leucocytes. There are many kinds of white blood cells and most fight germs and illness (see page 143). Some live a few days, others for many years.

• Between one and two million platelets, or thrombocytes, for blood clotting.

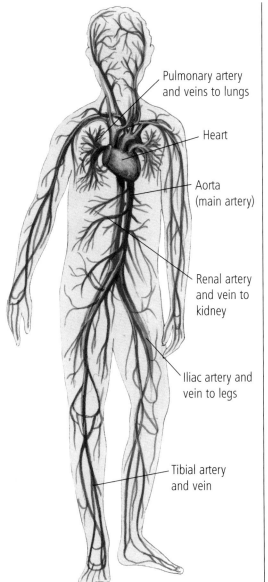

- Pulmonary artery and veins to lungs
- Heart
- Aorta (main artery)
- Renal artery and vein to kidney
- Iliac artery and vein to legs
- Tibial artery and vein

⬆ *The circulatory or cardiovascular ('cardio' for heart, 'vascular' for blood vessels) system includes a network of blood vessels which transport blood to every part of the body.*

How much blood is in the body?

About one-twelfth of the body's weight is blood. For most adults this means from 4–6 l. About 55 per cent of blood is a pale liquid, plasma, containing dissolved oxygen, nutrients and hundreds of other substances. The remaining 45 per cent of blood comprises microscopic cells.

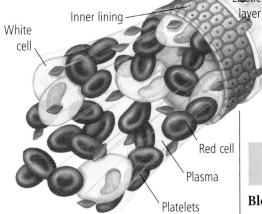

- Tough outer cover
- Muscle layer
- Elastic layer
- Inner lining
- White cell
- Red cell
- Plasma
- Platelets

⬆ *Red cells are the most numerous blood cells and have a rounded, dished shape. White cells can change their shape as they surround and attack germs. Platelets are much smaller, resembling pieces of cells.*

How many jobs does blood have?

Blood has more than 100 jobs to do. One of the most important is to carry oxygen in its billions of red blood cells. Blood also distributes nutrients, carries dozens of natural substances called hormones that control body processes, spreads warmth around the body, carries white cells that fight disease, and collects carbon dioxide and other wastes.

What is a clot?

Blood clots or goes lumpy to seal a cut or wound. At the damage site, a substance in blood, called fibrin, forms a tangled web of micro-fibres. Blood cells, known as platelets, help to form the clot, which stops blood leaking away. The clot hardens into a scab, which protects the area as the damage heals over the next few days, then falls off.

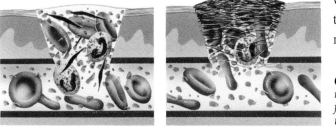

⬅ *Where there is a wound, red and white cells tangle in fibres (left). The lump hardens to seal the gap (right).*

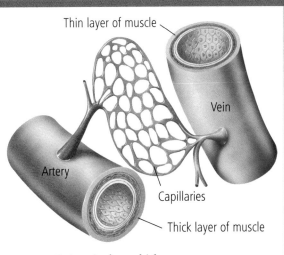

- Thin layer of muscle
- Vein
- Artery
- Capillaries
- Thick layer of muscle

⬆ *Arteries have thicker, stronger walls than veins.*

Types of **blood vessels**

There are five main types of blood vessels:
Arteries – carry blood away from the heart. They have thick walls to withstand the surge of high-pressure blood with each heartbeat. They carry blood to the major parts or organs, where they divide or branch into:
Arterioles – smaller versions of arteries, down to the thickness of human hairs. These divide more into:
Capillaries – the smallest blood vessels, less than 1 mm long and far too thin to see. Oxygen and nutrients seep from blood through their walls into surrounding tissues. Capillaries join to form:
Venules – which carry the slower-moving blood, now under much less pressure, as they join further into:
Veins – wide, thin-walled and floppy, which take blood back to the heart.

At any moment about 66 per cent of all the body's blood is in the veins, 29 per cent in the arteries and 5 per cent in the capillaries.

Wastes are produced by all living things, including the human body. Each day the body takes in 1–2 kg of foods, and 2–3 l of water. The unwanted parts and by-products from these 'inputs' must be removed daily, too. Otherwise after a year, the body would weigh more than one tonne and would be full of horrible, smelly wastes!

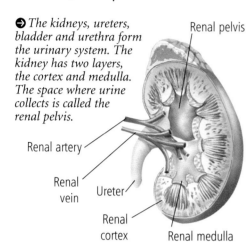

➜ *The kidneys, ureters, bladder and urethra form the urinary system. The kidney has two layers, the cortex and medulla. The space where urine collects is called the renal pelvis.*

Renal pelvis

Renal artery

Renal vein

Ureter

Renal cortex

Renal medulla

What do the kidneys do?

The two kidneys make the waste liquid, urine. Inside each kidney are one million microscopic filters called nephrons. Each has a tiny bunch of blood capillaries, which pass water and many substances into a long, looped tube. In the tube some of the water and substances are taken back into the body, leaving the unwanted water and wastes as urine. This flows from the kidney down a tube, the ureter, to the bladder.

How do wastes leave?

The body removes its wastes in three main ways – respiration, defecation and urination. Respiration (breathing), gets rid of carbon dioxide. Defecation, or bowel movements, removes the undigested and leftover parts of food and drink from the intestines. Urination gets rid of amounts of urine, a liquid containing urea and other unwanted substances filtered from the blood.

How much urine does the body make each day?

On average, the body makes about 1,500 ml of urine every 24 hours. The urine collects in the bladder until there is about 300 ml, when you feel the need to empty the bladder. This happens by urination along a tube to the outside, the urethra. However, the amount of urine varies hugely, depending on how much you drink, and if water is lost as sweat rather than as urine.

What do hormones do?

Hormones are natural body chemicals that control many internal processes and make sure the organs and systems work together. Hormones are made in parts called endocrine glands and travel around the whole body in the blood, but each hormone affects only certain parts, known as its target organs.

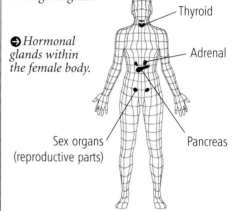

➜ *Hormonal glands within the female body.*

Thyroid

Adrenal

Sex organs (reproductive parts)

Pancreas

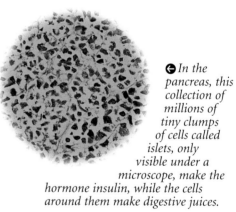

⬅ *In the pancreas, this collection of millions of tiny clumps of cells called islets, only visible under a microscope, make the hormone insulin, while the cells around them make digestive juices.*

Body chemistry

Renal dialysis

In some cases the kidneys do not work properly and wastes build up in the blood. Many such people can be treated by renal dialysis using an 'artificial kidney'. The blood is led along a tube from the body to the dialysis machine, which filters out the waste products and returns it to the body. This usually takes a few hours, several times each week. Other treatments include passing fluid through the abdomen to soak up wastes and then removing it, or a kidney transplant.

➜ *During dialysis the patient must stay still and rest, as blood is led to the machine and back into the body along tubes, which are connected to the body.*

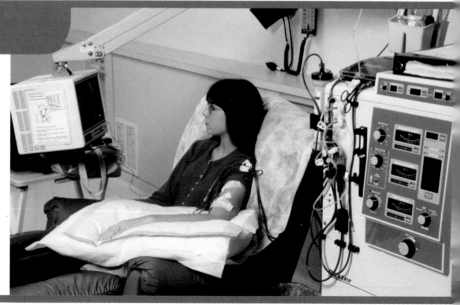

⬇ *Lymph nodes vary from less than 1 mm to about 20 mm across. They contain lymph fluid, which flows slowly around the body through lymph vessels. The nodes enlarge or swell greatly during illness as they fill with disease-fighting white cells.*

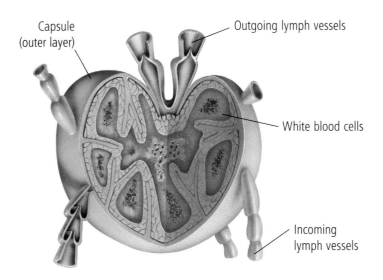

Capsule (outer layer)

Outgoing lymph vessels

White blood cells

Incoming lymph vessels

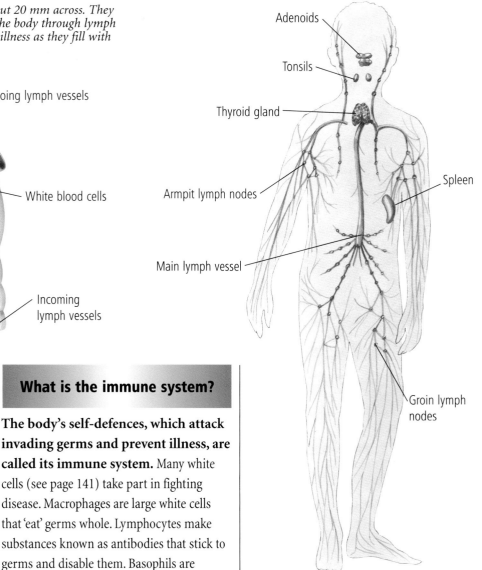

Adenoids

Tonsils

Thyroid gland

Armpit lymph nodes

Spleen

Main lymph vessel

Groin lymph nodes

Is blood the only liquid flowing around the body?

No, lymph fluid also flows through the body. Lymph fluid carries wastes of metabolism, and white blood cells, which destroy harmful substances such as germs. However, unlike blood, the fluid only moves one way. It begins as liquid around and between cells and tissues. It collects in small tubes called minor lymph vessels. These join to form major lymph vessels. The largest lymph vessels empty the lymph fluid into the main blood vessels near the heart. The body contains about 1–2 l of lymph fluid.

What is the immune system?

The body's self-defences, which attack invading germs and prevent illness, are called its immune system. Many white cells (see page 141) take part in fighting disease. Macrophages are large white cells that 'eat' germs whole. Lymphocytes make substances known as antibodies that stick to germs and disable them. Basophils are involved in allergic reactions and blood clotting. White cells are especially numerous in small areas called lymph nodes, which are sometimes called 'lymph glands'.

⬆ *The immune system includes many lymph nodes, found particularly in the neck, chest, armpits, lower body and groin. There are also lymph tissues in the adenoids, tonsils and the spleen, which sits behind the stomach.*

➡ *The pituitary gland is under the front part of the brain.*

Pituitary gland

⬅ *The thyroid gland is in the front of the neck.*

Hormones **and more hormones**

Adrenal gland – on top of each kidney produces hormones (adrenaline) for coping with stress, which prepares the body for action, and hormones to regulate the kidneys.

Pancreas – makes digestive juices, and produces the hormones insulin and glucagon, which control how quickly cells break down sugar for energy.

Pea-sized pituitary gland – just under the brain makes about ten hormones that control other endocrine glands, body growth and the reproductive (sex) organs.

Thyroid gland – in the neck makes hormones that control the cells' use of energy and the level of calcium in the blood.

Reproductive organs – make hormones, mainly oestrogen and progesterone in ovaries in women, and testosterone in testes in men.

Other hormone-making organs – stomach, intestines, heart and kidneys also make some hormones.

Are you a sensitive person? Of course – your body has senses! The five main ones are sight, hearing, smell, taste and touch. They provide information about what is happening around and on the body, and in the nose and mouth. There are also tiny sensors inside the body that give information about the positions of the muscles and joints.

Lachrymal tear gland

Retina

Lens

Sclera

Pupil

Iris

Lachrymal duct

Tear fluid is made in the lachrymal glands and drains from the inner eyelids through the lachrymal ducts into the nose. Inside the eye is the light-sensitive lining, the retina.

Outer ear flap

Cartilage in ear flap

Ear canal

Skull bone

The vibrations of sound waves pass along the ear canal to the eardrum, and along the tiny ear bones (ossicles) to the coiled cochlea, which converts them to nerve signals.

How do the eyes work?

The eye changes the brightness and colours of the light rays it sees, into a code of electrical nerve signals, which it sends to the brain. The light rays pass through the domed, clear front of the eye, the cornea, then through a hole, the pupil, in a ring of coloured muscle,

The eye's own lens, just behind the dark hole or pupil, can become thicker or thinner to focus on near or far objects. When the lens is not working properly, some people need extra lenses, so spectacles or contact lenses help them see clearly.

the iris. The iris makes the pupil smaller in bright conditions, preventing too much light from entering the eye and damaging the inside.

What numbers 125 million in the eye?

Microscopic light-detecting cells called rods and cones, which make nerve signals when light rays shine on them. The 120 million rods see well in dim light but not colours. Up to six million cones work only in brighter light, but see colours and fine details. All these cells are in a curved sheet, which is as big as your thumb-tip and thinner than this page, called the retina. The retina lines the inside of the eyeball.

Making sense

Colour vision
There are three kinds of cone cells. Red cones are not red, they are so named because they respond only to red light. Blue cones detect blue light and, likewise, green cones make nerve signals only when green light shines or them. All the thousands of different colours, shades and hues we can see are worked out by the brain from combinations of signals from these three types of cones. Occasionally, one type of cone is missing, which causes a problem with identifying some colours.

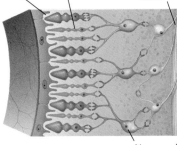

Cone cells

Rod cells

To optic nerve

Nerve cells

Rod and cone cells in the retina pass their signals along nerve cells to the optic nerve.

Amazing sense facts

- The taste buds of the tongue detect only four main flavours – sweet, salty, sour and bitter. The many tastes of different foods come from different strengths and combinations of these four.

- In contrast, the nose can detect more than 10,000 different smells and odours.

- As we eat, the tongue tastes – but the nose also smells the many different odours floating around the back of the mouth and up into the nasal chamber.

- What we think of as the 'taste' of a meal is not just flavours but also the sensation of many odours.

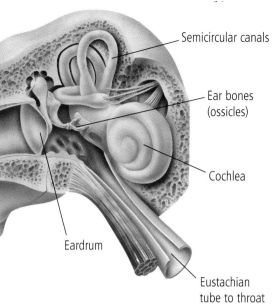

- Semicircular canals
- Ear bones (ossicles)
- Cochlea
- Eardrum
- Eustachian tube to throat

What is inside the nose?

An air space called the nasal chamber, as big as your two thumbs. In its roof are two patches, each about as large as a thumbnail, called olfactory epithelia. Each of these has more than 25 million microscopic olfactory receptor cells. Tiny smell-carrying particles called odorants float through on breathed-in air and land on the cells, causing them to send nerve signals to the brain. However, each of the millions of cells responds to only a few kinds of odorants.

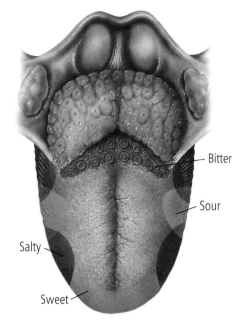

- Bitter
- Sour
- Salty
- Sweet

⬆ *The taste buds at the tip of the tongue sense mainly sweet flavours. Those at the sides detect salty and, behind them, sour, with bitter tastes sensed mainly across the tongue's rear.*

Can we hear every sound?

No, some sounds are too high-pitched (ultrasonic) or too low (infrasonic) for our ears – but some animals such as dogs and horses can hear them. Sound waves in air travel along the tube-like ear canal and hit the eardrum, making it vibrate. The vibrations pass along three tiny bones, the ossicles, into the fluid inside the snail-shaped cochlea, deep in the ear. The vibrations shake micro-hairs sticking up from delicate hair cells in the cochlea, and these produce nerve signals, which are sent to the brain.

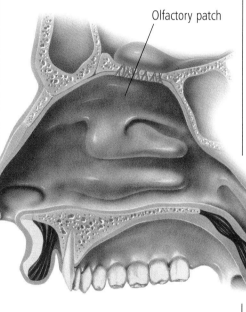

Olfactory patch

⬆ *The hairy-looking patches called olfactory epithelia, which detect smells, are in the top of the air space known as the nasal chamber, inside the nose and above the mouth.*

How does the tongue taste different flavours?

As we eat, about 10,000 taste buds scattered around the tip, sides and rear of the tongue detect tiny particles in foods called flavourants. Each taste bud has around 25 gustatory receptor cells. If a suitable flavourant lands on a cell, it sends nerve messages to the brain. The tongue tastes flavours similarly to how the nose smells odours.

| Jet take-off 120–140 dB | Motorcycle 70–90 dB | Vacuum cleaner 60–80 dB | Talking 40–60 dB | Whispering 20–30 dB |

⬆ *The loudness or intensity of sounds is measured in decibels, dB. Sound volumes of more than about 90 dB can damage the ears, especially if they are high-pitched and continue for a long time.*

⬅ *Sniffing helps the smell particles to swirl up into the roof of the nasal chamber within the nose, where the odour-detecting cells are situated.*

Direction of sounds

We know the direction of sounds, such as from the left or right, because we have two ears. This is known as stereophonic or binaural hearing.

- Sound waves travel through air at about 340 m/sec. A sound from the left reaches the left ear first, and the right ear less than one-thousandth of a second later.
- The ear facing the sound's direction hears sounds more loudly than the other ear because sounds fade as they travel.
- The brain works out these time and volume differences to tell the sound's direction.

The body has its very own 'Internet'. This sends millions of signals along thousands of routeways called nerves, to-and-fro between its hundreds of parts, and to and from the one part which controls all the others – the brain. The brain is linked to the body by the main nerve, the spinal cord.

Which body parts could stretch halfway to the Moon?

The body's complicated network of branching nerves. If all the nerves could be joined together end to end, including the tiniest ones visible only under a microscope, they would stretch this far! Nerves are like shiny, pale cords. They are made of bundles of even thinner parts, nerve cells or neurons, which pass messages between each other. Each nerve has a tough covering to prevent squashing or kinking.

Brain

Cervical nerves in neck and arms

Spinal cord

Abdominal nerves

Sciatic nerve to leg

➲ *The nervous system controls and co-ordinates all body processes and activities. Its main parts are the brain and main nerve, the spinal cord, which together are called the central nervous system, and the hundreds of nerves that branch from them all through the body, the peripheral nervous system.*

What is a motor nerve?

A motor nerve carries nerve signals from the brain, out to the rest of the body. Nerve signals or impulses are tiny bursts of electricity that travel along nerves, carrying information. Most of these go to the muscles, telling them when to contract, by how much and for how long. Some motor signals go to glands, such as the sweat, salivary and tear glands, instructing them to release their contents. Sensory nerves carry signals the other way, from the eyes, ears and other sense organs, to the brain.

⬇ *A single nerve cell or neuron has a wide part, the cell body, with branching parts known as dendrites, which receive signals from other nerve cells. One long fibre-like part, the axon, passes the signals to other nerve cells.*

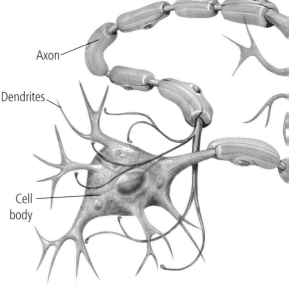

Axon

Dendrites

Cell body

How nerve **cells 'talk'**

Synapses

Nerve cells pass signals between each other at specialized links or junctions called synapses. However, the nerve cells do not actually touch at a synapse. They are separated by a very narrow gap, the synaptic cleft, which is 0.000025 mm (25 nanometres) across – less than one-hundredth the width of a hair. The signal passes across the fluid-filled gap as particles of chemicals known as neurotransmitters. However, this happens very fast, in less than one-thousandth of a second for each signal.

➲ *At a synapse, the axon end of one nerve cell almost touches the dendrite of another nerve cell. The nerve signal passes along the axon in electrical form but 'jumps the gap' as chemical particles, neurotransmitters, that slot into receptor sites on the receiving cell.*

Axon

Sending nerve cell

Neurotransmitters ready to be released

Synaptic cleft

Neurotransmitters cross the gap

Receiving nerve cell dendrite

Receptor site

↑ *Under the microscope, a nerve cell growing in a glass dish sends out tentacle-like dendrites to 'search' for other nerve cells.*

How many nerve cells are there?

Hundreds of billions, including about 100 billion in the brain itself. The optic nerve from each eye to the brain has more than one million nerve fibres, and other nerves also have huge numbers. Also some nerve cells pass messages to more than 10,000 others, at synapses (see panel below). So the possible number of pathways for nerve signals around the body is too big to imagine – and the connections continuously change, too.

➡ *As a person plays the guitar, the brain sends thousands of nerve signals every second along motor nerves to the muscles in the arms, hands and fingers, controlling movement with amazing speed and precision.*

How fast do nerves work?

The fastest signals, such as those from the skin, warning of damage and pain, go at more than 100 m/sec. This enables quick reflex action to protect the body from harm. However, the speed varies with the type of nerve it is and the information it carries. Other signals, such as those controlling how the stomach and guts work, can travel as slow as 1 m/sec.

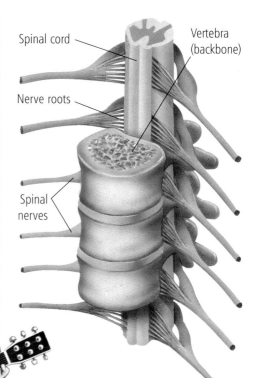

Spinal cord · Vertebra (backbone) · Nerve roots · Spinal nerves

↑ *The spinal cord is protected inside a tunnel, which is formed by a row of holes through the vertebrae (backbones).*

How is the brain 'wired' into the body?

By the spinal cord. This is the body's main nerve, and extends from the base of the brain down inside the backbone (spinal column). Thirty-one pairs of nerves branch from it, on each side, out into the body. There are also 12 pairs of nerves that branch from the brain itself, mainly to parts such as the eyes and ears. These are called cranial nerves and some extend down to the chest.

Amazing **brain facts**

- Ordinary or 'plain' X-rays do not show up softer parts very well, so they cannot reveal the details of the brain.

- A substance that shows up on X-ray, called a radio-opaque dye, can be injected into the bloodstream to show the blood vessels in and around the brain. This can reveal a blockage, as happens in a stroke.

- CT and MR scans (see page 129) show the brain in great detail, revealing the hollow fluid-filled chambers inside, called ventricles.

- PET (positron emission tomography) scans show how fast the various parts of the brain use energy, and so which parts are 'thinking' most.

↑ *A doctor studies brain or whole-body scans to check for illness, harmful growths or injury inside the body.*

The brain never truly 'sleeps'. Even while most of the body is relaxed and still at night, the brain is busy. It controls the beating of the heart, the breathing lungs, body temperature, the digestive system and many other internal processes. The more we find out about the brain and its processes, the more complicated it seems.

How does thinking happen?

Thinking seems to happen as a result of nerve signals passing between many different parts of the brain. There is no single part in the brain where thoughts occur. Especially important is the cortex, which is the wrinkled grey outer layer of the large, bulging parts known as cerebral hemispheres. Under these are the lower parts of the brain, which are concerned less with consciousness or awareness, and more with 'automatic' processes such as controlling heartbeat and breathing. The smaller, lower, wrinkled part at the rear of the brain is the cerebellum. It organizes nerve signals sent to muscles, to ensure that all the body's movements are smooth and co-ordinated.

Cortex of cerebral hemisphere

Sulcus (groove)

Corpus callosum (links two hemispheres)

Thalamus

Hyphothalamus

Hippocampus

Pons

Cerebellum

Brain stem

↑ *About nine-tenths of the brain is the large dome of the two cerebral hemispheres. The outer cerebral cortex is where many conscious thoughts happen. Inside are blob-like parts called ganglia.*

Where are memories stored?

As with thinking, there is no single 'memory centre' in the brain but many parts working together to store memories, as pathways for nerve signals through the incredible maze of nerve cells. However, a curved part called the hippocampus is important in changing short-term memories, such as a phone number we need for just a few seconds, into long-term memories that we can recall weeks or months later.

Brain **facts**

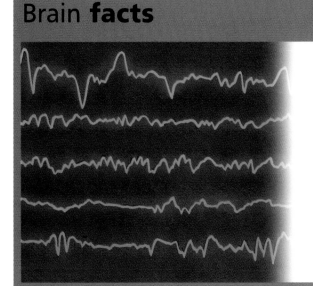

← *The spikes and dips of an EEG recording show the brain's level of activity at different times, revealing health problems such as a stroke or epilepsy.*

Amazing **facts**

- An average brain weighs about 1.4 kg and occupies the top half of the head.

- Men have slightly larger brains than women, because the average man is bigger than the average woman.

- Compared to body size however, women have slightly larger brains than men.

- The brain is surrounded by three sheet-like membranes, the meninges, under the skull bone. These contain a watery liquid called cerebro-spinal fluid. The brain floats in this fluid, which cushions it from knocks and jolts.

Are bigger brains more intelligent?

No, there is no link between brain size and intelligence. It also depends what we mean by 'intelligence'. Some people are not especially successful at mathematics or science, but they may be brilliant at music or painting, or making money, or developing friendships. Every person has different abilities, talents and ways of behaving.

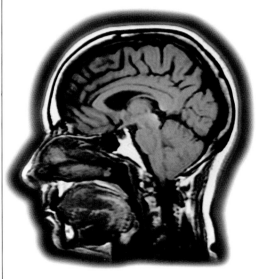

Touch centre **Movement centre**

Speech centre

Hearing centre

Visual centre

⬆ *Different parts of the cortex deal with nerve signals that are either coming from the senses or being sent to muscles.*

⬆ *Doctors examine brain scans to locate problems such as a stroke, when the blood supply to part of the brain fails and its nerve cells are damaged.*

What is the 'mind's eye'?

It is the place where we can imagine scenes and views that our eyes might see – even with our eyes closed. Different parts of the brain's cortex receive information from different senses. Information from the eyes goes to the lower rear of the cortex, called the visual centre, where the brain works out what is being seen. Other cortex centres are shown above. The movement centre is also called the motor cortex.

What happens during sleep?

EEG (electroencephalogram) recordings of the brain's nerve signals or 'brain-waves' suggest that, during sleep, the brain could be assessing recent events and memories, and deciding which ones are less important and can be forgotten. At certain times the body's muscles twitch and the eyes flick to-and-fro even though they are closed. This is called rapid eye movement or REM sleep and is when dreams occur.

⬆ *This MR head scan shows how the wrinkled cerebral hemisphere dominates the brain. The lower rear of the brain tapers into the brain stem and then into the spinal cord in the neck.*

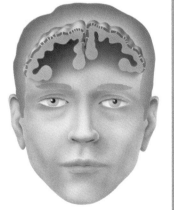

⬆ *Much of the brain is above eye level.*

Inside the **head**

Brainwaves

Sensor pads on the head pick up the very faint electrical pulses of nerve signals that are always passing around the brain, and display them on a screen or paper sheet.

These wavy lines are called EEGs (electroencephalograms).

The shapes of the waves change depending on whether the brain is fully alert and thinking hard, daydreaming, drowsy or fast asleep.

Even during sleep the waves change shape, especially between deep sleep, and lighter REM or 'dream' sleep.

The cortex and lobes

The brain's main outer surface, the cerebral cortex, contains billions of nerve cells linked together by trillions of connections.

If the wrinkled, grooved cortex was spread out flat, it would cover the area of a pillow-case, and be almost as thin – it is just a few millimetres in thickness.

The folds of the cortex reveal the main pairs of bulges or lobes of the brain. These are the frontal lobes under the forehead, the parietal lobes on the top of the head, the temporal lobes at the sides under the temples and the occipital lobes at the rear.

About four weeks after a new baby is born, we say it is 'one month old'. But really it has been ten months since its body began to form. After fertilization, the unborn baby spent nine months developing and growing inside its mother. People look carefully at babies to see who they resemble most, the mother or the father. This resemblance is due to the inheritance of genes.

How does the body begin?

In the beginning, every human body begins as a single cell. This is a tiny speck, smaller than the dot on this 'i', called the fertilized egg. It is made from the joining of two cells, the egg cell from the mother and the sperm cell from the father. As the human body develops over the following months and years, it is built up from billions and billions of microscopic cells, which are all formed by the splitting or division of other cells.

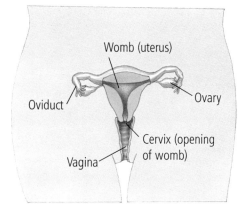

Womb (uterus)

Oviduct

Ovary

Cervix (opening of womb)

Vagina

Where do eggs come from?

Egg cells are contained inside a woman's body in rounded parts called ovaries, one in either side of the lower abdomen. Each ovary contains many thousands of egg cells. Each month one of these eggs develops and becomes ripe or ready to be fertilized. The ripe egg is released into a tube, the oviduct (fallopian tube), and passes slowly towards the womb, in a process called ovulation. The lining of the womb is thick and rich with blood, ready to nourish the egg if it is fertilized by a sperm cell (see page 151). If not, the egg and the womb lining are lost through the birth canal or vagina, as the monthly menstrual flow or period.

↩ The parts of the body specialized to produce a baby are known as the reproductive organs. In the woman, egg cells are contained in the two ovaries. Each month the menstrual cycle causes one egg to ripen and pass along the oviduct into the womb, where a sperm cell may join with it.

Where do sperm come from?

Sperm cells develop and are contained inside a man's body. They are made continually in rounded parts called testes, which hang below the lower abdomen inside a bag of skin called the scrotum. Millions of sperm cells are made each day. The sperm develop and are stored in a coiled tube called the epididymis. The sperm live for about one month. If they are not released from the body during sex, they gradually die and break apart as new ones are made.

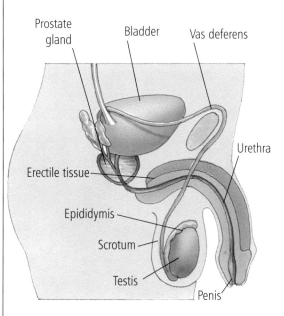

Prostate gland

Bladder

Vas deferens

Urethra

Erectile tissue

Epididymis

Scrotum

Testis

Penis

↪ In a man's reproductive organs, sperm are made in the two testes. During sex they pass along the vas deferens tubes, which join and continue as the urethra, to the outside.

Genes **and DNA**

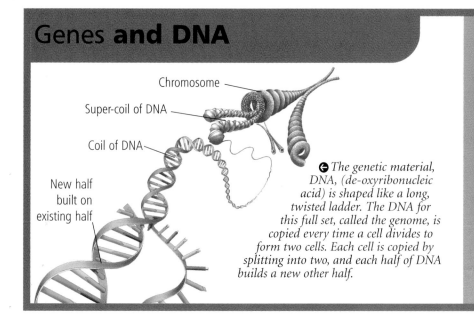

Chromosome

Super-coil of DNA

Coil of DNA

New half built on existing half

↩ The genetic material, DNA, (de-oxyribonucleic acid) is shaped like a long, twisted ladder. The DNA for this full set, called the genome, is copied every time a cell divides to form two cells. Each cell is copied by splitting into two, and each half of DNA builds a new other half.

Amazing **facts**

• The full set of genetic material for a human body to develop contains about 30,000 genes.

• The full set of DNA is found in every cell in the body, located in the cell's control centre, or nucleus.

• The full set of DNA is in the form of 46 separate lengths, and each length is coiled or wound up very tightly to form an X-shaped part, the chromosome.

• If all the DNA from all the 46 chromosomes in a single cell were joined together, it would stretch almost 2 m.

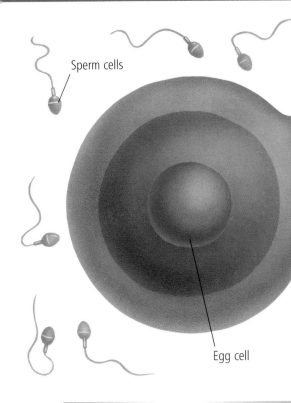

Sperm cells

Sperm cell fertilizing egg cell

Egg cell

Nucleus — Cap

Sperm tail —

Sperm cell

↑ A single sperm cell has a rounded head containing genetic material (DNA).

← Inside the oviduct of the woman, many sperm cells lash their tails to swim towards the egg cell. However, only one sperm cell can merge with the egg cell, adding its genetic material (DNA) to the egg's.

How do egg and sperm join?

During sex (sexual intercourse), sperm cells enter the woman's vagina, swim through the womb and into the two oviducts where a ripe egg may be present. The journey begins inside the man's body where millions of sperm cells pass from the testes and epididymis, along tubes known as the vas deferens, to another tube called the urethra, which is inside the penis. Fluid containing the sperm leaves the end of the penis, but only one sperm can join with the egg at fertilization to start the new baby.

What are genes and inheritance?

Genes instruct the human body how to develop and carry out its life processes, and inheritance is the passing of these genes from parents to offspring. Genes are in the form of a chemical substance called DNA (de-oxyribonucleic acid) (see panel below). The egg cell contains genes from the mother, and the sperm cell contains the father's genes. When egg and sperm join at the time of fertilization, the genes come together and the fertilized egg can begin to develop into a baby (see page 152).

Which kind of features are inherited?

Some physical body features are inherited from parents, such as the colour of the eyes, skin and hair, the shapes of the nose and ears, and overall body height. But some of these features can be controlled by several genes. This means a child's hair colour or ear shape is not always the same as either of the parents – it may be more similar to one of the grandparents. Even identical twins, with the same genes, have slightly different features.

↓ The full set of genes is contained in 23 pairs of chromosomes (below left). In reproduction the pairs split so that only 23 go into each egg or sperm (below centre). At fertilization, sets of 23 come together to form 46 (below right). The last pair of chromosomes determine the sex of the baby. The combination shown here is XY, with the large X and smaller x-like Y, and results in a boy. Two larger sex chromosomes, XX, would produce a girl.

IVF and assisted reproduction

Sometimes a woman and man wish to have a baby, but are unable to. There are many causes, such as previous illness, so that the reproductive parts do not work properly. In some cases medical techniques known as IVF, in vitro fertilization, can help. In one method, egg cells are removed from the woman's ovaries through a narrow telescope-like tube, a laparoscope, inserted through a small incision (cut) in the skin. The egg cells are added to sperm cells in a shallow dish and observed under the microscope. If an egg and sperm join and the fertilized egg begins to grow, it is put into the woman's womb to continue its development.

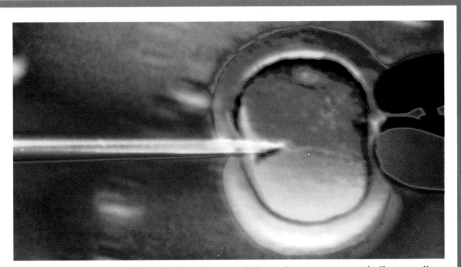

↑ Male genetic material is added to the egg cell through a very narrow hollow needle.

Each human body starts as a tiny speck, the fertilized egg. Nine months later it is six billion times bigger – a newborn baby, which can cry loudly when it is very tired or hungry! The time of development in the mother's womb is known as pregnancy.

→ *As the speck-like fertilized egg develops into a baby, most of the body parts form within the first two months. The mother's abdomen begins to bulge from about 16 weeks after fertilization. She can feel the baby moving from about 18 weeks, as it twitches its arms, kicks its legs and bends its neck and back.*

Which body parts develop first?

An unborn baby develops 'head-first', starting with the brain and head, then the main body, then the arms and legs. Life begins when the fertilized egg divides into two cells, then four, eight, and so on. After a few days there are hundreds of cells, and after a few weeks, millions. These cells build up the various body parts.

When does the heart start to beat?

The unborn baby's heart begins to beat after only four weeks, although it has not yet taken on its full shape. From the time of fertilization to eight weeks later, the developing baby is known as an embryo. The lungs, intestines and other parts are also taking shape around this time. In fact, by eight weeks all the main parts have formed, even the fingers and toes – yet the tiny body is only the size of a grape.

Can an unborn baby hear?

From before halfway through pregnancy, the unborn baby may be startled and move suddenly by a loud noise, indicating that it can hear. From eight weeks after fertilization until birth, the unborn baby is known as a foetus. It spends most of this time growing in size and developing smaller body parts such as eyelids, fingernails and toenails. In the womb it is dark, with nothing to see, yet the eyes are working, too, even though the lids are closed.

How does the unborn baby breathe?

It does not – it is surrounded and protected by bag-like membranes and fluids. However, it still needs oxygen to survive. This comes from the mother. The baby's blood flows along the twisted, rope-like umbilical cord to a plate-shaped part, the placenta, in the lining of the womb. Here the baby's blood passes very close to the mother's blood and oxygen can easily seep or diffuse into the baby's blood, which then flows back along the umbilical cord to its body. The baby is fed by nutrients in the same way.

Seeing the unborn baby

Ultrasound scans

In most regions of the world, a pregnant woman attends for regular check-ups at a medical centre or antenatal (before birth) clinic. The checks make sure that both she and the developing baby are healthy. One of the commonest tests is an ultrasound scan, which produces a picture of the baby in the womb. Tests on the mother's blood and urine, and checking her blood pressure, are also common. If there are problems, the medical staff may give the mother substances to start the birth process early, called induction, or decide to deliver the baby by Caesarean section. Babies born earlier than usual, before the nine months of pregnancy are complete, are known as premature.

→ *An ultrasound scan uses a pen-like probe moved over the skin to show an image of the unborn baby on a screen, which helps doctors to determine that the baby is healthy and developing well.*

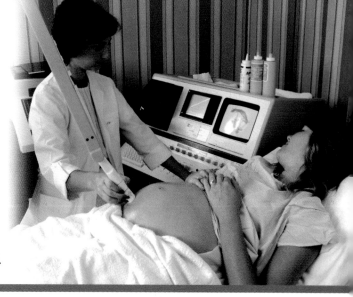

What happens at the start of birth?

As the time of birth approaches, powerful muscles in the wall of the womb begin to shorten or contract. This squeezes the baby through the opening or neck of the womb, called the cervix. The cervix was tightly closed during pregnancy but now widens, or dilates, to let the baby through. The contractions of the womb continue to push the baby along the birth canal, or vagina, until it emerges and is born.

⬆ *In order to keep fit whilst pregnant, and to prepare for birth, an expectant mother can undertake certain exercises and develop special breathing techniques.*

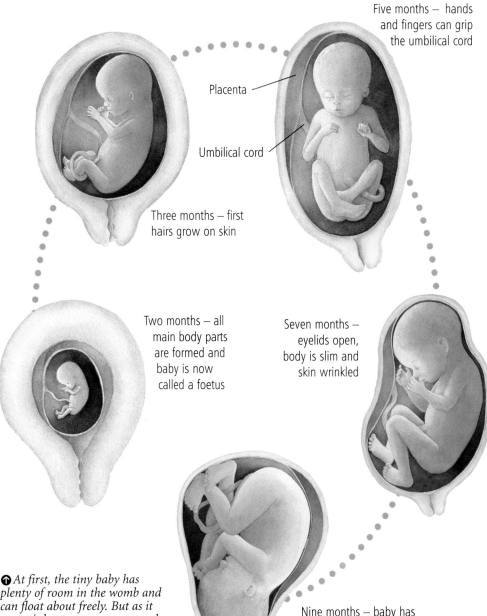

Five months — hands and fingers can grip the umbilical cord

Placenta

Umbilical cord

Three months — first hairs grow on skin

Two months — all main body parts are formed and baby is now called a foetus

Seven months — eyelids open, body is slim and skin wrinkled

Nine months — baby has 'turned' and is head-down, ready to be born

⬆ *At first, the tiny baby has plenty of room in the womb and can float about freely. But as it grows it becomes more cramped and has to bend its neck, back, arms and legs.*

Problem **births**

- Most babies are born head-first, known as cephalic presentation. This is the safest way, since the baby's head is its widest part and gently makes the cervix open wide, so the rest of the body follows easily.

- Some babies are not in the right position in the womb to be born this way. For example the baby may be born positioned bottom-first, known as breech presentation.

- It may be possible for a doctor to turn the baby from outside, by pushing or massaging the mother's abdomen, so it can be born head-first.

- In some cases the baby gets stuck. One option is to use a spoon-like device called forceps which fit around the baby's head and help to ease it out of the womb.

- Another option is to make an incision (cut) in the mother's abdomen and womb wall, remove the baby through this, and stitch or fasten the incision so it heals. This is known as a Caesarean birth.

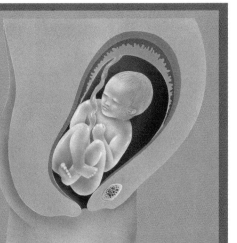

⬆ *In a breech birth, the baby's bottom may get stuck in the cervix.*

A newborn baby is about one-twentieth of the size of a fully-grown adult. But growth is about far more than getting bigger. Body shape and proportions change, muscles become stronger and movements more skilled. From the moment of birth, the baby learns an incredible amount almost every day.

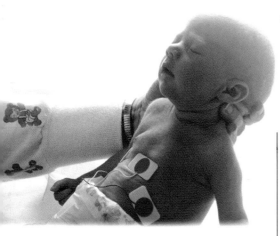

⬆ *A newborn baby is given an extensive medical check-up, in this case with sensor pads to monitor heartbeat rate. The baby's head is so large and heavy compared to its neck and body muscles, it needs to be carefully supported to prevent damage.*

What does a newborn baby do?

A new baby seems to do little except cry, feed on its mother's milk and sleep. At first it probably sleeps for about 20 hours in every 24. But the baby can carry out various automatic actions, or reflexes. It grips something that touches its hand and turns its head towards anything that touches its cheek. If startled by a loud noise, it throws out its arms and cries. And when its bladder and bowels are full, it empties them straight away!

When does walking start?

On average a baby can walk at around one year of age. Most babies learn to do more complicated actions, such as walking and talking, in the same order. But the times may differ widely, and being early to talk or late to walk is rarely a problem. Most babies can sit up by themselves at five to six months, stand whilst supported at seven to eight months, crawl at eight to nine months, and walk at about one year old. These movements are called motor skills.

⬆ *Babies can smile as young as a few weeks old, and can laugh within the first year. On average, babies start to talk from about ten months old.*

When does talking begin?

Like motor (movement) skills, the process of learning to talk happens at widely varying ages in different babies. Some can say several simple words like 'dada', 'mama' and 'cat' by the age of ten months, while others may not begin to form words until 13 to 14 months. Putting words together, like 'teddy bear' starts at about 14 to 15 months. By 18 months old the average toddler knows 20 or more words.

⬅ *Some babies crawl at six months – but some never do. They may use other methods such as rolling over or shuffling along on their bottoms to move about, before they begin to walk.*

Years of change

Puberty
The age at which puberty begins varies, from eight to nine years old up to 14 to 15 years. This depends on features such as body size and availability of healthy food, while illness can delay or slow the process. In general, the changes take two to three years in girls and three to four years in boys. The changes occur, on average, two years earlier in girls than in boys.

⬆ *Girls go through both a physical and mental change during puberty.*

Changes at puberty

- During childhood, girls and boys are similar in height. During puberty, both sexes rapidly become taller. But, on average, boys grow more, and so usually end up taller adults than girls.

- Girls develop a more rounded body outline, especially on the shoulders and hips, while boys become more angular, with broader shoulders.

- The reproductive or menstrual cycle begins in girls, while the reproductive organs in the male body begin to make sperm cells.

When does the body grow fastest?

After birth, the fastest time of growth is during the first year, when body weight increases about three times. Then growth gradually slows until the age of about 9 to 12 years, when it speeds up again. This time of fast growth through the early teenage years is known as puberty. It includes rapid development of the reproductive or sexual parts, as these begin to work.

🔽 *Teenagers may interact with one another to develop social skills, which can become the basis for future relationships in life.*

🔼 *Young children often think little about risks and dangers, such as falling over during play – which could cause a serious injury and even life-long harm. Adults need to point out the hazards and the need for safety precautions such as protective clothing and equipment.*

When is the body fully-grown?

Most people reach their full height by about 20 years of age. The muscles reach their full development at about 25 years. However, some physical activities involve co-ordination, training, practise and mental preparation as well as simple muscle power. Some sports people do not reach their peak until 30-plus years of age. Body weight is more variable – certain people alter their body weight, up and down, throughout life.

🔽 *The body grows not only physically, but also mentally – in the mind. This involves social skills such as making friends, respecting the opinions of others, understanding right and wrong and working out risks.*

Changes **in later life**

The changes of ageing are even more varied in their timing, than development when young. Some people begin to show signs of age from 40 years old, while others continue to look youthful at 60. In general, the changes in later life include:

- Hair becomes lighter, grey or perhaps white. Hair loss is also common, especially in men.

- Skin becomes less flexible and more wrinkled.

- Senses become less sharp, so that spectacles may be needed for eyesight, and a hearing aid to clarify sounds.

- Muscles begin to lose power from about 35 to 40 years old.

- Reactions become slower – about half the speed at 65 years of age compared to their speed at the age of 20.

- The heart and lungs gradually lose efficiency, with less stamina or 'staying power' for lengthy exercise.

- A century ago, the average lifespan for a person in a developed country was 50 years. Today, it has increased to 72 to 75 for men, and 76 to 79 for women.

🔼 *Some people enjoy good health at 80 years old or more.*

M atter is anything and everything in the Universe. It includes all substances, items and objects, whether solid, liquid or gas – and not only here on Earth, but deep into space, to the Sun and beyond, in fact, all through the entire Universe. So there is plenty of matter! Studying what it is made of is one of the great quests of modern science.

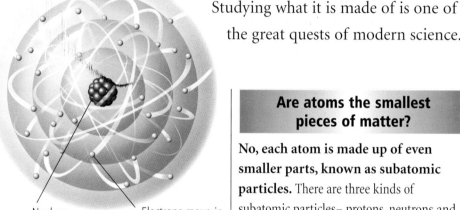

● Neutrons
● Protons
● Electrons

Nucleus   Electrons move in
                 areas called 'shells'

⬆ *Uranium is a very hard, heavy metal. Its atoms, such as this one above, are among the largest of all atoms, with 92 protons and about 146 neutrons in the nucleus, and 92 electrons to balance the protons.*

What are substances made of?

All substances consist of atoms. If you could chop up any substance smaller and smaller, the pieces would become too small to see. But if you could keep chopping, under the most powerful microscope, eventually you would reach the tiniest pieces or atoms of the substance. All matter is made of atoms.

Are atoms the smallest pieces of matter?

No, each atom is made up of even smaller parts, known as subatomic particles. There are three kinds of subatomic particles– protons, neutrons and electrons. Protons and neutrons clump together at the centre of the atom, called the nucleus. Electrons whizz round and round the nucleus. If an atom is split, it no longer has the features of the original substance.

➡ *The simplest and lightest atom of all is hydrogen. It has just one proton as the nucleus and one electron going around it. Helium is next, with a nucleus of two protons and two neutrons, and two orbiting electrons. Oxygen is more complex, with eight of each particle – protons, neutrons and electrons.*

What are quarks?

Some scientists believe that subatomic particles are made of even tinier pieces of matter known as quarks. For example, a proton is composed of three quarks. Other scientists believe that atoms, quarks and all other matter are made of far smaller vibrating lengths of energy called 'strings'. If an atom was the size of planet Earth, a 'string' would be the size of a shoelace. These 'strings' may join into 'superstrings' that could even stretch past lots of atoms. Scientists are beginning to investigate whether 'strings' really exist.

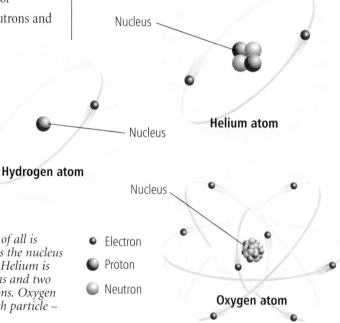

Nucleus

Helium atom

Nucleus

Hydrogen atom

Nucleus

● Electron
● Proton
● Neutron

Oxygen atom

Atomic facts

Key dates

2500 BC Empedocles from ancient Greece suggested that all matter was made of mixtures of four elements – earth, air, fire and water.

2400 BC Greek philosopher, Democritus, developed the idea that matter could be cut so small that it could not be cut any more. He named these pieces of matter 'atoms', meaning 'uncuttable'.

340 BC Greek thinker and scientist Aristotle added ether to the elements

1661 English scientist Robert Boyle described elements as "simple or perfectly unmingled bodies".

1787 French chemist Antoine Lavoisier defined a chemical element as "the last point which analysis can reach". He listed all the known elements and introduced chemical symbols, such as O for oxygen, which we still use today.

1808 English physicist John Dalton suggested that each pure chemical element had its own kind of atom. This was the forerunner of modern ideas about matter and atoms.

1868–9 Russian scientist Dmitri Mendeleév listed all the known elements, and devised a chart called the Periodic Table (see above) to categorize them all by their similar weights and properies.

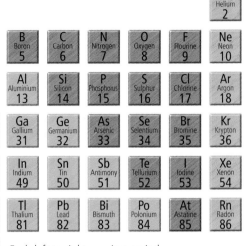

H Hydrogen 1																															He Helium 2

⊕ *All the known pure substances are arranged in a chart called the Periodic Table of chemical elements (see panel below). They are arranged by their properties and weights. The lightest elements are upper left, the heaviest ones are lower right. The different colours represent the different type of element. For example, all the elements known as noble gases are shown in turquoise (first column on right). Each of the elements in this column are extremely stable, which means that they do not react dangerously with other elements.*

Periodic table:

H Hydrogen 1																He Helium 2
Li Lithium 3	Be Beryllium 4										B Boron 5	C Carbon 6	N Nitrogen 7	O Oxygen 8	F Flourine 9	Ne Neon 10
Na Sodium 11	Mg Magnesium 12										Al Aluminium 13	Si Silicon 14	P Phosphorus 15	S Sulphur 16	Cl Chlorine 17	Ar Argon 18
K Potassium 19	Ca Calcium 20	Sc Scandium 21	Ti Titanium 22	V Vanadium 23	Cr Chromium 24	Mn Manganese 25	Fe Iron 26	Co Cobalt 27	Ni Nickel 28	Cu Copper 29	Zn Zinc 30	Ga Gallium 31	Ge Germanium 32	As Arsenic 33	Se Selentium 34	Br Bromine 35	Kr Krypton 36
Rb Rubidium 37	Sr Strontium 38	Y Yttrium 39	Zr Zirconium 40	Nb Niobium 41	Mo Molybdenum 42	Tc Technetium 43	Ru Ruthenium 44	Rh Rhodium 45	Pd Palladium 46	Ag Silver 47	Cd Cadmium 48	In Indium 49	Sn Tin 50	Sb Antimony 51	Te Tellurium 52	I Iodine 53	Xe Xenon 54
Cs Caesium 55	Ba Barium 56		Hf Hafnium 72	Ta Tantalum 73	W Tungsten 74	Re Rhenium 75	Os Osmium 76	Ir Iridium 77	Pt Platanium 78	Au Gold 79	Hg Mercury 80	Tl Thalium 81	Pb Lead 82	Bi Bismuth 83	Po Polonium 84	At Astatine 85	Rn Radon 86
Fr Frankium 87	Ra Radium 88		Rf Rutherfordium 104	Db Dubnium 105	Sg Seaborgium 106	Bh Bohrium 107	Hs Hassium 108	Mt Meitnerium 109	Ds Darmstadtium 110	Uuu Unununium 111	Uub Ununbium 112

Each left-to-right row is a period of elements with similar weights

Each top-to-bottom column groups elements with similar properties

La Lanthanum 57	Ce Cerium 58	Pr Praseodymium 59	Nd Neodymium 60	Pm Promethium 61	Sm Samarium 62	Eu Europium 63	Gd Gadolinium 64	Tb Terbium 65	Dy Dysprosium 66	Ho Holmium 67	Er Erbium 68	Tm Thulium 69	Yb Ytterbium 70	Lu Lutetium 71
Ac Actinium 89	Th Thorium 90	Pa Protactinium 91	U Uranium 92	Np Neptunium 93	Pu Plutonium 94	Am Americium 95	Cm Curium 96	Bk Berkelium 97	Cf Californium 98	Es Einsteinium 99	Fm Fermium 100	Md Mendelevium 101	No Nobelium 102	Lr Lawrencium 103

What holds the parts of an atom together?

Protons and neutrons are held together in the nucleus by a basic attraction called the strong nuclear force. Protons have a type of electrical force called electric charge, which is positive. Electrons have a negative charge and neutrons have no charge. The positive protons attract the negative electrons and hold them near the nucleus. Most atoms have the same number of protons and electrons, so their charges balance each other. The atom has no charge – it is neutral.

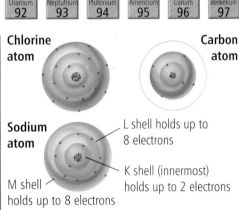

Chlorine atom

Carbon atom

Sodium atom

L shell holds up to 8 electrons

K shell (innermost) holds up to 2 electrons

M shell holds up to 8 electrons

⊕ *Scientists once thought that electrons orbited the nucleus at a different distance, like planets orbiting the Sun. Then the idea of 'shells' arose, where groups of electrons stay at a set distance from the nucleus. The modern view is that electrons move from one shell to another.*

Are all atoms the same?

Each kind of pure substance, known as a chemical element, has its own kind of atoms, which differ from the atoms of all other elements. So in an element, such as carbon, all the atoms are the same, with the same number of subatomic particles. Oxygen atoms are also all the same, but they differ from carbon atoms, with a different number of subatomic particles. There are more than 100 chemical elements as shown in the table above. About 30 of these are manufactured.

Amazing **atom facts**

⊕ *Dalton studied gases as well as chemistry, and from the age of 15, he kept daily records of the weather.*

- A nanometre is an incredibly small unit – one billionth of a metre. So 10 million atoms in a row would stretch just 2 mm.

- A typical atom is about 0.2 to 0.3 nanometres across.

- The nucleus at the centre of an atom is tiny compared to the size of the whole atom.

- If the whole atom was a massive sports stadium, with the outermost electrons whizzing around the farthest seats, the nucleus would be the size of a human thumb in the middle.

- In a solid substance, the atoms are about 0.3 nanometres apart, so their outermost electrons almost touch.

⊕ *Lavoisier began the system of using symbols for chemicals in 1787.*

All matter in the Universe is made of the atoms of pure substances, called chemical elements. These atoms join together or can be linked in countless ways to form the common objects and materials that we see and use every day – metals, wood, plastic, glass, water, rocks, soil and even the air around us.

⊕ *Molecules of sodium chloride form crystals of salt, such as table salt, sea salt or rock salt.*

Shared electrons

⬆ *When atoms join by covalent bonds, electrons orbit in one atom for part of the time, and the other for the rest of the time. The three atoms of a water molecule, two hydrogen and one oxygen, H_2O, have covalent bonds, as shown above.*

Do atoms join together?

Atoms usually join or bond with other atoms to form groups called molecules. In some cases the atoms come very close together and 'share' electrons, so that the electron sometimes goes around one nucleus and sometimes around the other. This is a covalent bond. Oxygen atoms floating in the air are joined in pairs by covalent bonds to form oxygen molecules O_2.

Are atoms ever alone?

On Earth, atoms are rarely found alone. Among the few examples are the 'inert gases' – helium, neon, argon, krypton and xenon. 'Inert' means 'inactive'. These gases form a tiny proportion of the air. Their atoms have all the electrons they need, with no need to share or swap. So they hardly ever join or bond, even with each other.

Sodium atom

⊙ *In an ionic bond, one or more electrons pass from one atom to another. Molecules of common salt, sodium chloride, form in this way.*

How else do atoms join?

One or more electrons may 'jump' from one atom to a nearby one. This is known as an ionic bond. Atoms of the elements sodium and chlorine are linked by ionic bonds to form molecules of sodium chloride, NaCl, which we know as salt (table or cooking salt). Electrons are negative, so the sodium atom that loses its electron becomes a positive ion. The chlorine atom which receives an electron becomes a negative ion. Positive and negative attract and the sodium and chlorine stay close together.

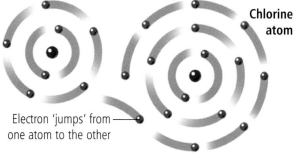

Chlorine atom

Electron 'jumps' from one atom to the other

Key **dates**

1800s Chemists had studied matter as much as possible. Physicists carried on the search, using methods such as electrical pulses.

1897 English scientist J. J. Thomson discovered particles smaller than atoms, which he called corpuscles. Streams of the particles were known as cathode rays. Today we call them electrons.

1911 New Zealand-born physicist Ernest Rutherford suggested that each atom had a tiny, heavy nucleus at its centre, with electrons circling it.

1912–13 Danish scientist Niels Bohr devised the 'shell' idea of an atom, that electrons move at certain distances from the nucleus of the atom, within separate 'shells'.

1919 Rutherford succeeded in breaking apart the nucleus, a process called 'splitting the atom'.

1932 English physicist James Chadwick discovered the neutron particle inside the nucleus of an atom.

1942 A team led by Enrico Fermi carried out the first 'chain reaction' of atomic fission – where nuclei split apart, releasing huge amounts of energy, causing more nuclei to split.

1945 The science of splitting atoms was used to make two atomic bombs, which were dropped on the Japanese cities of Hiroshima and Nagasaki, ending the Second World War.

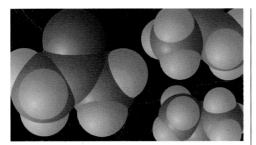

⬆ *The substance called acetone, also known as propanone, is commonly used in nail varnish remover. Each molecule of acetone has three carbon atoms (orange), one oxygen (pink) and six hydrogen (light green). It is written as the formula CH_3COCH_3.*

What is a compound?

A compound is a molecule with atoms from different chemical elements, rather than from the same chemical element. For example, an oxygen molecule, O_2, is not a compound. However, a salt molecule, NaCl, is a compound, because it consists of two or more different chemical elements (see page 160). Most everyday substances are made from compounds.

⬆ *The tall towers at an oil refinery split crude oil into all its 'fractions'.*

How many atoms are in a compound?

The number varies from a few, to millions. Some substances, such as salt, have molecules with just two atoms each. If each sodium chloride molecule in a tiny grain of salt was increased to the size of the dot on this 'i', then the salt grain would be more than 2 km high. Other substances, such as plastic and wood, have giant molecules consisting of millions of atoms. Many of these are based on the element carbon. Carbon can join with up to four other atoms, so that it forms thousands of different compounds. Especially common are combinations of carbon and hydrogen, called hydrocarbons (CHs), and those of carbon, hydrogen and oxygen known as carbohydrates (CHOs).

➡ *Crude oil or petroleum, straight from the ground, is a mixture of hundreds of compounds. In an oil refinery it is heated so that it splits up into the gases of these compounds. These gases are turned back into liquids at various temperatures, at different levels in a tall tower called a fractionation column.*

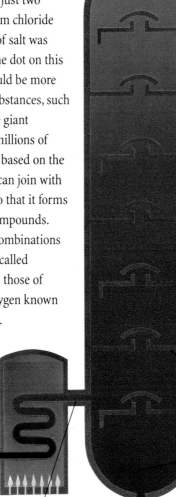

Crude oil turned into gases inside boiler

Fuel gases

Petrol and light fuels

Kerosene and jet fuels

Heavier fuels and oils

Waxes, tars, asphalts and bitumens

Hottest part of tower

Take off pipes

Condensation trays

Coolest part of tower

⬆ *Rutherford worked on radioactive rays and energy as well as atoms and nuclear fusion.*

⬅ *A nuclear explosion's vast energy comes from energy within atoms.*

Bigger and bigger

Natural gas and petroleum oil contain many compounds of the type known as hydrocarbons. They form larger and larger molecules. The simplest is methane, with one carbon and four hydrogen atoms, written as CH_4. It is also given off by decay and known as 'marsh gas'. Next simplest is ethane, with two carbon and six hydrogen atoms (CH_3CH_3). Ethane is found in natural gas and used for refrigeration. Propane has three carbon and eight hydrogen atoms ($CH_3CH_2CH_3$). It is a common fuel in tanks and 'bottle' cylinders. Also relatively simple is butane, with four carbon and ten hydrogen atoms ($CH_3CH_2CH_2CH_3$). It is also a valuable fuel gas. There are many more compounds.

⬇ *In about 1912, Niels Bohr devised the beginnings of what scientists now call quantum theory.*

Science plays a huge part in the items we use every day – cars, televisions, tools, appliances, buildings, even furniture and clothing. They are all made from specially chosen materials, ranging from natural wood or stone to high-tech composites. Materials scientists specialize in putting together atoms, molecules and substances to create the right material for each job.

⬆ *Copper is especially efficient at carrying or conducting electricity, it is second only to silver. It is braided so that it can be bent many times without cracking.*

How is a material's strength measured?

It depends, because there are different kinds of 'strength'. Tensile strength resists pulling or stretching, compression strength resists pressing or squeezing, and torsional strength resists twisting. These different kinds of strength are measured by putting pieces of a material into a very powerful machine, a hydraulic test rig, which pulls, squashes or turns them until they crack and break. Every substance or material has a different combination of these strengths, suitable for different purposes.

What are other features of materials?

Another feature is flexibility or bendiness, which is the opposite of stiffness or rigidity. This is linked to elasticity – whether a material springs back to its original shape after being bent. Weight is another feature, especially density, which is the amount of weight in a certain volume. Durability is how long a material can last. A material is also categorized by its ability to conduct electricity (see page 166).

What are natural materials?

Natural materials are found around us, as part of nature, rather than being artificial or manufactured. Wood is a natural material and is important in making furniture, utensils and structures such as houses and bridges. Various kinds of rock and stone are also widely used, especially in the construction of larger buildings. Natural fibres, such as cotton, are woven into fabrics for clothes, curtains and other items.

⬆ *Wood is often used in the construction of houses or boats, because it is a strong and durable material that can last against elements, such as strong winds and rain.*

◀ *Materials that carry heat or electricity, such as a metal spoon in a cup of hot liquid, are thermal or electrical conductors. Those that do not are insulators, such as a ceramic mug.*

More about materials

Glass as a material

Glass is among the most useful of all materials. Various types of glass are made by heating the natural substances of sand (silica), limestone and soda-ash, with other ingredients. Glass is sometimes used as a structural material, to take strain, but it is very brittle, and under too much strain it can crack or shatter. It is widely-used as an insulator for heat and electricity – and for windows because it is see-through or transparent.

Plastics as polymers

Many plastics are polymers. A polymer molecule is a large molecule made by joining or stringing together many identical smaller molecules, known as monomers, like the links in a chain.

➡ *Glass is known as an amorphous material, meaning its atoms do not have a regular arrangement or pattern.*

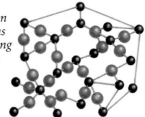

Polymers

Polyethylene – often known by the trade name Polythene. It is slightly 'waxy' to touch. It is used for packaging, toys, pipes, tubes and wire covering.

Polystyrene – It is 'expanded' or 'blown' to contain bubbles of air and used for lightweight packaging and heat insulation, or in solid form for kitchen utensils.

Polyurethane – This is also blown or foamed with air bubbles and used for lining materials and padding in furniture.

What material is most commonly used?

One commonly-used material is steel, an alloy (combination) of various substances based on the metal, iron. Pure metals are also widely used, such as very light aluminium, for items ranging from aircraft to drink cans. Copper is used as a conductor of electricity in wires. Most materials in modern products are made by various industrial processes rather than being obtained from nature.

Iron ore, coke and limestone

➡ *Iron is obtained by heating iron ore in a blast furnace, and pouring off the wastes or slag. Pure iron is often combined with carbon and other substances to make steel.*

Super-heated iron ore and limestone (the coke burns to create the heat)

Super-heated air blows into furnace

Hot gases to super-heater

Slag

Molten iron ore

⬆ *Specialist metals are heated in furnaces and carefully hand-poured into moulds, where they cool and solidify into the required shape. Brass is an alloy (mixture) of copper and zinc.*

Is a tin can really made of tin?

Only the outer coating is made of tin. A 'tin' can is mainly steel, but steel can rust. So the steel can is coated with a thin layer of the metal, tin, which does not rust and so protects the steel beneath it.

⬅ *Many metals and minerals form crystals as they cool from liquid to solid. The cooling process must be carefully controlled so the crystals lock together well for strength. Random-sized crystals would cause weakness in the material. Most crystals are tiny, only visible under a magnifying glass or microscope.*

➡ *Bullet-proof vests are woven from an immensely strong fibre, called kevlar, to withstand the impact of bullets.*

⬇ *Fast vehicles, such as racing cars, speedboats and jet planes contain many composites, each manufactured to have the right mix of strength, weight, stiffness and other features.*

Amazing **facts**

- Composites are combinations of single materials, which combine the best features of each material, in order to create materials specialized for certain jobs.

- One common example of a composite is GRP, glass-reinforced plastic, commonly called 'glass-fibre'.

- GRP has strands or fibres of glass, for rigidity and toughness, surrounded by a resin of plastic for some flexibility and resistance to shattering and corrosion.

- Many composites contain the material called carbon fibre, which is very thin, silky-black strands of pure carbon.

- Carbon fibre has four times more tensile strength than steel and is mixed with plastic resins to make some of the strongest and lightest of all composite materials.

Our world is driven by energy. Without energy the world would be dark, cold, still and silent. We use it in many forms, including movement, sound, chemical bonds, electricity, heat, light, waves and rays. Energy is needed for anything to happen and it can be converted from its current form to various other forms to be used.

○ *A typical power station changes chemical energy in the fuel into heat, then movement and then electricity. But some of the fuel energy is converted into excess heat, which is spread into the air by huge cooling towers.*

Where is energy?

Energy is everywhere and exists in everything. It has many forms. Chemical energy is released during chemical reactions. Food is a store of chemical energy, and when eaten can be used to power the movements of the human body. Potential energy is stored energy, ready to be used and converted into kinetic (movement) energy. Electrical energy is when a form of energy is converted into electricity. Solar energy comes from the Sun. There are many forms of energy.

○ *Wind turbines convert the kinetic energy of moving air into electricity. The wind obtained its energy in the form of heat from the Sun. In fact, nearly all the energy we use on Earth, in one form or another, comes from the Sun. Wind turbines generate their energy in a sustainable way, without using up valuable fuel resources.*

Can energy be made or destroyed?

A basic law of science says that energy cannot be created from nothing and equally cannot disappear. This applies throughout the Universe. However, energy can be changed from one form to another. For example, when a rocket takes off, the chemical energy in its fuel is changed into other forms of energy, such as heat, light, sound and movement energy. Energy can also be spread out so that it becomes weaker. When we say we 'use' energy, we mean that we convert some of it into the type we need. This generally converts the rest into a less useful type of energy that we cannot use. However, scientists say that energy is 'conserved' because the total amount of energy is always the same.

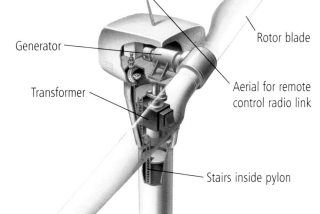

Generator

Transformer

Rotor blade

Aerial for remote control radio link

Stairs inside pylon

Using energy

Changing energy

In science, energy is the ability or capacity to do work or to cause change. Work is usually described as the changing of energy from one form or system to another, often resulting in some type of movement. In everyday life we think of 'work' as something useful, with a purpose. But this is not so in science. For example, an apple hanging on a tree has the type of energy known as potential energy, because of its position high above the ground. If the apple falls, its potential energy is changed into the energy of movement, known as kinetic energy, and 'work' has been done in the process, as it fell from the tree. This work happens whether the apple falls to the ground, or if it hits something on its way down.

○ *Potential energy is found in a bird as it sits on a perch before flying away. The potential energy becomes kinetic energy once the bird takes off into the air.*

What happens in an energy chain?

An energy chain is the conversion of different forms of energy into a form that can be used. For example, coal, which is found deep underground, has a store of chemical energy. When burnt, this chemical energy becomes heat energy, which is used to make steam by heating water. The steam turns turbines to produce kinetic energy. This kinetic energy is converted in a machine called a generator in the power station to become electrical energy. Electrical energy is sent to homes and offices (see page 167) where it is used for light, and to power applicances, such as televisions and computers.

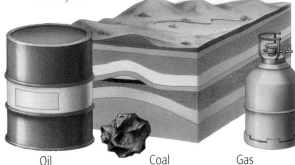

Common fuels we burn for energy include oil, coal and gas. These were formed by the fossilization of decayed plants and other life-forms long ago. Their energy came as light from the Sun. Oil and coal are extracted from deep in the ground, formed beneath rock layers.

Oil   Coal   Gas

A waterwheel changes the kinetic energy of running water into useful mechanical energy, to drive machines such as millstones, which grind grain into flour.

Can energy be created from atoms?

Energy can be made in one way – from matter or mass. Atoms, or usually parts of atoms, can be changed into energy. The different parts of atoms, such as neutrons, cease to exist in their current form and instead there is a large amount of energy in their place. The scientific law regarding the conservation of mass and energy states that any process or event has the same amount of mass and energy at the end as there was at the beginning of the process.

What is nuclear energy?

Nuclear energy is created in reactors inside nuclear power stations, nuclear-powered submarines, some spacecraft, and also in nuclear explosions. Nuclear fuel, such as uranium, generates enormous amounts of heat energy from the 'destruction' of the parts of its atoms. The energy produced is called nuclear energy because it comes from splitting the nucleus of an atom.

Nuclear energy comes from the splitting or fission of the nuclei (centres) of atoms in nuclear fuel, such as uranium or plutonium. A fast-moving neutron smashes apart the nucleus, releasing heat, other forms of energy, and also more neutrons, which enable the fission process to continue.

Fast-moving neutron

Nucleus of fuel atom

Nucleus splits in two

More neutrons released

Measuring **energy**

About 100 billion joules of energy is needed to launch a spacecraft.

- The main unit for measuring both energy and work is the joule.

- An older unit was the calorie, which was used especially to measure heat energy and the chemical energy contained in foods.

- One calorie equals 4.2 joules, and one kilocalorie or kcal (also written as 'Calorie' with a capital 'C') equals 4,200 joules (4.2 kJ).

- A 100-watt light bulb requires one joule of electrical energy each second.

- A typical light bulb left on for 24 hours takes about 5 million joules.

- An average person needs about 5 to 10 million joules of energy each day from foods, to stay active and healthy.

- A split-second bolt of lightning releases 2,000 million joules.

- A large earthquake releases about 10 million million million joules in just a few seconds.

When we switch on a light, turn on the computer, listen to the radio or watch television, we rely on our most convenient form of energy – electricity. It is convenient because it can be sent easily along wires and cables. Also it is readily changed into many other forms of energy, including light, heat, sound and movement.

Electrical energy or charge does not always flow. It can build up on the surface of an insulator, for example, after rubbing a plastic comb. This charge is called 'static electricity' and it attracts very light items, such as bits of tissue paper.

What is electricity?

Electricity is the movement or flow of the tiny parts of atoms called electrons, which have an electric charge. Electrons move around the central nucleus of an atom (see page 158). But if an electron receives enough energy it can break away from its atom and 'hop' to the next one, where an electron has also broken away and jumped to the next atom, and so on. These moving electrons represent energy. As billions of them hop in the same direction from atom to atom, they cause a flow of electric current.

Electric current only flows if it has a pathway or circuit of conductors, from its source and back again. Here, the circuit includes two wires and a bulb. The wires move the current to the bulb and back again.

Ceramic discs are stacked and used as insulators, to stop the very powerful electricity of power lines from leaking or jumping into the ground. However, if the strength of the electricity is too high, half a million volts or more, and conditions are very wet (water being a good conductor of electricity) then the electricity may leap as sparks into the earth.

Do all substances carry electricity?

No, only certain substances carry electricity. These substances are called conductors. Most metals, especially silver and gold, carry electricity well. Many other substances do not carry electricity. Instead, they have a high resistance to its flow and are known as insulators. They include wood, glass, plastic, paper, card and ceramics, such as pottery. Electrical wires usually have a conducting core of metal strands surrounded by a plastic sheath for insulation, which prevents the electricity from leaking.

Electrical units

A portable multimeter can be adjusted to measure volts, amps, ohms and other electrical units. It is a vital piece of equipment for electricians and electrical engineers. The meter is used to check safety equipment and ensure that electricity is not flowing to parts of machines that people touch, which would make the machines unsafe.

How **long**?

For the same amount of electricity, these gadgets and appliances would run for the following lengths of time:

'Instant' hot-water shower	10–15 mins
Electric heater (convector)	1–1.5 hrs
Hair-dryer on maximum setting	1–1.5 hrs
Washing machine	2 hrs
Large freezer	3 hrs
Standard television	3–5 hrs
Electric blanket	6 hrs
100 watt light bulb	10 hrs
Electric shaver	70 hrs

How do batteries work?

Batteries change chemical energy into electrical energy. The links or bonds between atoms in chemical substances contain energy. As these break down in a chemical reaction, their energy passes to the electrons in the atoms and makes them move. This happens in a battery, but only when the electrons have somewhere to go, such as along a pathway or circuit of wires and components.

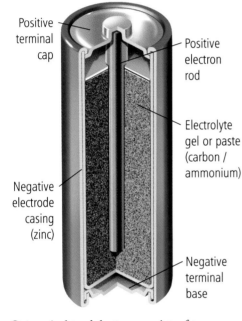

↑ *A typical torch battery consists of two contacts or electrodes: the positive anode and negative cathode, with chemicals between them called the electrolyte. Chemical reactions between the electrodes and electrolyte cause the current to flow.*

Sheath or cover

High-voltage power line

Transformers

Electrons jump from atom to atom in conductor

Pylon

Generators at power station

↑ *The flow of electricity is the movement of millions of electrons, which jump between atoms in the conductor – usually copper wire.*

What happens inside a power station?

In some power stations fuels such as coal, oil or gas are burned to make heat. This boils water into steam, which blasts past the fan-shaped blades or rotors of a turbine and makes them spin. The turbine is linked to a generator, inside which is a magnetic field, which rotates near a coil of wire, and this makes electricity in the wire (see page 169). In hydro-electric power stations, running water spins the turbine blades. In wind turbines the propeller-like blades are whirled around by the wind to generate electricity.

What are DC and AC?

DC is direct current electricity and AC is alternating current electricity. Direct current electricity flows steadily in the same direction while alternating current electricity rapidly changes direction and flows one way then the other, 50 or 60 times each second. Batteries make DC. The mains electricity from wall sockets and light fittings is AC.

Transformers

← *Electricity from power stations is sent along huge cables, high above the ground, or buried below the surface. Its voltage is reduced by transformers, from hundreds of thousands of volts to only a few thousand for large factories, and just hundreds for homes, offices and schools.*

Measuring **electricity**

Electricity is measured in various ways by special scientific units.

- Amps (amperes, A) are the amount or quantity of electrical flow. One amp is about 6 billion billion electrons flowing past each second.

- Volts (v) is the pushing strength or force of electricity, also called EMF, electromotive force. A typical torch battery is 1.5 volts, a car battery 12 volts, mains electricity in many countries such as France and the USA is 110 volts, and in the UK it is 220–240 volts.

- Ohms (Ω) measure the resistance of flow to electricity. A 1-m length of a good conductor, such as copper wire, has almost no ohms, while the same length of a good insulator, such as wood, has millions.

- Watts measure power, which in science is the rate at which energy is changed or converted. One watt is one joule of energy per second.

- An ordinary light bulb is 60 or 100 watts, and a room heater 1,000 watts.

- Watts can be used to measure any form of energy use, not just electrical energy. For example, a person jogging along requires about 500 watts, while a family car produces about 100,000 watts.

- An older unit for power is horsepower, hp. One unit of horsepower is equivalent to 746 watts.

- When generating electricity, a typical wind turbine produces about one megawatt (millions of watts). The biggest hydro-electric power stations produce more than 10,000 megawatts.

Magnets have no effect on many substances, such as wood, paper, plastic and even some metals, such as the aluminium used in drink cans. Yet when they are near an iron-based object, they pull it towards them with an invisible force. And when two magnets are near each other, they may attract (pull each other together) or repel (push each other apart).

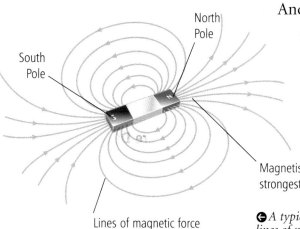

South Pole

North Pole

Lines of magnetic force

Magnetism at its strongest at the pole

◔ *A typical bar magnet is made of steel. Its lines of magnetic force curve from one pole to the other at each end. But a magnet can be any shape, including a u-like horseshoe, a disc with a pole on each side, or a ring with one pole on the outer rim and one on the inner.*

What is a magnet?

A magnet is an object that produces a force called magnetism. The area where the force is felt is called the magnetic field. The force is strongest at two places in the magnet, called poles. The two poles are not the same, in fact they are opposites. One is called north or + and the other is called south or –. When two magnets come near, the north pole of one pushes or repels the north pole of the other, but pulls or attracts the south pole. The basic law of magnetism is that like poles repel, unlike poles attract.

How is magnetism made?

It is due to the movements of the same particles that cause electricity – the electrons of atoms. Electrons orbit their atom's nucleus, and spin around while the nucleus spins, too. Normally electrons spin in random ways, at different angles. But in a magnet it is believed that the electron spins are lined up, so their tiny forces combine to create the force of magnetism.

Which substances are magnetic?

A magnetic substance is one that is attracted by a magnet. The most common magnetic substance is iron. Steel contains mainly iron, so steel is magnetic too. A few less common metals are slightly magnetic, such as nickel and cobalt, and the much rarer metals, such as neodymium, gadolinium and dysprosium.

◔ *The type of iron-rich rock called magnetite or lodestone has natural magnetism. Long, slim pieces of it were used for the first direction-finding magnetic compasses.*

◔ *A maglev (magnetic levitation) train 'floats' above its track, held in place by the attraction of magnetic forces.*

Magnets in train

Magnets in track

Magnetic attraction

The Earth as a magnet

Planet Earth is itself an enormous magnet. It has a core of iron-rich rocks at its centre, at immense pressure and temperature. The core is so hot that it flows like treacle. As the Earth spins around once each day the core flows and swishes, too, and the moving iron generates a magnetic field. This field extends around Earth's surface and out into space. Like all magnetic fields, it becomes weaker with distance. The magnetic poles of the Earth are actually some distance from the geographic poles, the North and South Poles. These geographic Poles mark the line of axis around which the planet spins.

◔ *Earth's natural magnetism is generated in its core. But the magnetic field extends hundreds of kilometres out into space. The magnetic north pole is near Bathurst Island in northern Canada, more than 1,000 km from the geographic North Pole. The magnetic south pole is in the ocean near Wilkes Land, Antarctica, more than 2,000 km from the geographic South Pole.*

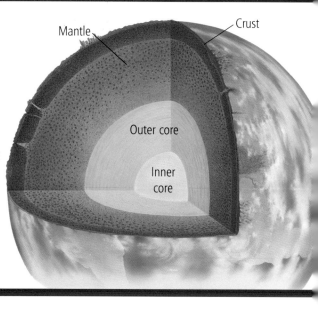

Mantle

Crust

Outer core

Inner core

↑ *Big electromagnets can lift up heavy loads, such as car engines. They are also used at scrapyards for sorting iron-based or ferrous metals from other metals when recycling.*

Can magnets be switched on and off?

They can if they are electromagnets.
Electricity and magnetism are two parts of the same basic or fundamental force, known as electromagnetism. Whenever an electric current flows in a wire, it creates a magnetic field around itself. If a wire is wound into a coil, with a piece of iron in the middle, this makes the magnetic field stronger and is known as an electromagnet. The magnetic field is present when the electricity flows, but when it is switched off, the magnetism disappears in an instant.

Are magnets common?

Very common. They are used in a simple way for holding paper onto appliances such as fridges, as knife-holders, for gathering and holding pins and nails, and as magnetic catches for doors. Large magnets are found in loudspeakers. Electromagnetism is used in many devices, such as remote-control cars, locks, electric generators and motors, videotapes, television sets, computers and their magnetic disc drives. Magnets are used in hundreds of different devices.

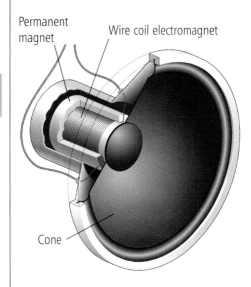

Permanent magnet

Wire coil electromagnet

Cone

↑ *A loudspeaker is a device that changes an electric current into sound. Electrical signals flow through a wire coil and turn it into an electromagnet, which pushes and pulls against a permanent magnet to produce sound.*

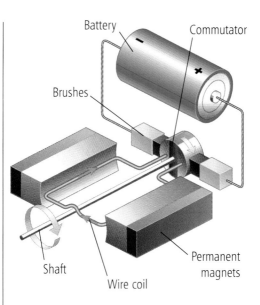

Battery

Commutator

Brushes

Shaft

Wire coil

Permanent magnets

↑ *A simple DC motor (see page 167) consists of a wire coil on a shaft between two magnetic poles. As it turns, the electric current flowing through the spinning wire coil is reversed by a barrel-shaped commutator switch.*

How does an electric motor work?

Using the push and pull of magnetism.
A coil of wire inside an electric motor is positioned near two magnets. As the current flows, the wire becomes an electromagnet and its field interacts with the magnetic field of the surrounding magnets. The pushing and pulling forces produced by the magnets move the wire and so the motor spins. A rotating switch, the commutator, makes the flow of current through the coil change each turn to keep the motor spinning.

Magnets save lives!

The device called a compass is a long, slim magnet that can turn or swivel freely. It follows the basic law of magnetism so that each of its poles attracts the Earth's opposite magnetic pole. This makes the compass line up with the Earth's magnetic field and point north-south. Countless lives have been saved as explorers, sailors, pilots, mountaineers and numerous travellers have used the magnetic compass to find their way to safety. Today, travellers may use satellite navigation receivers, but they may break or run out of electricity so the magnetic compass is still carried as a standby.

◗ *The dial of a magnetic compass is turned around so that its north lines up with the compass needle. A map held next to the compass is then also moved around so that it lines up too. Maps are usually produced with north at the top.*

Flipping poles

As certain types of rocks melt and then cool and solidify in the Earth's crust (outer layer), tiny amounts of magnetism are 'frozen' into them. This magnetism is lined up with the Earth's natural magnetic field. Different layers of rock, formed over millions of years, show how the Earth's magnetic poles have moved about, and even 'flipped' or reversed, so that north became south, and south turned into north. This has happened many times throughout Earth's history. This type of information helps to determine the age of rocks and the fossils of dinosaurs and other prehistoric animals found within the rocks.

Electronic gadgets are all around us, from televisions, computers and mobile phones to washing machines and cars. Electronics is one of the fastest-growing areas of science, as the electronic chip becomes smaller and smaller, yet faster and more powerful.

Magnetic and optical (CD) disc slots

Electron guns   Aerial

Camera

Flat screen monitor

The mouse contains sensors, which move the on-screen cursor

Keyboard

The computer is equipped with a 'Read-only memory' (ROM)

All instructions and commands, known as programs, are interpreted and carried out in the CPU

Phosphor dots on inside of screen

Focusing and scanning coils

Glass vacuum tube

⬆ *In a standard TV set, 'guns' fire streams of electrons at the inside of the screen. The electrons hit tiny dots of phosphor chemicals whose glow can be seen from the other side of the screen as the image. There is one electron gun for each set of coloured dots – red, green and blue. The beams pass electromagnetic coils or plates, which make the beams bend or deflect to scan the screen line by line.*

⬆ *One of the smallest components in a typical personal computer is the central processing unit (CPU), where microprocessors interpret commands. The items connected by wires, called peripherals, include the keyboard, mouse, screen (monitor) and additional devices, such as scanners or cameras.*

How do electronic devices work?

Electronic devices use electrons, or electricity to work. Electrical devices such as hair-dryers, car central-locking systems, food processors and microwave ovens often have moving parts, such as motors, electromagnets and gears, that we can usually see. They are electromechanical and so are powered by electricity. Electronic devices, such as transistors, have no moving parts except electrons, which are too small to see.

Do electronic devices use much electricity?

The electrons in an electronic device flow as an electric current, which is usually tiny. They measure from a few volts in strength down to only thousandths of a volt, and only fractions of an amp (measure of electrical amount). The electrons are mainly controlled by other electrons, as tiny electrical pulses or by magnetic effects.

Electronic advances

⬇ *Apple iMac computers were purpose-designed for electronic information transfer (e-mail and the Internet).*

Key dates

1904	Ambrose Fleming made one of the earliest electronic devices, the diode valve.
1906	Lee de Forest developed the triode valve, which worked as an amplifier.
1923	Vladimir Zworykin developed early versions of the electron-scanning television camera and screen.
1946–7	A team, led by William Shockley, invented the transistor, which could amplify electrical signals.

1958	Jack Kilby made several transistors on one piece of semiconductor – an early intergrated circuit.
1962	The first 'microchips' or integrated circuits were mass produced.
1971	The first central processing unit microchips were developed.
1981	Early versions of the IBM PC (personal computer) were introduced.
1988	Mobile phones were introduced.
1996	Playstation computer games.
1998	Apple iMac computers.

What are ICs?

An IC – integrated circuit – is a circuit board where all the components and connections are made at the same time, fully joined together or integrated. Microscopic in size, the circuit can be made up of thousands of individual components. The components, such as switches, resistors, capacitors and transistors, are connected by wires or metal strips on the circuit board.

A PCB, printed circuit board, is made with all the metal connectors in position or 'printed' onto the insulator board. Microchips and other components are connected by inserting their metal 'legs' into sockets.

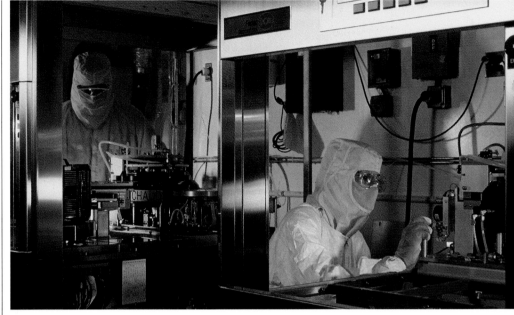

What is a microchip?

The 'chip' is a slice of a semiconductor material such as silicon and 'micro' means that all the components and connections of the integrated circuit on the chip are microscopic in size. Tiny parts of this material either carry electricity or not, depending on conditions such as changing temperature, or the presence or absence of electricity or magnetism nearby.

Integrated circuit

Plastic casing for insulation

'Leg' connecting pins

Electronic components must be made in extremely clean conditions. A few specks of dust could get inside the components and ruin the manufacture of microchips and electrical circuit boards.

What are CPUs?

Central processing unit microchips are the 'brains' of electronic devices, such as computers. Information is fed into the CPU as patterns of millions of tiny electrical signals per second. The microcircuits in the CPU analyze or process the signals and 'decide' what to do according to a set of rules built into the circuit design. The results are fed out as more electrical signals to various other parts of the equipment.

Electronic **components**

Capacitor – stores electrical energy and charge.
Diode – allows electrical flow one way only.
Photovoltaic cell – turns light energy directly into electricity.
Potentiometer – resistor adjusted to control, measure or compare voltages.
Resistor – resists the flow of electricity, and reduces its voltage.
Transformer – changes voltage (up or down) and alters current to flow in the opposite way.

Transistor – adaptable component which can be an amplifier, switch or an oscillator, which makes current flow one way then the other very rapidly.

Computer-aided special effects can be extended into entire animated adventures.

Amazing **electronic facts**

• In the early 1970s, the CPUs or microprocessor chips inside the first home computers contained about 8,000 transistors each.

• By the early 2000s, over 40 million transistors can be found in the same-sized chip, and work a thousand times faster than the first ones.

• In general, computing ability doubles in speed and power every 18 months. This is called Moore's law, named after Gordon Moore who suggested it would happen in 1965.

The air around us is full of rays and waves. We can only see one kind of them – light. The others include radio waves, microwaves, heat rays and even tiny amounts of X-rays. These are invisible, yet they are very similar to light rays in every feature, except for the length of each actual wave.

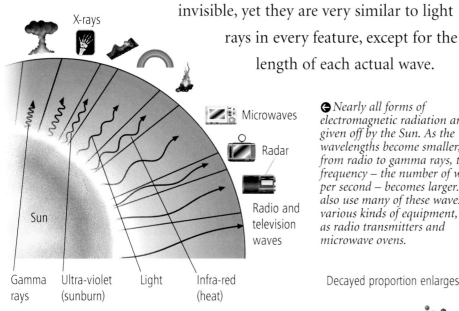

X-rays

Microwaves

Radar

Radio and television waves

Sun

Gamma rays

Ultra-violet (sunburn)

Light

Infra-red (heat)

⊙ *Nearly all forms of electromagnetic radiation are given off by the Sun. As the wavelengths become smaller, from radio to gamma rays, the frequency – the number of waves per second – becomes larger. We also use many of these waves in various kinds of equipment, such as radio transmitters and microwave ovens.*

Can radiation be emitted as particles, not waves?

Some types of radiation are emitted as particles. One type is known as alpha radiation, which is a stream of particles from inside atoms. Each alpha particle consists of two protons and two neutrons (similar to the nucleus of an atom of the very light gas, helium, which also contains two protons and two neutrons). Another type is beta particles, where each particle is an electron (or its 'opposite', a positron).

Nuclei of atoms become lighter

Alpha particles

Beta particles

Decayed proportion enlarges

Decayed mineral

What is radiation?

Radiation is energy that is given out, or radiated, from a source. One type of radiation is a combination of electricity and magnetism, as electromagnetic waves. These are like up-and-down waves of energy. The different lengths of waves have different names, but they are all the same form of energy. We use them in hundreds of different ways, in communications, medicine, industry and scientific research.

Undecayed mineral

⊙ *Tiny amounts of radioactivity, in the form of particles such as electrons, are given off by most substances, including rocks in the ground. This is known as radioactive decay. In some rocks, measuring the proportions of decayed and non-decayed minerals shows when the rock was formed.*

Waves and rays

⊙ *As the length of electromagnetic waves become shorter, their frequency (number of waves per second) becomes higher. More waves per second can carry more information, for example, as the on-off pulses of digital code in a computer.*

⊙ *X-ray images show up the denser or harder parts of the body, such as bones and teeth, as white or pale against the dark background of softer, fleshy parts.*

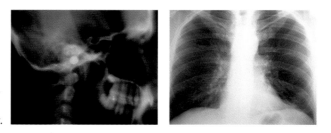

Long radio waves

Shorter radio waves (used in radio and televison)

Microwaves

Light waves

X-rays

Short X-rays

Gamma rays

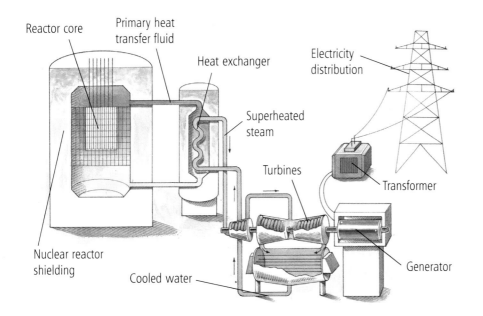

Reactor core
Primary heat transfer fluid
Heat exchanger
Electricity distribution
Superheated steam
Turbines
Transformer
Nuclear reactor shielding
Cooled water
Generator

Is 'radioactivity' radiation?

Yes, radioactivity is energy given off by atoms that are not stable or 'settled', because their subatomic particles are out of balance. Substances that naturally have a proportion of unstable atoms include

radium, uranium and plutonium. These substances give off alpha and beta particles (see page 172) and gamma rays, which are extremely short electromagnetic waves.

🔆 *In a nuclear power station, the radiation given out by the splitting of fuel atoms (see page 165) includes vast amounts of heat. This boils water into high-pressure steam that spins turbine blades linked to the generator.*

How fast does radiation travel?

Radiation travels faster than anything else in the Universe. Its electromagnetic waves include light, and nothing can exceed the speed of light in a vacuum (such as the nothingness of space) – which travels about 300,000 km/sec. Many electromagnetic waves travel this fast – equivalent to seven times around the world in less than one second.

🔆 *If an electron beam is fired at certain metal objects, the beam gives off X-rays, which can penetrate solid objects, such as a hand, and cast an image of the interior, such as the bones inside a finger.*

Is radiation harmful?

Generally, no, but some types can be in certain amounts. Ultra-violet rays from the Sun can cause sunburn and skin cancers. Too many X-rays can damage the microscopic cells of living things and lead to illness, tumours and cancers. However, used very carefully, X-rays can also destroy growths and cancers: this is known as radiotherapy. Radioactivity may cause burns, sickness and many other ill effects. Too much of any radiation can be damaging. But in daily life, most forms of radiation are controlled in their amounts and strengths so as not to cause harm to living things.

🔆 *The magnetron in a microwave oven produces the type of radiation known as microwaves. The waves are up to 20 cm in length. They bounce or reflect off the paddles of the stirrer to spread evenly inside the oven.*

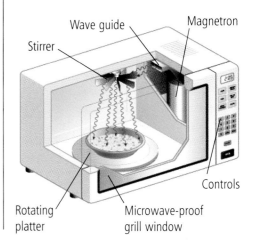

Wave guide
Magnetron
Stirrer
Controls
Rotating platter
Microwave-proof grill window

The EM **spectrum**

The full range of electromagnetic waves and rays is known as the EM spectrum. The parts differ in the lengths of their waves:

Radio waves – Each wave more than 1 km long to less than 10 m.
Radio waves – (very short, used for television) 10 to less than 1 m.
Microwaves – About 1 m to 1 mm.
Infra-red waves or rays – (carry heat energy) 1 mm to less than 1 micrometre (one-thousandth of 1 ml).
Light waves or rays – (visible light) About 0.8 to 0.4 micrometres.
Ultra-violet rays – 0.1 to 0.001 micrometres.
X-rays – 0.001 to 0.00001 micrometres.
Gamma rays – Less than 0.0001 micrometres (0.1 millionths of a mm).

Amazing **radiation facts**

Different types of radiation pass through different substances, depending on their power:

• Most kinds travel through air easily.

• Radio waves hardly travel through water.

• Light waves are stopped by most solid objects unless they are transparent, such as glass.

• X-rays can travel through fleshy parts of the body, but not through teeth and bones, and so these show up on a medical X-ray image.

• A thick sheet of metal, such as lead, stops most forms of radiation.

A simple description of light is that it is something we see with our eyes! Light is actually a form of energy, which is made up of electromagnetic waves. It is essential to our lives, so that we can look around to move about, eat, drink, learn and stay safe. We cannot survive in darkness, nor can most animals and plants.

What is light?

Light is a type of energy. We can imagine it as up-and-down waves of the form of energy known as electromagnetism. This is a combination of electricity and magnetism (see page 172). So light waves are very similar in form to radio waves, microwaves, infra-red, ultra-violet and X-rays. Light waves are so short that about 2,000 of them would stretch just 1 mm.

⊙ Light bounces or reflects off very smooth surfaces, in the same pattern and at the same angle as the rays hit the surface. This produces what we call a mirror-image. In this image, left and right are reversed. So in a mirror, we do not see our faces as other people see them.

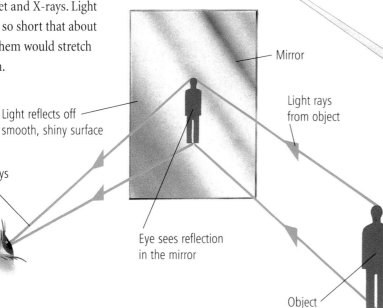

Mirror

Light rays from object

Light reflects off smooth, shiny surface

Light rays to eye

Eye sees reflection in the mirror

Object

Is light always in the form of waves?

Not always. Light energy also seems to be in the form of tiny 'packets', which are pieces of light energy known as photons, like the stream of bullets from a machine-gun. For some purposes scientists view light as a continuous form of energy, that moves in up-and-down waves. For other purposes, they view it as units of energy called photons. This is known in science as the 'wave-particle duality' of light.

⊙ Different wavelengths or colours of light are bent or refracted by slightly different amounts as they pass at an angle into a glass prism. The waves spread out and reveal that ordinary 'white' light is really a mixture of all colours, known as the visible light spectrum.

Glass or clear plastic prism

White light

Beam hits surface at an angle

Longest light waves are red

Light fantastic

Making laser light

'Laser' means 'light amplification by stimulated emission of radiation'. A laser beam is made by putting pulses of energy into a substance called the active medium. The input energy can be electricity, heat or even ordinary light. The atoms of the active medium gain more and more energy, which suddenly reaches a certain limit or threshold, and is given off as a burst of laser light.

➲ In one type of laser, energy is put into the active medium of a ruby rod as flashes of ordinary light.

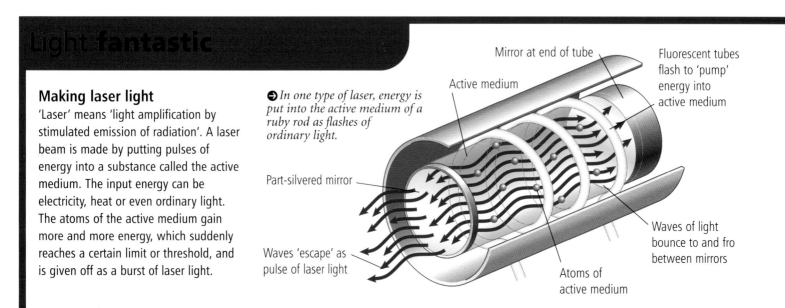

Mirror at end of tube

Fluorescent tubes flash to 'pump' energy into active medium

Active medium

Part-silvered mirror

Waves of light bounce to and fro between mirrors

Waves 'escape' as pulse of laser light

Atoms of active medium

Why are there different colours of light?

The colour of light depends on the length of its waves. The longest ones are each about 770 nanometres (0.00077 mm) in length. Our eyes detect these as red. The shortest light waves are 400 nanometres (0.0004 mm) and our eyes see these as violet. The wavelengths in between form all the other colours, from orange and yellow to green, blue and indigo. This range of colours is known as the light spectrum.

Shortest light waves are violet

Medium length waves are green

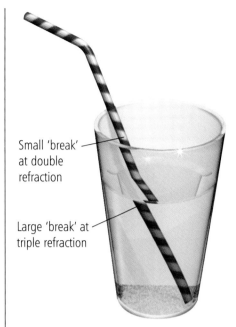

Small 'break' at double refraction

Large 'break' at triple refraction

⬆ *Light rays from the lower straw (beneath the surface of the water) are refracted as they pass through water, glass and air. From the upper straw they pass through only air and glass, so the path of light is different and makes the straw appear broken.*

Does light always travel in straight lines?

If nothing gets in its way, yes. But if light hits any objects or substances, various things can happen. If the object is see-through or transparent, such as a glass window or water, then the light carries on. It may bend where it goes from one transparent substance to another, known as refraction. If an object is opaque (not clear), such as a wooden door, then the light bounces or reflects off it.

How fast is light?

Light has the fastest known speed in the Universe – almost 300,000 km/sec. All electromagnetic waves (see page 172) go at this speed. But this is their speed in a completely empty space or vacuum. The speed of light is affected as it travels through different materials or substances. It travels slower through transparent substances, such as water and glass (see panel below).

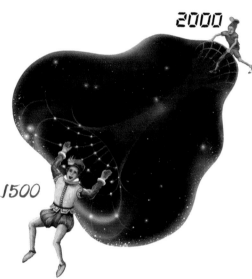

2000

1500

⬆ *One theory about space and time says that as an object moves faster and approaches the speed of light, then the passage of time for that object slows down. At light speed, time stops. Perhaps if the object went faster than light, time would go backwards. 'Short-cuts' in space called wormholes might make faster-than-light speed possible. So travelling through a wormhole could take you back in time, maybe 500 years or more!*

Amazing **facts**

The light of a laser is the same type of electromagnetic wave energy as ordinary light. But it differs in three ways:

Laser light

1 All the light waves are the same length. This means they are the same colour. A laser gives out light of one pure colour only.

2 All of the peaks and troughs of the waves are level or aligned, like the equal 'waves' of corrugated sheet metal.

3 The waves are all parallel, which means they stay the same distance from each other, no matter how far they travel.

Ordinary light

1 Even what seems to be a single colour of light has a mixture of wavelengths, and therefore a mixture of colours.

2 The peaks and troughs are mixed up and not aligned.

3 Waves of ordinary light spread out or diverge so the whole beam gets wider.

Slower **light**

Light speed varies greatly with the substance or medium through which it passes.

Medium	Speed (km/sec)
Vacuum	299,792
Air	299,700
Water	225,000
Window glass	195,000
Decorative (lead crystal) glass	160,000
Diamond	125,000

Loud shouts, soft whispers, repetitive noise, beautiful music, warning sirens, different voices, the crash of thunder – sounds are a huge part of our daily lives. The science of sound is known as acoustics, and it affects the design of modern buildings, as well as a vast variety of products, from televisions and water plumbing to cars, trains and planes.

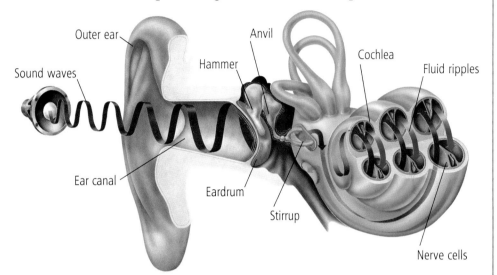

Outer ear

Sound waves

Anvil

Hammer

Cochlea

Fluid ripples

Ear canal

Eardrum

Stirrup

Nerve cells

What is sound?

Sound is energy in the form of movements of a substance or object. The to-and-fro movements many times each second are known as vibrations. Vibrating objects such as a loudspeaker make ripples of waves of high and low air pressure, which travel through the air to our ears. Since sound involves motion, it is a type of kinetic energy.

Invisible sound waves travel through the air and vibrate the eardrum, which passes the vibrations along the tiny ear bones into the cochlea. The vibrations cause ripples in the fluid within the cochlea, which make nerve signals that are sent to the brain to be processed.

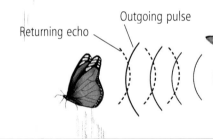

Outgoing pulse

Returning echo

Can we see sounds?

We cannot see sound waves in the air, but we can see big vibrations in solid objects that produce sounds, such as loudspeakers or engines. We can also see the ripples on a liquid such as water, through which sound passes. However, the sounds we hear come from vibrations at the rate of more than 20 per second, known as 20 Hz. Our eyes cannot follow such fast movements so we see just a blur. A butterfly's wingflaps, at 10 Hz (ten per second), are too slow to produce sound for us to hear. A hummingbird's wingbeats at 100 Hz are fast enough to make a buzzing hum, but can only be seen as a blur.

A bat's squeaks and clicks are mostly ultrasonic – too high for our ears to detect. The sounds reflect from objects around and the bat works out whether the echoes indicate leaves and twigs to be avoided when flying or prey to be caught. This system is called echolocation and allows the bat to fly and feed – even in total darkness.

Acoustic information

Mach speed
Very fast planes can exceed the speed of sound, known as Mach 1. This causes pressure waves to build up around the craft, which travel away as the loud, deep, dull thud known as sonic boom. The boom would give away the presence of 'stealth' planes, such as this B-2 bomber, which usually flies at just below Mach 1.

The B-2's cruising speed is about 700 km/h.

Amazing **Mach facts**

The speed of sound is measured on the Mach scale. This does not give a speed in m/sec or similar. It gives a comparison number to the speed of sound in certain conditions. The Mach scale is named after German scientist Ernst Mach (1838–1916).

• The speed of sound through air at 20°C and standard air pressure at sea level is about 1,238 km/h. So an object moving this fast would be travelling at Mach 1, while one moving at 1,857 km/h is going at Mach 1.5.

• Very high in the air, where temperature and pressure are lower, the speed of sound is nearer 1,062 km/h. So Mach 1.5 up there is 1,593 km/h.

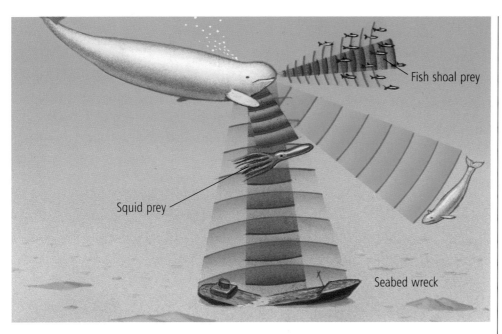

Fish shoal prey

Squid prey

Seabed wreck

Can we hear all sounds?

No, our ears only respond to sounds with vibration speeds between about 20 and 20,000 Hz. The vibration speed or frequency, in Hz, affects the pitch of a sound. Low frequency sounds, such as the roar of a truck or rocket, are very deep and booming. High frequency ones, such as birds singing, are shrill. Sounds lower than about 20 Hz or higher than 20,000 Hz may be all around us, but we cannot hear them.

⊙ *Some birdsong can exceed 100,000 Hz.*

⊙ *Hunting whales such as the beluga send out sonic clicks (similar to the bat on page 176). These pulses bounce back as echoes to tell the whale about nearby objects.*

How fast does sound travel?

The speed of sound depends on what it has to travel through. Its speed in the air varies with air temperature, pressure and humidity (moisture content), travelling an average of 344 m/sec. Sounds move at about 1,500 m/sec through liquids, such as water. It travels even faster through solid objects: 2,500 m/sec through hard plastic, 5,000 m/sec through steel, and about 6,000 m/sec through some types of glass.

Can sound reflect, like light?

Yes, sound waves reflect or bounce off hard, smooth, flat surfaces, such as walls and doors, just as light waves bounce off a mirror. If the returning sound or reflection is more than about one-tenth of a second after the original sound, we hear it separately and call it an echo. If the time gap for the reflection is less, it mixes with the original sound and makes it seem longer, which is known as reverberation.

⊙ *Special 'acoustically insert' rooms have shapes of soft substances on the walls, ceiling and floor. These absorb almost all sound energy. So there are no reflections of sound such as normal reverberations or echoes. It is sometimes called a 'deadroom' because all sounds inside it seem 'dead'.*

The decibel **scale**

⊙ *In the decibel scale, each gap of 10 dB means a ten-fold increase in energy. For example. 60 dB represents ten times more sound than 50 dB.*

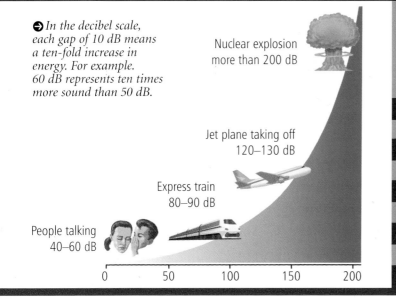

Nuclear explosion more than 200 dB

Jet plane taking off 120–130 dB

Express train 80–90 dB

People talking 40–60 dB

0   50   100   150   200

The energy content of sound is measured in decibels, dB. Sound above 90 dB, especially if high-pitched and long-lasting, can damage hearing.

10 dB	Quietest sounds our ears detect, such as a ticking watch
20 dB	Average whisper
40 dB	Quiet talking with people nearby
50 dB	Television or radio at average listening volume
60 dB	Fairly loud conversation
70 dB	Appliance such as vacuum cleaner or food processor
80 dB	Train passing through station
100 dB	Very loud machine or tool-like road drill
120 dB	Jet plane at take-off

Machines are all around us, and are often used in everyday life. Jet planes roar overhead, cars whizz past on the road, cranes lift loads, gears are changed on cycles, vacuum cleaners suck and swings and seesaws are used in playgrounds. Machines work because forces make movements.

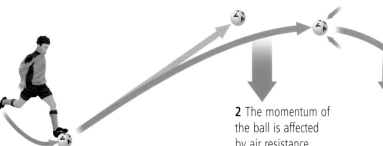

1 Kinetic energy is passed from the foot to the ball, applying a force to make the ball move

2 The momentum of the ball is affected by air resistance

3 The ball is pulled back down by gravity

⬆ *The tendency of a moving object to carry on moving in a straight line is counteracted by other forces. For example, air resistance and gravity may act upon a moving object to break its momentum.*

What is a force?

It is a push, pull or other action that makes an object move, or tries to make it move. If you kick a ball, the force from your foot makes the ball move. The kinetic (movement) energy of your foot is passed, or transferred, to the ball. If you kick a wall, the kinetic energy of your foot does not make the wall move, but it is changed into energy that squashes against your foot.

⬇ *The basic forms of matter (solid, liquid, gas and plasma) depend on the motion of atoms. Most pure substances can change their form as their temperature changes. For example, water (liquid) becomes ice (solid) when cooled enough, or steam (gas) when heated enough.*

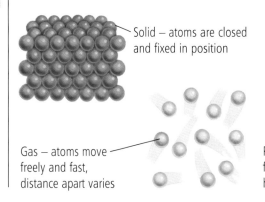

Solid – atoms are closed and fixed in position

Gas – atoms move freely and fast, distance apart varies

Do atoms move?

It depends on the substance or object they are in. If it is a solid, such as iron, or wood, the atoms are almost still and just move or vibrate slightly around a central point. In a liquid, such as water or oil, the atoms can move about, but they stay the same distance from each other, so the liquid keeps the same volume. In a gas, like the air around us, atoms can move even faster and also change their distances, so the volume of the gas can increase or decrease.

➡ *There is movement even at the subatomic scale. Electrons spin and whirl around the nucleus of an atom. The proton and neutron particles in the nucleus vibrate or oscillate (move from side-to-side) slightly.*

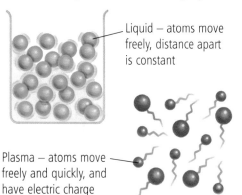

Liquid – atoms move freely, distance apart is constant

Plasma – atoms move freely and quickly, and have electric charge

World in motion

➡ *Gravity is the force of attraction that pulls everything in the Universe together. It acts on any object to pull it to the ground. The more mass an object has, the more the pull of gravity. A parachute or similar flat surface opens up to form a larger area for air to press against. Air resistance acts in the opposite direction to gravity and so slows the rate of fall back down to the ground.*

Amazing facts

• A force is measured in units called newtons (N).

• One newton of force will give an object of 1 kg an increase in speed of 1 m/sec.

• Pushing a car needs a force of about 500–1,000 N.

• The four jet engines of the retired airliner Concorde produced more than 700,000 N.

• When we measure the weight of an object, we measure the force of Earth's gravity pulling down on it. For example, a 100 g medium-sized apple is equivalent to about 1 N.

Are there different kinds of motion?

Yes, depending on the direction or path of the moving object. The simplest kind of motion is movement in a straight line, known as linear motion. Angular motion is in a bend or curve, such as a car going around a corner. A special case of this is circular motion, where the object stays the same distance from a central point, like a wheel on an axle. Reciprocating motion is a to-and-fro movement from a middle point, such as pistons in an engine or the vibrations in a loudspeaker.

❷ As a motorcycle travels in a curved pathway, the rider must lean into the corner. This counteracts the natural tendency of a moving object to keep going in a straight line. Otherwise the motorcycle would topple outwards, away from the corner.

A nutcracker is a form of lever that provides the effort (squeezing force) to break the load (nut)

An axe is a form of wedge

A screw is a turning type of wedge

A wheelbarrow enables heavy loads to be lifted using a wheel and axle, which reduce friction to make the task easier

What is a machine?

In basic science, a machine is a device that allows a small force, the effort, to move a large object, the load. There are six types of simple machine – the ramp (slope or inclined plane), lever, wedge, pulley, screw, and the wheel and axle. Examples of four of these are shown above. Of the other two machines, the ramp eases the movement of heavy objects over a distance. Pulleys move loads by changing the direction and distance of the force, to be pulled down, rather than lifted up. All other machines work by using a combination of these simple machines.

Do machines give us extra energy?

No, machines cannot create energy or motion from nothing. As you pull out a nail with a crowbar, your hands move a long way with less force, while the other end of the lever moves a little way with great force. This is known as mechanical advantage. It breaks a task down into smaller, easier stages. Many machines have motors or engines, which provide the force, rather than our own muscles, so the task becomes even easier.

❷ The Solo Trek XFV has two propellers that push air downwards (the action). The reaction creates an upwards force. When this is equal to the downwards pull of gravity, the craft hovers in mid-air.

Newton's **laws of motion**

❷ Sir Isaac Newton (1642–1727) developed his ideas about gravity and motion in 1665–6. According to records, he began to form his theories after he saw an apple fall from a tree and wondered what force had pulled it to the ground.

The laws

1 An object keeps moving in a straight line in the same direction (or keeps still if it's already still), unless a force acts on it.

2 A force makes an object change its movement in the direction of the force, with an acceleration (increase in speed) that depends on the size of the force.

3 For every action caused by a force, there is an equal and opposite reaction.

Examples

1 A spacecraft heading into outer space will keep going straight, unless it is affected by gravity from a planet or star, and pulled towards it.

2 Kick a football and it changes from being still to moving in the direction of the kick. Apply more force, which means a harder kick, and the ball gains speed faster and goes farther.

3 The engines of a jet-car blast hot gases backwards, which is the action. The reaction is to push the car forwards.

Many people wear wristwatches, and there are clocks in most rooms, which are there to tell us the time. We need to know the date and time so that we can arrive at school or work promptly, meet friends on agreed dates and at certain times, and in order to catch a bus, train or plane. However in science, there is much more to time than the tick of a clock.

↑ *The ancient Egyptians made sundials more than 3,000 years ago. The marks showed hours. The length of the hours varied with the seasons, but people were used to such an idea and called them 'temporary hours'.*

When did people start measuring time?

At least 10,000 years ago, and probably well before that. Ancient peoples recorded sunrise and sunset each day, the changing phases of the moon each month, and the seasons of the year. They used these natural occurrences to devise calendars and predict important events, such as when a river might flood or the time to worship a certain god.

When were clocks first developed?

Ticking clocks similar to today's were devised in the 1300s. For centuries before, people had relied on simpler methods of timekeeping, such as hourglasses, or sundials. From the 1400s, however, explorers sailed on great voyages to find new lands. In order to track their positions, they needed to measure time precisely. In the 1700s, engineer John Harrison developed a series of very accurate clocks called chronometers (special clocks for use at sea to measure longitude). Accurate to less than 30 seconds in a year, even on a swaying ship, these began a new era of precise timekeeping.

Could time stand still?

Modern science predicts that yes, it might. We are used to time passing regularly, with every minute the same length, day after day, year after year. But Albert Einstein's theories (see panel below) said that time could change speed. The faster an object moves, the slower time passes. However, the speeds involved are enormous. If an object could move at the speed of light, then time might actually stop (see page 175).

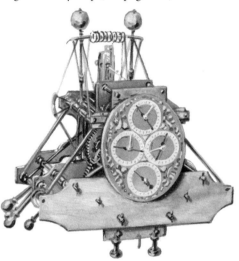

↑ *John Harrison's 1759 version of the chronometer won a £10,000 prize. The prize had been devised by the British government in 1714 to promote research into the development of accurate timekeeping devices.*

← *Simple timekeepers, such as hourglasses of trickling sand remained common until the 1300s when mechanical clocks were developed.*

Relativity

Albert Einstein

The theories of relativity developed by scientist Albert Einstein in 1905 and 1915 make some amazing predictions. From our everyday experience they seem to be impossible. But the predictions happen in extreme conditions out in the Universe, at incredible speeds and with vast objects such as stars and galaxies. In normal life here on Earth, the effects of Einstein's theories of relativity are so tiny that they can be measured, and they do not affect daily life. But out in the Universe, when travelling between the stars, the effects would be much more important. One effect is that as an object goes faster and faster, it shrinks in the direction that it is travelling.

↑ *A rocket would get shorter lengthways, even though its width stays the same. To an observer on the outside, the rocket and the people in it would become shorter and fatter, and their clocks would become slower. To the people inside the rocket, everything seems normal within. But the Universe outside would look longer and thinner and clocks outside would tick much faster.*

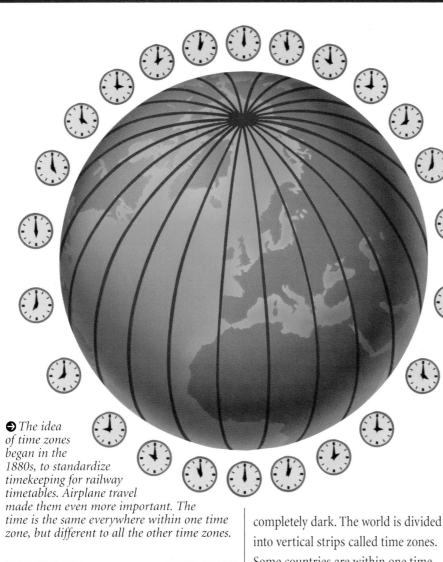

→ *The idea of time zones began in the 1880s, to standardize timekeeping for railway timetables. Airplane travel made them even more important. The time is the same everywhere within one time zone, but different to all the other time zones.*

Is it the same time everywhere in the world?

No, because of the way the Earth spins around once every 24 hours. Otherwise at 8 a.m. the Sun might have risen in the UK, yet be setting in Australia, while the USA is completely dark. The world is divided into vertical strips called time zones. Some countries are within one time zone while others encompass several. Travellers need to adjust their watches or clocks as they move between zones to know the 'local' time. Some time zones 'bend' around islands or national borders.

Are time and space linked?

Yes, in modern science they are four parts or dimensions of the same whole. Three of these dimensions are in physical space – length, width and height. The fourth dimension is time. For example, to describe dangerous rocky rapids in a river, the length and width of the rapids, and the height that the water falls need to be measured. But the time of the measurement should also be recorded. Otherwise someone might arrive to see them in the dry season when the river and rapids have gone, and so the other measurements become irrelevant.

↓ *Atomic clocks use the movement of atoms from substances such as caesium, which vibrate more than nine billion times each second, and are accurate to less than one second in a million years.*

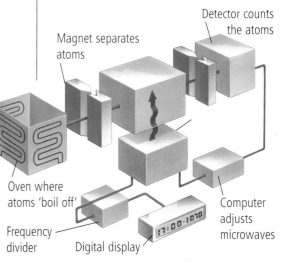

Detector counts the atoms

Magnet separates atoms

Oven where atoms 'boil off'

Frequency divider

Digital display

Computer adjusts microwaves

Amazing **facts**

• Time is relative. That is, it changes under different conditions, especially with speed of motion. The faster you move, the slower time passes.

• The only constant in the Universe, which is always the same, is the speed of light. This has the symbol c.

• Einstein showed that mass or matter, m, such as parts of atoms, could be changed into Energy, E.

• Einstein's famous equation was $E = mc^2$. This says that the amount of energy in a piece of mass, such as an atomic particle, equals the amount of mass times the speed of light multiplied by itself. Since light speed is huge, when multiplied by itself it is far greater. So a tiny bit of mass equals a vast amount of energy.

→ *Albert Einstein (1879–1955) altered science greatly with his ideas about space and time. He showed they were relative – that is, they can change according to different conditions.*

Long ago, people travelled by foot and communicated face to face. It may have taken days to transport heavy goods just a few kilometres. Advances in transport and communication technology mean that we can now converse with a person on the other side of the world, using a videophone, or travel to be with that person within a day.

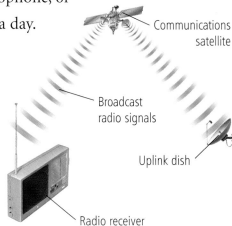

Communications satellite

Broadcast radio signals

Uplink dish

Radio receiver

Is the world really 'shrinking'?

Planet Earth itself is not getting smaller. But a 'shrinking world' means we can travel and communicate much faster than previously. In the late 1700s, a journey halfway round the world by sailing ship might have taken three months. In the late 1800s, a similar journey by steamship took six weeks. In the 1920s, pioneering aeroplane flights over the same distance took just two weeks. Today the journey time halfway round the world has 'shrunk' to less than 24 hours.

↻ *Mobile phone technology has progressed to enable people to send better-quality still images and even moving images.*

Will travel times continue to shorten?

In the near future, probably not. There are various plans for 'space-planes' that could travel around the world in just a few hours. However, the costs of developing such a massive project are phenomenal. In the 1960s, many people thought that supersonic (faster-than-sound) aircraft travel would become widely-used. But the only supersonic passenger plane was Concorde, which first flew in the same year as the subsonic Boeing 747 'Jumbo'. Concorde could fly from Paris to Washington in a record time of 3 hrs 32 mins.

What is a comsat?

A communications satellite is designed to receive information such as radio programmes, telephone calls and television channels, usually sent to it in the form of 'uplink' radio waves. The satellite then strengthens or amplifies the signals and beams them back down again as radio waves. These satellites can be used as repeaters or relays to pass on information over great distances, or to broadcast to many receivers over a huge area. Most satellites are in geosynchronous orbits (see page 183).

↻ *Broadcast communications satellites send radio signals direct to many receivers over a wide area, for radio programmes and television channels.*

Inventions on the move

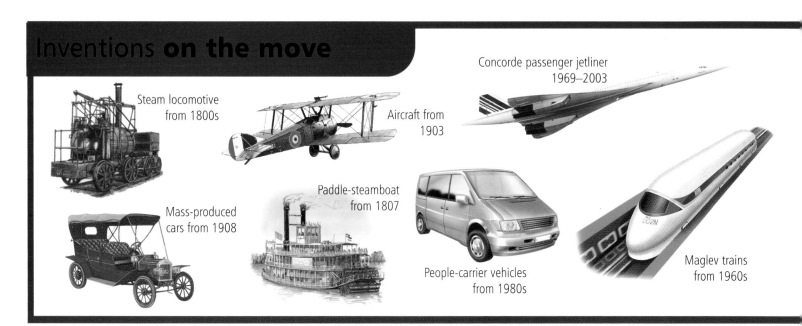

Steam locomotive from 1800s

Aircraft from 1903

Concorde passenger jetliner 1969–2003

Mass-produced cars from 1908

Paddle-steamboat from 1807

People-carrier vehicles from 1980s

Maglev trains from 1960s

What are the fastest forms of transport?

Rockets and spacecraft are the fastest, with the space shuttle travelling at more than 24,000 km/h. The fastest jet warplanes travel at more than 3,000 km/h, but a passenger jet plane moves at about 900 km/h. On land, electric-powered 'bullet trains' exceed 300 km/h. Passenger hovercraft on the sea reach 70–80 km/h and fast passenger ships around 40–50 km/h. Most cars reach up to 150 km/h but speed restrictions and crowded roads mean that journeys are often much slower and safer.

⊕ *The world is encircled by communications satellites and criss-crossed by telecom wires, fibre-optic cables, and radio and microwave links. The telecom network links telephone calls, radio, television and computer data.*

⊕ *The luxurious* Queen Mary II *is 345 m long and weighs 150,000 tonnes.*

Which form of travel is most luxurious?

Cruise liners offer amazing comfort and luxury, as 'floating hotels'. The biggest cruise liner in operation at present is the *Queen Mary II*, which went into service in January 2004. It can carry 2,700 passengers at a top speed of 30 knots (equivalent to 55 km/h). The on-board facilities available to the passengers include 14 bars and clubs, six restaurants, a casino, theatre, swimming pools and even a planetarium.

Will we have personal jump-jets or helicopters?

In the near future, probably not. There is only one working type of 'jump-jet' – the British Harrier multirole strike fighter. A newer US / British design, the JSF or Joint Strike Fighter, is taking years and costing billions to develop. Many important or wealthy people have personal helicopters. But the skills needed to fly a helicopter, and the strict limits on engineering, maintenance and safety mean that they are unlikely to become as common as cars in the near future.

⊕ *'Jump-jets' such as the Harrier and JSF are VTOL – vertical take-off and landing aircraft. The jet blasts come out of tilting nozzles, which can point down for take-off and landing, or to the rear for forward flight.*

Amazing **facts**

GPS or satellite navigation

The Global Positioning System is a series of 24 NAVSTAR satellites circling Earth at an average height of 17,500 km. Of these satellites, 21 are active and three are spares.

Each satellite is about 5 m long and takes about 10 hours for each orbit.

➲ *GPS satellites continuously circle the Earth in groups.*

The satellites are in six groups, with four in each group that follow the same orbit one after the other.

At any time or place on the Earth, at least four satellites should be above the horizon, when their radio signals can be detected by a GPS receiver.

Each satellite's signals include its own identification and position, and the exact time from its on-board atomic clock.

The receiver works out the time delay for the signals from each satellite and compares them to find the receiver's location, usually to the nearest 20–30 m.

GEO for communications satellites

Many comsats are in GEO – geostationary or geosynchronous Earth orbit. In this position the satellite is 35,840 km above the Equator. It takes 24 hours to complete one orbit – which is the same time as the Earth beneath takes to spin around once.

So the satellite seems to 'hover' high in space above the same spot on the surface.

It means dishes sending and receiving signals can be aimed at the satellite and then left. They do not have to be continually adjusted to 'track' the satellite as it passes over.

Science and technology have filled our lives with machines, devices and gadgets. It seems incredible that just a few decades ago there were no CD players, satellite television or games consoles. Technical advances are moving at a tremendous rate with better and more efficient machines being constantly developed.

Controls

Drive belt

Motor

Hydraulic suspension

Detergent and additive trays

Door

Drum

Pump

Filter

How do CDs and DVDs store information?

CDs (compact discs) and DVDs (digital versatile discs) hold information in the form of tiny bowl-like pits in the shiny underside surface. In a CD there are over 3,000 million pits in a spiral path or track about 5 km long. They can store about 70 minutes of high-quality music, over 700 megabytes of computer data or similar amounts of information. A DVD has more, smaller pits in different vertical layers and stores 4.7 gigabytes (4,700 megabytes) – enough for a full-length movie and its soundtrack. These pits are 'read' by a laser beam.

⊕ *Personal music players can store sounds on tape, compact disc (like this version), minidisc (similar to CD but smaller) or electronic microchip.*

⊕ *A powerful microscope reveals the bowl-like pits and flat areas between them, in the surface of a CD (compact disc).*

⊕ *In western countries, such as the UK, about one household in two has a washing machine. About one in three households has a dishwasher.*

Which labour-saving devices are most popular?

One of the most popular machines in daily life is the washing machine. In most developed countries, many households have one. Some people use industrial versions in launderettes. The machine washes clothes inside a revolving drum with hot water and soap, which are then rinsed away with clean water. A fast spin gets rid of excess water, so that the clothes can be hung to dry.

Technical **developments**

Key **dates**

The second half of the 20th century saw an explosion in technology:

1950 First commercials or 'adverts' shown on colour television.
1953 Heart-lung machines in medicine.
1955 Development of optical fibres.
1958 Ultrasound scans check babies in the womb.
1959 Photocopiers are first sold commercially.

1960 First laser developed.
1961 Live television by satellite.
1963 Audio cassette introduced.
1965 Development of holograms.
1967 UK begins colour television broadcasts.
1969 First Moon landing.
1970 Removable floppy discs for computers.
1972 Early home computer games with tennis-like bats and ball.

⊕ *Holograms show 3-D images, with depth as well as width and height, on a flat surface.*

Can mobile phones get much smaller?

The main limits on mobile phone size are the rechargeable battery bulk and the size of the buttons so they are easy for our fingers to press. Also, screens for photos and videos cannot be too small. In the future mobile phones may become voice-operated so that they do not need buttons. For security it will only respond to the unique voice of its owner.

◀ *Mobile phones have shrunk amazingly in the past 10 years, from the size of a housebrick to almost as small as a thumb.*

Does medicine benefit from technology?

Yes, technology is very important in many aspects of modern medicine. For example, an endoscope is a flexible tube that can be inserted into the body to view its insides to achieve a more detailed and accurate diagnosis. Light to illuminate the interior is carried to the tip along optical fibres, which are bundled, flexible rods of transparent glass or plastic, thinner than human hairs. The image is carried from the tip to the eyepiece and screen by another set of optical fibres. There are also many kinds of scanners that can see inside the body.

◖ *Doctors can see inside the body using various kinds of scanners, or directly by looking through an endoscope. The endoscope can also carry out treatments, such as sealing a cut using a laser beam.*

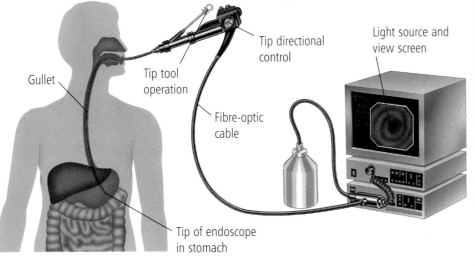

Gullet

Tip tool operation

Tip directional control

Fibre-optic cable

Light source and view screen

Tip of endoscope in stomach

Main unit feeds images to monitor or television

Hand console with controls

◐ *Games consoles become more realistic every year, with faster action and better graphics, as well as more imaginative challenges. Some games can be played 'live' over the Internet with people anywhere in the world.*

How fast does technology become out-of-date?

Technology is frequently updated, making existing versions out-of-date. For example, vinyl discs were used to play back recorded sound for more than 50 years. Cassette tapes also became popular for about 30 years. About 20 years later, CDs took over. Some 10 years after that, MP3-players arrived, storing sounds in electronic microchips. The world of technology continues to produce faster and more efficient machines.

1975	First commercial 'flat screen' LCDs, liquid crystal displays.
1977	Mass-produced pocket televisions.
1979	Personal music players (audio cassette).
1981	First PCs (personal computers) as we now recognize them.
1982	Audio CDs, compact discs, go on sale.
1984	Camcorders developed.
1987	DAT, digital audio tape.
1988	Colour laser photocopiers; early mobile phones.
1989	'Gameboy' early hand-held games console.

1990	Bag-less vacuum cleaners.
1992	Superbike cycles with many composite materials.
1993	Early videophones.

1994	Internet users exceed 30 million.
1995	A standard format for the DVD is agreed.
1996	'Playstation 1' games.
1998	Apple introduces iMac computers.
1999	International Space Station construction under way, bringing the idea of 'holidays in space'.
2000	DVDs begin to sell in commercial quantities.

◐ *The camcorder is a personal movie camera and videotape recorder. Some models can now fit in the palm of the hand.*

Our world is a varied landscape with diverse countries and cultures. Mountains, rivers, deserts, seas, oceans, rainforests, grassland and extreme weather are just some of the Earth's features. For more than two million years humans have populated the Earth, building towns and cities to live in, and working the land to produce food and materials to sustain life.

↑ *Beaches in the Mediterranean are packed during the summer, when mostly European holidaymakers head for the sea.*

Where are Asia's high and low points?

Asia has the highest mountain on Earth, Mount Everest, and the lowest point, the Dead Sea. In fact, the ten highest peaks (all more than 8,000 m high) are in the Himalayas, the greatest mountain range in Asia. But not all Asia is mountainous. There are huge areas of flat grasslands and desert, and the lowest point on Earth is the shore of the Dead Sea (in Israel and Jordan) – 400 m below sea level.

Where is the world's largest desert?

The world's largest desert is the Sahara, in northwest Africa. The Sahara Desert covers an area of over 9 million sq km, stretching across the northern third of the African continent. It continues to grow as the areas surrounding it are overgrazed by animals and so turn to dust. Temperatures during the day can reach 50°C and yet drop to freezing during the night. Despite years without rain in the Sahara, certain animals and plants have adapted to be able to live in these conditions.

← *The Himalayan mountain range has formed over 25 million years, and continues to grow at a rate of 5 cm every year.*

Which is the most densely populated continent?

More than 700 million people live in Europe, which is only slightly bigger than Australia, making Europe the most densely populated continent for its size. The most densely populated area stretches from southeast Britain, through northern France and into the Netherlands, where there are approximately 410 people per sq km. This figure is in vast contrast to a country such as the USA in North America, where there are about 27 people per sq km.

Facts and **statistics**

International organizations
Many countries of the world have joined together to create international organizations that provide law, order, aid and support throughout the world. These organizations use resources from the member states of the international community to help those in need, during periods of war or natural disasters. The United Nations (UN) is one such organization, set up in 1945 to try to resolve disputes between countries.

↑ *Red Cross workers travel around the world to regions of war, drought, famine or flood, to provide shelter, food and medicine for the victims.*

Vital **statistics**

Circumference	40,075 km
Population	More than 6 billion
No. of countries	194
Largest continent	Asia – 17,400,000 sq km
Largest country	Russia, in Asia and Europe – 17,075,184 sq km
Highest mountain	Mount Everest, Asia – 8,863 m
Longest river	Amazon River, South America – 6,750 km
Largest lake	Caspian Sea, Asia – 371,000 sq km
Largest desert	Sahara Desert, Africa – 9.3 million sq km
Major religions	Christianity, Islam, Hinduism, Buddhism, Other – see page 213 for statistics

Where is the world's largest rainforest?

The Amazon rainforest of Brazil, Peru and Bolivia, in South America, covers more than 6 million sq km. It is home to more than 1,500 varieties of fish, more than 22,000 species of plants and a vast variety of insects, birds, reptiles and mammals. Local people and scientists use as many as 2,000 of the plant species found in the Amazon for use in medicine. Natural resources, such as gold, diamonds and rubber can also be found in the rainforest.

⊙ Spider monkeys are just one of the many mammal species that are found in the Amazon rainforest.

Where is the world's longest coral reef?

Covering more than 350,000 sq km, the Great Barrier Reef is found off the northeast coast of Australia. More than 2,000 species of fish live among the many thousands of individual reefs, which are built from the remains of marine life. Some parts of the reef are up to 25 million years old.

Where is the world's coldest place?

In July 1983, a record −89°C was recorded near the Vostok Scientific Station in Antarctica. The average annual temperature on the continent is −57°C, and 98 per cent of the land is covered in ice, which accounts for 90 per cent of the world's ice.

⊙ The Great Barrier Reef has been made a World Heritage Centre in order to protect it from pollution and damage caused by tourists and divers. Overfishing, mining, or tourists taking coral away from the Reef as a 'souvenir' of their trip, are some of the threats to the Reef.

Which continent experiences extreme weather conditions?

North America has some of the worst hurricanes, deepest snowfall and is home to one of the hottest places on Earth. In 1998 Hurricane Mitch reached 290 km/h, killing 11,000 people and destroying more than 93,000 buildings. The greatest snowfall ever recorded was 11.5 m, measured in California in 1911. In contrast, Death Valley in California can reach a temperature of 57°C. Furthermore, an average of 800 tornadoes a year rage across U.S. states such as Kansas, Missouri, Iowa and Nebraska.

Amazing **facts**

- The population of the world is estimated to grow at a staggering rate – approximately 360,000 babies are born every day.

- Approximately 150,000 people die every day.

- There are about 1,000 minor earthquakes every day, in various regions of the world.

- The Aral Sea, between Kazakhstan and Uzbekistan, is disappearing as a result of its water being used to irrigate crops. Today it is only one-third of its original size.

- Sweden in Europe has at least 90,000 lakes, which were formed during the last ice age, more than 100,000 years ago.

- In a region in northern Scandinavia, in Europe, it stays constantly light throughout summer, and constantly dark during winter.

- Maine is the first of the US states to see the sunrise each day.

- The Grand Canyon is the largest gorge in the world, at 349 km long.

- The highest temperature was recorded in 1922 in Libya, at 58°C in the shade.

- In the Nazca region of Peru, patterns have been scraped into the surface of the desert. They were created more than 2,000 years ago.

- There could be as many as 30,000 islands scattered around the Pacific.

- McMurdo is a community in Antarctica, which has cafés, a cinema and a church, for people visiting during the summer.

- The plates of the Earth's crust are moving the ocean floor at between 1.25 and 10 cm a year.

Asia is the world's biggest continent, both in land area and in the number of people who live there. It fills about one-third of the planet's land area. About six in every ten people on Earth are Asian. Asia's terrain is vast and varied and includes the world's highest mountain range, the Himalayas, as well as desert, steppe grassland, tundra, boreal (northern) forest and jungle.

Which country is also a subcontinent?

India is a subcontinent and is home to about one-fifth of the world's population. The Indian subcontinent comprises India itself, which has more than one billion people, plus the countries of Pakistan, Bangladesh, Bhutan, Sri Lanka, Nepal and the Maldives. India also has 14 major languages and more than 400 other languages and regional dialects. Over the last 5,000 years the land has been invaded many times, and as migrating people have settled there a varied and diverse culture has emerged. India is now the world's largest democracy (see page 210) and has given rise to some of the world's most popular religions. The climate is hot and dry, but the monsoon season bring heavy rains and often flooding.

map key

1	Armenia	15	Myanmar (Burma)
2	Azerbaijan	16	Nepal
3	Bahrain	17	North Korea
4	Bangladesh	18	Oman
5	Bhutan	19	Qatar
6	Cambodia	20	Singapore
7	Cyprus	21	South Korea
8	Georgia	22	Syria
9	Israel	23	Tajikistan
10	Jordan	24	Thailand
11	Kuwait	25	Turkmenistan
12	Kyrgyzstan	26	UAE
13	Laos	27	Uzbekistan
14	Lebanon	28	Yemen

Facts and statistics

United Arab Emirates (UAE)

The UAE is a federation of seven independent Arab states or emirates, the most well-known of which are Dubai and Abu Dhabi. An emirate is a region that is ruled by an emir or prince. About 96 per cent of the population are Muslim. Before the mid-1900s most Arabs made their living through pearl fishing or herding camels. Oil was discovered here in the 1950s, and by the 1970s the UAE had one of the world's richest economies.

⬆ *Bahrain's Emir is Sheik Isa bin Salman Al-Khalifa.*

Vital statistics

Area	44,389,400 sq km
Population	More than 3.8 billion
Major cities	Kuala Lumpur (Malaysia), Mumbai (India), Seoul (South Korea)
Largest country	Russia* – 17,075,352 sq km
Highest mountain	Mount Everest – 8,848 m
Longest river	Chang Jiang – 6,380 km
Largest lake	Caspian Sea – 378,400 sq km
Largest desert	Arabian Desert – 1,250,000 sq km
Main religion	Islam – c. 807 million

* Russia is partly in Europe: Asiatic Russia is 13,119,582 sq km

⬆ *Hanoi in Vietnam is modernizing rapidly, and its trade is increasing with Europe and the US. Traditionally, sampans, boats are used to transport goods to market.*

Where is Hanoi?

Hanoi is the capital of Vietnam, in Southeast Asia. It is in the north of this long, narrow country. Ho Chi Minh City is the major city in the south. It used to be called Saigon until in 1976 it was renamed after Ho Chi Minh, who led North Vietnam in a long and bitter civil war against South Vietnam and their American allies.

What is a zen garden?

A zen garden is a simple outdoor space containing natural materials, neutral colours and clean lines designed to promote peace and serenity. Zen is a form of Buddhism, which developed in China from about AD 500. Zen Buddhism was introduced to Japan in about AD 1100 and became influential in Japanese culture and has since become very popular in western countries.

⬅ *Zen gardens often contain one flower, such as a lotus, and small, pruned trees, such as bonsai.*

Where do Sinhalese people live?

Sinhalese people live in Sri Lanka, the island at the southern tip of the Indian subcontinent. About 72 per cent of the population are Sinhalese, who are mainly Buddhist. The largest minority group in Sri Lanka are the Tamils who originated in southern India and are mostly Hindu. Sri Lanka was a British colony from 1802 until 1948 and was called Ceylon until 1972. Sinhalese and Tamil are the country's two official languages and tea is one of its most profitable exports.

⬇ *Many Sri Lankan people are employed on plantations to pick tea leaves. Tea is one of Sri Lanka's main exports.*

Amazing **Asia**

- Russia is the largest country in the world, in land area, and is partly in Europe, partly in Asia.

- Japan and Indonesia are at risk from volcanoes. A ring of volcanoes called the Ring of Fire surrounds the Pacific Ocean.

- Asia has the world's largest bat, the Bismarck flying fox from Indonesia, and the smallest bat, Kitti's hog-nosed bat from Thailand.

⬅ *In some parts of China, couples have been limited to having only one child in an attempt by the Chinese government to control population figures.*

- Garden plants native to Asia include tulips (Turkey) and rhododendrons (India).

- The Japanese call their country Nippon, meaning 'source of the Sun'. The red disc on the Japanese flag represents the Sun.

- The most common family name in the world is probably Zhiang – as many as one in ten Chinese people are called Zhiang.

- Temperatures in Asia can range from −68°C in Verkhoyansk, Russia, to 54°C in Tirat Zevi, Israel.

Asia was the home of great ancient civilizations, such as those of the Indus Valley and the Tigris-Euphrates region. The greatest imperial power in Asia was China, but by the 1800s much of Asia had come under European colonial rule. Japan was the first Asian country to 'westernize' its industries, and by the 1950s it had become one of the world's leading economic powers.

The Forbidden City in Beijing was once the emperor's private world, kept a secret from the people and foreigners. Beijing has been China's capital since 1421 when the emperor Yung Le made the city his base.

Why does Asia have some of the world's richest countries?

Much of Asia's wealth comes from its manufacturing nations such as Japan, China, South Korea, Malaysia and India; and its oil-producers, such as Saudi Arabia, Brunei and Kuwait.
The manufacturing countries have large populations, many of whom work for low wages, so the average income per person is less than in Europe or North America. The oil-rich states have smaller populations, so average incomes are higher. The two richest rulers in the world are the King of Saudi Arabia and the Sultan of Brunei. The Middle East possesses more than 65 per cent of the world's oil reserves.

Oil has made some Asian countries, such as Kuwait, immensely wealthy.

Where is the Forbidden City?

The Forbidden City is the old imperial section of Beijing, in China. It forms a square that is surrounded by a moat and wall. Inside the boundaries are palaces that were once used by the Chinese emperors, but they are now open to the public as museums. Ordinary Chinese people and foreigners were once banned from entering the city. Only officials and nobles could gain entrance. One million workers took ten years to build the walled city, with its great halls, temples, pagodas and gardens.

Asia **facts**

Marco Polo and China
The Italian traveller, Marco Polo (1254–1324) wrote first-hand accounts of China that gave Europeans some of the first detailed reports about the Chinese way of life. After an long and intrepid journey from Venice, across Europe and Asia, Polo reached the palace of Kublai Khan (1216–94), founder of the Mongol dynasty in China, where he received a warm welcome.

When Marco Polo travelled to China, he wrote many books, such as Description of the World, *in which he told of Kublai Khan's advanced society. His work also encouraged European interest in the east and may have motivated other explorers.*

Mahatma Gandhi led peaceful protests to campaign for India's independence. He saw this achieved in 1947, but was assassinated a year later by a fanatic of the Hindu religion.

Why is Korea divided into North and South?

At the end of the Second World War (1945) Korea was occupied by Russia and America, who divided the country into communist North Korea and democratic South Korea. Korea is a peninsula, or strip of land, on the east coast of Asia, bordering China. Its old name was Joseon. The Korean War (1950–53) failed to settle disputes, and the two Koreas remain separated by a heavily guarded border control.

↑ *Seoul in South Korea is a busy, modern city. South Koreans enjoy a much higher standard of living than people across the closely guarded border, in the North.*

↑ *Singapore skyscrapers rise from a small island linked to the mainland by a causeway.*

Which is the only city situated on two continents?

Istanbul, in Turkey, lies in both Europe and Asia. It stands on both banks of the strait called the Bosporus, which separates the two continents. The Asian part of the city is one and a half times smaller than the European part. Istanbul had been called Byzantium and (from AD 330) Constantinople, and was the capital of the eastern half of the Roman Empire. It became Istanbul in 1453 when the Turks captured it.

Who founded Singapore?

Singapore was founded in 1819 by Sir Stamford Raffles. He built a British trading base on what had been a small fishing village, which then flourished as a small republic at the tip of the Malay peninsula. It became a major port, and is now a busy trade centre. The people are mostly Chinese and Malay.

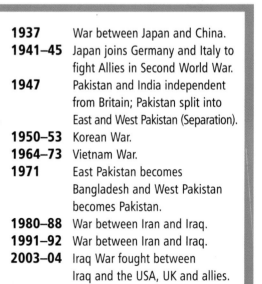

⬇ *Istanbul is the gateway between Europe and Asia. Because the continents are joined, it is a super-continent known as Eurasia.*

Key dates

c. 30,000 BC	Stone Age people live in Asia.
8000 BC	First farm and towns form in Asia.
3500–500 BC	First writing in Sumer (Iraq); rise of first Asian empires (Assyria, Babylon, Persia).
c. 1760 BC	Shang dynasty founded in China.
c. 660 BC	Jimmu Tenno is first emperor of Japan.
269 BC	Asoka rules India.
221 BC	Shih Huangdi is first emperor to rule all China.
c. 800 BC	Khmer empire in Cambodia.
AD 1096	First Crusade (war for Holy lands) – the last one ends 1291.
1200s	Mongols conquer much of Asia. Marco Polo visits China.
1299	Ottoman empire founded in Turkey.
1483	Russians explore Siberia.
1500s	Regular trade contacts by sea with Europe. Mogul Empire in India. Japan united by Hideyoshi.
1700s	Britain and France fight for control of India.
1800s	China and Japan became open to western trade.
1912	China becomes a republic.
1937	War between Japan and China.
1941–45	Japan joins Germany and Italy to fight Allies in Second World War.
1947	Pakistan and India independent from Britain; Pakistan split into East and West Pakistan (Separation).
1950–53	Korean War.
1964–73	Vietnam War.
1971	East Pakistan becomes Bangladesh and West Pakistan becomes Pakistan.
1980–88	War between Iran and Iraq.
1991–92	War between Iran and Iraq.
2003–04	Iraq War fought between Iraq and the USA, UK and allies.

Africa is a huge continent, covering about 20 per cent of the Earth's land surface. Only Asia is bigger. Africa comprises 53 different countries and more than 600 different tribal or ethnic groups. Africa's landscape is varied, with the world's largest desert, the Sahara, and the world's second longest river, the Nile. It has vast expanses of tropical grasslands or savanna, as well as rainforest.

map **key**

1	Benin	11	Liberia
2	Burkina Faso	12	Malawi
3	Burundi	13	Republic of Congo
4	Central African	14	Rwanda
	Republic	15	Senegal
5	Djibouti	16	Sierra Leone
6	Equatorial Guinea	17	Swaziland
7	Gambia	18	Togo
8	Ghana	19	Tunisia
9	Guinea-Bissau	20	Western Sahara
10	Lesotho		

Which is Africa's largest city?

Cairo, in Egypt, is Africa's largest city, with more than 15 million people living there. It outranks other big cities in the continent, such as Algiers (Algeria), Lagos (Nigeria) and Johannesburg (South Africa). Like other cities of northern Africa, Cairo has Islamic mosques, open-air markets (bazaars) and tall, modern buildings. All over Africa cities are growing rapidly, as people leave the countryside to look for work in towns.

🔽 *Cairo has grown into a large, modern city, but old mosques (Muslim places of prayer) remain.*

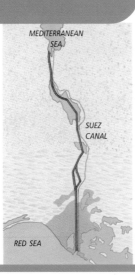

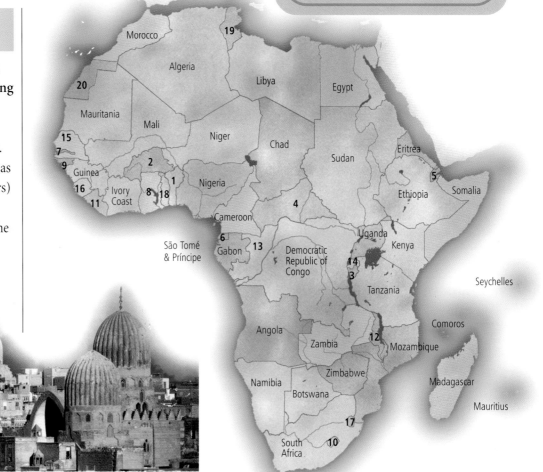

Facts and **statistics**

The Suez Canal

Completed in 1869, the Suez Canal soon became one of the world's largest artificial waterways. Before it was built, ships from Europe had to sail around Africa to reach East Asia. In 1956, the Egyptian government took control of the canal. Tolls paid by ships that use the canal provide a major source of income for Egypt.

➡ *The 165-km long Suez Canal runs from the Red Sea to the Mediterranean Sea, linking Europe to India and East Asia.*

Vital **statistics**

Area	30,303,000 sq km
Population	More than 840 million
Major cities	Algiers (Algeria), Cairo (Egypt), Casablanca (Morocco), Johannesburg (South Africa), Lagos (Nigeria)
Largest country	Sudan – 2,505,5,810 sq km
Highest mountain	Mount Kilimanjaro, Tanzania – 5,895 m
Longest river	River Nile – 6,670 km
Largest lake	Lake Victoria – 69,484 sq km
Largest desert	Sahara Desert – 9 million sq km
Main religion	Christianity – *c.* 350 million

Which are Africa's most valuable minerals?

Gold, diamonds, coal, oil and gas are among the many valuable minerals that are mined in various parts of Africa. South Africa is mined for gold, diamonds, coal and cobalt. Algeria, Libya and Nigeria provide oil and gas. Diamonds are mined in Sierra Leone and copper is found in Zambia. Africa also produces iron ore, tin, bauxite (aluminium ore) and manganese.

Which is the highest mountain in Africa?

At 5,895 m high, Mount Kilimanjaro, a dormant volcano in Tanzania, is the highest mountain in Africa. It is so high that, even though it is very near the Equator, its peak is always snow-covered. Its name in Swahili is *Uhuru*, which means 'freedom'.

➔ *This section of the Victoria Falls is called the Devil's Cataract. The falls were named after Britain's Queen Victoria by 19th-century explorer David Livingstone, who travelled across much of Africa, and mapped out various parts of the continent.*

How much of Africa is desert?

About 40 per cent of this hot continent is desert. The Equator crosses the middle of Africa and in most places it is hot all year round. There are great rivers and lakes in Africa but, in contrast, large areas of it are very dry and this has led to the spread of deserts. The Sahara is the biggest desert in the world, and stretches across north Africa. In the southwest of Africa are the smaller Namib and Kalahari deserts.

⊙ *Mount Kilimanjaro rises above the savanna in northern Tanzania, close to the Kenyan border. It formed over one million years ago.*

What is 'the smoke that thunders'?

Victoria Falls is Africa's most famous waterfall and its African name Mosi-oa-tunya, means 'smoke that thunders'. This refers to the cloud of spray that rises above the Victoria Falls as the Zambezi River tumbles over a sheer rock wall. The rumble of the falls can be heard far away and sounds like distant thunder. The falls are 108 m high and 1,500 m wide.

Amazing **facts**

- Approximately half the population of Africa is under the age of 15.

- Liberia was founded as a land for freed African slaves from the USA.

- Fossils found in Africa's Great Rift Valley show that humans originated in Africa.

- Millet is an important crop in much of Africa. The seeds are ground into flour to make flatbread or a kind of porridge.

- When European leaders split the countries of Africa between them, only Ethiopia and Liberia remained independent and ruled by Africans.

- The world's biggest gold-field is in the Witwatersrand in South Africa.

⊙ *African athletes, especially those from the highlands of Ethiopia and Kenya, dominate world athletics in the long-distance events with their speed and agility.*

By 1900 Africa was almost completely colonized by European countries. The colonial boundaries became the boundaries of new independent African nations, as African peoples sought self-government from the 1950s. Libya was the first African country to win its independence in 1951. In South Africa, the white minority controlled the government until the 1990s, under a system known as apartheid.

⬆ *A Zulu from South Africa wears traditional warrior dress, comprising of a short spear, or assegai, and an ox-hide shield. A regiment of Zulu soldiers is known as an impi.*

Who are the Zulus?

The Zulus are a people who live in South Africa. In the early 1800s, they were a small tribe, mainly cattle-herders, but a chief named Shaka led a powerful army to fight against the Boers (Dutch settlers) who were taking their land. In 1879, the Zulus were defeated by the combined armies of the Boers and British in the Zulu War. Today the Zulus are citizens of the Republic of South Africa.

Where do the Masai people live?

The Masai are a tribal group of people in Kenya, East Africa. Traditionally, they lived as cattle-herders. Masai men were famous for their skill at hunting lions, armed only with spears. Many African countries have a mixture of tribal groups. There are about 50 ethnic groups in Kenya alone, including the Kikuyu, who are the biggest tribe.

What causes famine in some parts of Africa?

Famine can be caused by drought or civil war. The regions hit hardest by drought include Ethiopia, Chad and Mali, which may go for a year or more without rain. Farmers rely on the seasonal rains to make their crops grow and so the lack of rain means that the soil becomes dry and vegetation dies. This leaves the local population with very little to eat. Civil wars are also responsible for famine because they disrupt farming and trade, thus increasing the risk of famine in some areas.

⬆ *Masai women wear colourful headbands and beaded collars for tribal ceremonies. Many other traditional African costumes are now seldom seen except for tourist displays.*

Africa **facts**

Key **dates**

900 BC	Kingdom of Kush founded.
100 BC	Niger-Congo languages spread from West Africa to other regions.
AD 641	Invading Arabs introduce Islamic faith.
c. 1000	The kingdoms of Benin and Ife are created.
1100	Great Zimbabwe culture founded in southeast Africa.
1450	Portuguese develop trading posts in parts of Africa.

c. 1510	First African slaves taken to USA.
1652	Dutch set up colony in South Africa.
1795	British take Cape Colony from Dutch.
1835	Boers (Dutch settlers) set off on Great Trek from the Cape.
1847	Liberia becomes independent.
1869	Suez Canal is opened.
1879	The Zulus are defeated by the British and Boer armies.
1884	Africa is divided between European leaders.

1889	Boer War break out in South Africa.
1902	British defeat the Boers to seize their lands as part of the British Empire.
1948	Apartheid begins in South Africa.
1951	Libya becomes indepedent.
1957	Gold Coast independent from Britain, as Ghana. Many colonies become independent over the next 15 years.
1963	Organization of African Unity formed.
1994	Nelson Mandela elected South Africa's first black president.

Why are Africa's game parks so important?

Tourism is a major source of income for African countries, as tourists flock to the game parks to see the amazing variety of wildlife. Lions, giraffes, rhinos, elephants, hippos, antelope and many more animals are found in game reserves across Africa. The reserves protect the animals from poachers, who shoot elephants for their ivory tusks and rhinos for their horns. People used to go to Africa on safari to shoot 'big game', but now many of these animals have become endangered and so are protected inside game parks, such as the Kruger in South Africa and the Tsavo in Kenya.

↑ Big cats, such as the cheetah, can be spotted by tourists travelling through game reserves in South Africa, Tanzania and Kenya.

Which African leader fought for an end to apartheid?

Nelson Mandela was imprisoned for 26 years for campaigning for the end of apartheid. Apartheid was a social system in place in South Africa that separated black and white citizens. Mandela was jailed in 1964 for being a senior member of the ANC (African National Congress). In 1990, South African president, F. W. de Klerk, released Mandela.

➔ Mandela became the first black president of South Africa in 1994. Under his leadership, apartheid gradually began to break down.

Where is Timbuktu?

Timbuktu is an ancient trading city south of the Sahara Desert in the African country of Mali. The name means 'place of Buktu'. According to legend, a slave named Buktu was left there to guard her master's goods. Timbuktu was once rich and prosperous, a stopping place for camel travellers crossing the Sahara, carrying gold and salt. It later fell on hard times.

← Many people in Timbuktu live in traditional mud-brick houses.

← This sculpture of the Sphinx was relocated to avoid damage when the Aswan Dam was built and the Nile was flooded. The 1,951-m long Aswan Dam was built across the River Nile in 1902. The Nile flows through the countries of Uganda, Sudan and Egypt, providing water for farming, fishing, homes and industry.

➔ The San people, or Bushmen, are hunters and gatherers who live in the Kalahari Desert. They collect honey from wild bees' nests, and bee grubs are considered a delicacy. They live and work in small, close communities. They were originally nomadic, moving around the country in order to search for food and to hunt animals. But today they usually settle in one area.

Europe is the smallest continent, not counting Australia, and the most densely populated. It has the longest coastline of all the continents (more than 60,000 km), with mountains in the north and south enclosing a central plain. There are 42 independent countries in Europe, some are large (Russia, Ukraine, France and Spain) and others, such as Liechtenstein, are tiny.

Where does Europe end?

Europe has sea on three sides (north, west and south), but it merges with the Asian landmass on the eastern side. There are natural land barriers forming a boundary between Europe and Asia. These boundaries include the Ural Mountains and the Caspian Sea, in Russia. Europe is separated from the continent of Africa by the Strait of Gibraltar, which lies between Morocco in Africa, and Spain in Europe.

Where is Scandinavia?

Scandinavia is the region of northern Europe with a shared geography and history. The countries of Scandinavia are Norway, Sweden, Denmark, Finland and Iceland, which is an island in the Atlantic Ocean. The Scandinavian countries are famed for their landscapes of fjords (Norway), lakes (Sweden), forests (Finland), busy fishing ports (Denmark) and hot springs (Iceland).

map key

1	Albania	9	Lithuania
2	Andorra	10	Luxembourg
3	Belgium	11	Macedonia
4	Bosnia-Herzegovina	12	Moldova
5	Croatia	13	Netherlands
6	Estonia	14	Slovenia
7	Latvia	15	Switzerland
8	Liechtenstein	16	Yugoslavia

Facts and statistics

◐ *Denmark's flag is Europe's oldest national flag, first flown in 1219. The Danish king at the time is said to have seen a white cross in a red sky before winning a battle.*

◑ *The white cross on the Greek flag represents the Christian faith. The blue represents the sea and sky, and the white symbolizes the people who fought for Greece's independence in the early 19th century.*

◐ *Sweden, like all other Scandinavian countries, has an off-centre cross on its flag, based on the same legend as Denmark's flag. Sweden's flag may date back to 1449.*

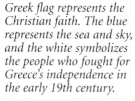

Vital statistics

Area	10,534,600 sq km
Population	More than 700 million
Major cities	Berlin (Germany), London (UK), Madrid (Spain), Milan (Italy), Moscow (Russia), Paris (France)
Largest country	Russia – 4.7 million sq km (European area only)
Highest mountain	Mount Elbrus, Russia – 5,633 m
Longest river	Volga River, Russia – 3,531 km
Largest lake	Caspian Sea, Russia – 438,695 sq km
Main religion	Christianity – c. 552 million

⬆ *St Petersburg is Russia's second largest city, and boasts the world's biggest art gallery, the Hermitage Museum (shown above) and a famous opera and ballet theatre.*

Which is the biggest country in Europe?

Russia is so big that it is shared between Europe and Asia, so strictly speaking only part of Russia is 'European'. Even so, at 4.7 million sq km, the European region of Russia is seven times bigger than the next biggest country in Europe, the Ukraine. Next come France, Spain and Sweden.

How many countries make up the British Isles?

The British Isles is made up of two independent countries: the United Kingdom and the Republic of Ireland. The United Kingdom consists of Great Britain (the island containing the nations of England, Scotland and Wales) and Northern Ireland (part of the island of Ireland).

Where do people walk on land that was once sea?

The Netherlands. The name Netherlands means Low Countries, and this region is very low-lying. Sea walls or dykes have been built to stop the sea flooding the land, and water has been pumped from flooded parts to turn salt marshland into fertile agricultural land. The reclaimed land is known as polders. About 40 per cent of the country has been reclaimed from the sea and 25 per cent of this is used for housing and roads. It takes about eight years after draining the land for it to be suitable for farming and building on.

➡ *Merchants built the network of over 100 canals that cross the Dutch city of Amsterdam.*

⬆ *The Tower of London is in the capital city of England. Building of the Tower was begun by William the Conqueror in 1078, when London was already 1,000 years old.*

⬆ *The Alps is the highest mountain range in western Europe, running through southeastern France, Switzerland, Italy and Austria. The range started to form more than 15 million years ago.*

Amazing **Europe**

- Less than 3 per cent of mountainous Norway is cultivated.

- The UK is Europe's biggest island, at 229,850 sq km.

- The highest volcano in Europe is Mount Etna in Sicily, at more than 3,300 m.

- Turkey and Russia are each situated partly in Europe and partly in Asia.

- The highest peak in the Alps is Mont Blanc, at 4,807 m, but Mount Elbrus in the Caucasus mountain range is even higher, at 5,633 m.

Europe was the birthplace of ancient Greek and Roman culture, and later European ideas and technology were spread by explorers, traders and empire-builders to other continents. Europe was the first continent to undergo the Industrial Revolution, in the 1700s. It was also the cradle for two terrible world wars, 1914–18 and 1939–45. Since 1950, the European Union has become the dominant economic force in Europe.

In which city is the Kremlin?

The Kremlin is the medieval centre of Moscow, which is the capital of Russia, and used to be the home of the Russian tzar (emperor). The name kremlin means fortress, and the first wooden fortress was built on this spot more than 800 years ago. The walls now in place date from the 1400s. Cathedrals and palaces were built around the Kremlin fortress. In 1917, the Kremlin became the headquarters of the world's first communist government, which then collapsed in 1991.

St Basil's Cathedral, with its cluster of domes, is one of Moscow's landmarks.

The Rock of Gibraltar is a 426-m high mass of limestone. Gibraltar was once an important naval base, but is now a favourite tourist location.

Where is the Rock of Gibraltar?

Gibraltar is a rocky landmark at the southern tip of Spain, at the point where the Mediterranean Sea and Atlantic Ocean meet. About 30,000 people live there. The Rock (as Gibraltar is known) was held by the Arab and Berber Moors and the Spaniards until 1713, when it was ceded to Britain by treaty. Spain wants Gibraltar back, but local people voted to stay British.

The colony of Gibraltar is represented by this flag and covers an area of 6.5 sq km.

Europe facts

Key dates

c. 8000 BC	End of last ice age.	1066	The Normans conquer England.	1871	Germany united.
4000 BC	Farming reaches northern Europe.	1236–41	Mongols invade Russia.	1914–18	First World War.
2000 BC	Minoan civilization on Crete.	1300	Renaissance (re-birth in the arts) begins in Italy.	1939–45	Second World War.
c. 480 BC	Hunters mark out territories; Celts spread. Greece at peak of power.	1338	Black Death (bubonic plague) hits Europe.	1957	European Economic Community (now European Union) set up.
AD 50	Rome is world's biggest city (one million people).	1400s	Portuguese start overseas exploration.	1961	Berlin wall is erected, dividing Germany.
285	Roman Empire splits in two.	1700s	Industrial Revolution begins in Britain.	1990	Collapse of Communism in Eastern Europe. Collapse of Berlin Wall reunites Germany.
476	Collapse of western Roman Empire.	1804	Napoleon becomes emperor of France.	2004	Expansion of EU to 25 member states.
711	Spain invaded by Moors.				

➜ *Some members of the European Union have discussed the creation of a European federal state, represented by the current European Union flag. However, most member states prefer their national independence and wish to keep their own flags and currencies.*

Which is Europe's smallest country?

Europe's, and the world's, smallest independent state is the Vatican City, official home of the Pope (the head of the Roman Catholic Church). Fewer than 1,000 people live in the Vatican City. It has its own police and the Pope's bodyguard force, the Swiss Guard, who wear traditional uniforms. It also has a national anthem, stamps, coins, flag and a radio station.

➜ *The Vatican's main buildings are St Peter's (shown below), one of the world's largest churches, and the Vatican Palace.*

How did the European Union begin?

The European Union evolved from a series of economic agreements, such as the common market, set up by various European nations, from the 1950s. The founder members of the EU were France, Germany, Italy, Netherlands, Belgium and Luxembourg. More countries joined and by 2004 the EU had 25 member-states and its own parliament. A common currency (the euro) is shared by some member states.

➜ *The Colosseum in Rome is the biggest Roman amphitheatre (open-air arena): 49 m high and 157 m across. Inside there was room for 80,000 spectators.*

Which European city was once the heart of the Roman Empire?

The city of Rome, in Italy, was once the heart of the Roman Empire. The Romans conquered most of Europe over 2,000 years ago, and imposed their laws and culture on the peoples who lived under their rule. This had an enormous effect on later European history. The remains of some buildings from ancient Rome, such as the Colosseum and the Pantheon, still stand today in Rome, the capital of Italy.

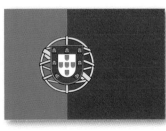

➜ *The flag of Portugal dates from 1910. The shield in the centre dates from the 12th century, and the nautical instrument behind it celebrates Portugal's exploration and maritime past.*

➜ *The Swiss flag, which dates from the 14th century, is the only other completely square flag (the other is the flag of the Vatican City). In honour of its founder, Swiss, Jean Dunant, the flag of the International Red Cross organization is a red cross on a white background, the reverse of the Swiss flag.*

Queen Victoria

European **rulers**

Queen Elizabeth, the Queen Mother – (1900–2002) The first member of the British royal family to reach the age of 100.

Louis XIV of France – One of the longest reigns in European history, of 72 years.

Louis XIX of France – Shortest reign (15 mins, before abdicating in 1830).

Queen Victoria of Britain – Longest reign in Britain of 63 years (1837–1901).

The third largest continent, North America extends from Greenland and Alaska in the Arctic north, through Canada and the United States, to Mexico in the south and the islands of the Caribbean Sea. The landscape of North America includes bleak polar regions, towering mountain ranges such as the Rockies, vast grassy plains or prairies (now ploughed for cereal crops), forests, mighty rivers and the Great Lakes.

Greenland

Alaska (USA)

Canada

Hawaii (USA)

USA

Mexico

Cuba

Jamaica

Honduras

Guatemala

Nicaragua

Costa Rica

Panama

6

3

20 1

12 8 15 16

11

5

9

2

14 17

13 7 4

18 10

19

US states

Alabama	Louisiana	Ohio
Alaska	Maine	Oklahoma
Arizona	Maryland	Oregon
Arkansas	Massachusetts	Pennsylvania
California	Michigan	Rhode Island
Colorado	Minnesota	South Carolina
Connecticut	Mississippi	South Dakota
Delaware	Missouri	Tennessee
Florida	Montana	Texas
Georgia	Nebraska	Utah
Hawaii	Nevada	Vermont
Idaho	New Hampshire	Virginia
Illinois	New Jersey	Washington
Indiana	New Mexico	West Virginia
Iowa	New York	Wisconsin
Kansas	North Carolina	Wyoming
Kentucky	North Dakota	

map key

1	Antigua & Barbuda	12 Haiti
2	Aruba	13 Martinique
3	Bahamas	14 Montserrat
4	Barbados	15 Puerto Rico
5	Belize	16 St Kitts & St Nevis
6	Bermuda	17 St Lucia
7	Dominica	18 St Vincent & the
8	Dominican Republic	Grenadines
9	El Salvador	19 Trinidad & Tobago
10	Grenada	20 Virgin Islands
11	Guadaloupe	

Which is North America's largest country?

Canada, with an area of more than 9.97 million sq km, is North America's largest country. The United States is a little smaller, at 9.37 million sq km, but the population of Canada is only 11 per cent of that of the USA. Canada shares a 6,400 km long land border with its southern neighbour, the USA. The Rocky Mountains stretch almost 5,000 km southwards from Canada, south into the United States.

Facts and statistics

The Rocky Mountains
Thousands of visitors flock to the Rocky Mountain range each year to see the vast array of fauna and wildlife, such as bears, deer, mountain lions, squirrels and minks. The Rockies stretch more than 4,800 km from Alaska to New Mexico. In the Canadian Rockies, the snow-capped mountains reach more than 3,600 m above sea level and the tallest peak is Mount Robson, at 3,954 m high. The Rockies are also a good source of lead, coal, silver and zinc.

⬇ *The brown grizzly bear once roamed much of North America, but is now less common. The biggest bears live on Kodiak Island, Alaska.*

Vital statistics

Area	23,497,000 sq km
Population	505 million
Major cities	Chicago (USA), Mexico City (USA), New York (USA), Philadelphia (USA), Toronto (Canada)
Largest country	Canada – 9,976,162 sq km
Highest mountain	Mount McKinley – 6,194 m
Longest river	Mississippi – 3,779 km
Largest lake	Lake Superior – 82,103 sq km
Largest US state	Alaska – 1.5 million sq km
Main religion	Christianity – c. 250 million

⬆ *Red rocks rise hundreds of metres out of the otherwise flat Monument Valley, which is situated in both Utah and Arizona.*

Why is the USA called the land of the skyscraper?

The USA is home to some of the world's greatest cities, and many of the world's tallest buildings. In many US cities, such tall buildings create dramatic skylines, particularly in Chicago, along the shore of Lake Michigan and in New York City, on Manhattan Island. Chicago once boasted America's tallest building, the Sears Tower, which has 110 floors and stands 1,707 m high with its topmost masts.

Where is Monument Valley?

Monument Valley is in the dry, western American state of Utah but also crosses into Arizona. In the valley can be found some of the most spectacular scenery in the United States. Over thousands of years, the huge crags of sandstone have been eroded by the wind and rain, making the valley an ideal location for shooting 'western' films.

Where are four presidents cut into stone?

In the Black Hills of South Dakota, in the midwest United States. A sculptor named Gutzon Borghum carved the heads of four US Presidents into the granite rock of Mount Rushmore. Each head is about 18 m high and can be seen from almost 100 km away. Work started on the monument in 1927 and lasted until the 1960s.

⬅ *The four presidents on the Mount Rushmore National Memorial are (left to right): George Washington, Thomas Jefferson, Theodore Roosevelt and Abraham Lincoln.*

⬆ *The Niagara River tumbles into a gorge. Spray and foaming water rise into the air, often forming rainbows.*

Where are the Niagara Falls?

There are two falls on the Niagara River: the Horseshoe Falls on the Canadian side and the American Falls on the US side. The Horseshoe Falls are 792 m wide and 51 m high. The American Falls are 305 m wide and about 54 m high. The most water (about 85 per cent) crashes over the Horseshoe Falls. Each year millions of tourists head for Niagara Falls, which have been an attraction ever since European explorers first saw them in the late 1600s.

Amazing **facts**

- The Big Muddy is the name given to the Missouri, the second longest river in North America. It carries with it huge quantities of mud.

- The most important waterway in North America is the St Lawrence Seaway. Ships use it to move inland for 3,500 km from the Atlantic Ocean to the Great Lakes.

- The highest waterfall in the USA is the Yosemite Falls, Yosemite National Park, California, at 739 m high.

- North America's hottest spot is Death Valley, California, where a temperature of 57°C was recorded in 1913.

⬆ *Bridalveil Fall has a 436 m high drop and is the first waterfall seen by visitors to Yosemite National Park.*

⬆ *Toronto is Canada's biggest city. Canada has far fewer people than the USA – 31 million compared to the USA's 287 million.*

North America includes countries with diverse cultures and traditions. Canada and the United States have historic ties with Britain, but Canada also has a large French-speaking minority. Both countries have populations of Native Americans, who retain many of their traditional cultures and languages, as well as people of African, Asian and European origin. In Mexico, people speak Spanish – this is also a legacy of the country's past.

⬆ *Chichén Itzá is an ancient sacred site of the Maya of Central America. The Maya people built stepped-pyramid temples in their cities.*

Who were the first Americans?

The first people to live in North America were the Native Americans and Inuit, whose ancestors came from Asia, probably before the last ice age. When Europeans invaded in the 1500s, the natives fought a fierce battle to keep their land. However, today Native Americans form less than one per cent of the population of the USA. Most Americans today are those whose ancestors came from Africa, Asia and Europe.

⬇ *Today, about one-fifth of Native Americans live on land known as reservations, which has been given back to them by the government.*

Who were the Aztec and Maya?

The Aztecs were a native people living in what is now Mexico, around AD 1300: the Maya were a native people living in Central America around the same time. The Aztecs built a city called Tenochtitlán, upon which Mexico City now stands. The Aztecs were conquered by the Spaniards in 1521, who destroyed their temples. Each of the Mayan Kingdoms had a capital city that was built entirely from stone.

North America **facts**

Key **dates**

c. 30,000 BC	First hunters arrive from Asia.
c. 10,000 BC	People spread south across North America.
AD **c. 250**	Mayan culture in Mexico.
c. 500	Farming in Mississippi region.
c. 900	Caribs conquer Arawaks in the Caribbean.
c. 950	Toltec culture in Mexico.
1000	Vikings reach North America.

1492	Christopher Columbus reaches the Caribbean.
1521	Spanish conquest of Mexico.
1534	French explorers move into Canada.
1570	Spanish set up a colonial rule centre in Guatemala.
1607	First English colony in North America, in Virginia.
1620	Pilgrims land from the English ship *Mayflower*.
1626	Dutch found New Amsterdam, later renamed New York.

1682	French claim Louisiana territory.
1775–83	American Revolutionary War.
1803	USA buys Louisiana from France, doubling its size.
1821	Central American colonies break away from Spanish rule.
1823	United Provinces of Central America formed, but does not last.
1840s	Settlers and wagons move west.
1848	Gold rush in California, USA.
1861–65	American Civil War; slavery abolished in 1865.

⬆ *The Caribbean Sea is in the Atlantic Ocean. Caribbean islands have a tropical climate. Many of the islands are formed from volcanic rock and contain vast coral reefs.*

Where is the Panama Canal?

The Panama Canal opened in 1914, providing a shipping short cut between the Atlantic and Pacific oceans. The Panama Canal is 81 km long, and using it saves ships more than 12,000 km travelling around the tip of South America. The Canal was dug across the isthmus (narrow neck of land) of Panama. The area was so jungle-covered and hot that, after work started in 1881, it had to be halted after eight years because so many workers died of disease and exhaustion. The canal cuts through the continent at its narrowest part.

How did the Caribbean Sea get its name?

When Spanish explorers arrived in the New World from Europe in 1492 they called the sea in which they discovered the islands, 'Mar Caribe', after the Caribs who lived there. The Caribs were Native American people who had settled on the islands we now call the 'West Indies' and on the mainland of South America (see page 206). Within a few years the Caribs were completely wiped out by wars, enforced slavery and diseases brought by the Europeans. Most Caribbeans today are the descendants of Africans and Europeans.

How did Greenland get its name?

When Viking sailors first saw the island, they were encouraged when they saw the green grass and so settled. Most of Greenland today looks white, not green, because the island is almost entirely covered by ice and snow. Only the coast has a small amount of vegetation in summer. The name Greenland also encouraged others to follow and start settlements. Greenland today actually belongs to the European country of Denmark.

⬆ *Inuit people of the Arctic traditionally make ice-houses as temporary hunting lodges. They hunt and fish in the sea for food.*

1898	Spanish–American war.
1909	Robert Peary reaches North Pole.
1914	Panama Canal is completed.
1939–45	Second World War.
1948	Organization of American States founded.
1959	Revolution in Cuba.
1969	US astronauts walk on the Moon.
1979	Rebels overthrow government in Nicaragua, leading to civil war.
1991	Collapse of Soviet Union leaves the USA as the only world superpower.

Amazing **facts**

- Powerful tropical storms, known as hurricanes, affect the Caribbean between May and October.

- In 1943 a new volcano appeared in Mexico. It was given the name Paricutín. Red-hot lava poured out of the ground and within one year the volcano had risen to 300 m high.

- Trinidad's Pitch Lake is strange because it doesn't contain water and it is possible for people to walk over it. The lake contains hot, sticky, black tar, which covers about 57 ha to a depth of about 40 m.

- The Caribbean islands are famous for beaches of white sand, but on the island of Montserrat they are grey, brown or black.

The fourth largest continent, South America, is almost twice as big as Canada. It has the world's largest tropical rainforest, the world's longest river, and the Andes Mountains, as well as areas of grasslands. It has a rugged, forested interior, and volcanic eruptions and earthquakes are frequent. Most South Americans are descendants of the ancient civilizations, such as Aztec and Maya, or of European, African or Asian descent. The main languages spoken on the continent are Spanish and Portuguese.

What is Latin America?

The name Latin America is used for Mexico, Central America and South America. Most people living here speak Spanish or Portuguese – languages that developed in Europe from Latin. The settlers and explorers who sailed to America from the late 1400s took these languages with them, and they became widespread, although some Native American languages have survived. Many of the customs of Latin America also show signs of Spanish or Portugese influence. Many of the people, for example, are Roman Catholic Christians. European missionaries converted the local people to Christianity but some traces of pre-Christian religions remain in local customs and rituals.

What is Argentina's biggest city?

Argentina's biggest city is its capital, Buenos Aires. The city has a population of more than ten million people and a very busy port. It was founded in 1536 as a port on the Rio de la Plata, and the name is spanish for 'fair winds'. Buenos Aires is famous for its broad streets and wide plazas, or squares, such as the Plaza de Mayo. Many people have moved from the countryside to live in towns or cities, such as Buenos Aires, where more employment and higher wages can be found.

⊕ *Residential districts are called barrios, and one called La Boca is noted for its colourful painted houses. Many of the city's poorest inhabitants live in shanty towns on the outskirts of the city.*

Facts and **statistics**

Key **dates**

c. 10,000 BC	Hunters spread south from North America.
c. 2600 BC	Mayan culture in Central America.
AD 200	Nazca culture in Peru.
1438	Inca empire in the Andes.
1500	Pedro Cabral claims Portugal.
1532	Spanish conquer Incas.
1776	Spain sets up the Viceroyalty of La Plata, a colony in South America.
1809	Wars of independence against Spanish rule in South America.
1817	José San Martín leads an army across the Andes during wars with Spanish.
1819	Simon Bolívar of Venezuela becomes first president of Gran Colombia.
1821	Peru becomes independent.
1822	Brazil becomes independent.
1825	Bolivia declared a republic.
1860	Argentina takes its modern name.
1888	Slavery is abolished in Brazil.
1889	Brazil becomes a republic.
1898	Spanish–American War.
1914	Panama Canal opens.
1932–35	Bolivia and Paraguay at war.
1959	Fidel Castro becomes Cuba's Communist leader.
1979	Civil wars in Nicaragua and El Salvador.
1982	Falklands War between Argentina and Britain.
1990	Chile becomes a democracy again.

Why do people visit Machu Picchu?

One of the most amazing insights into South America's past is the lost city of Machu Picchu, built by the Incas in the 1400s. The terraced city high in the Andes Mountains was one of the last refuges for the Inca people after their empire was conquered by Spain in the 1500s. It had stone houses, a royal palace and army barracks, and around it were fields cut into the mountain slopes. The city was abandoned and forgotten, until it was rediscovered by an American archaeologist in 1911.

⊕ *The ruins of Machu Picchu lie northwest of the city of Cuzco, Peru, in mountains more than 2,000 m high.*

⊕ *The statue of 'Christ The Reedemer' overlooks Rio de Janeiro. Founded by the Portuguese in 1565, this Brazilian city is a busy port, famous for its music, beaches and vibrant carnivals.*

Where do most South Americans live?

About 75 per cent of South Americans live in cities. Many of the cities are badly overcrowded like São Paulo in Brazil, which has some of the worst slums in the world. However, much of South America is thinly populated. Few people live in the high Andes Mountains or in the Amazon rainforest – though settlement there is being encouraged.

Where can you see Sugar Loaf Mountain?

Sugar Loaf is a curiously-shaped mountain overlooking Rio de Janeiro, the second biggest city in Brazil after São Paulo. Sugar used to be sold in solid blocks of this shape. On Corcovado Mountain, another peak across Guanabara Bay, stands a 30-m statue of 'Christ The Redeemer', which can be seen from most parts of the city.

Vital **statistics**

Area	17,871,000 sq km
Population	More than 350 million
Major cities	Buenos Aires (Argentina), Lima (Peru), Rio de Janeiro (Brazil), Santiago (Chile), São Paulo (Brazil)
Largest country	Brazil – 8,511,957 sq km
Highest mountain	Aconcagua, Argentina – 6,959 m
Longest river	Amazon River – 6,448 km
Largest lake	Lake Maracaibo, Venezuela – 13,511 sq km
Main religion	Christianity – c. 474 million

Amazing **facts**

- Not all of South America is forest or mountain. There are also vast regions of grasslands, such as the Pampas of the south and the Llanos of the north.

- Nicaragua is named after a Native American tribe called the Nicarao.

- Chile is the world's longest country, about 4,300 km from end to end.

- Balsa wood, from a tree grown in South America, is one of the lightest woods known – a third of the weight of cork.

- Brazil has one of the world's largest dams, the Itaipú, which dams the Paraná River to produce electricity.

Australia, New Zealand, Papua New Guinea and the Pacific island groups of Melanesia, Micronesia and Polynesia form Oceania. Australia is the world's sixth largest country and is populated by people of mostly aboriginal, European and Asian descent. It is the only country that is also a continent in its own right. To the south of Oceania lies the much bigger and uninhabitable landmass of Antarctica.

Papua New Guinea

Solomon Islands

Australia

Tasmania

New Zealand

Which country is the biggest wool producer?

Australia produces more wool than any other country in the world. More than one-quarter of the world's wool is shorn from sheep roaming the sheep stations (farms) of Australia. Australia has a vast and dry interior, but is also rich in pasture ideal for sheep-grazing. There are approximately 150 million sheep in Australia. Some sheep stations can reach up to 15,000 sq km in size. The sheep that produce most wool are Merino, a breed originally from Spain and able to thrive in an arid climate.

What is it like in Antarctica?

The ice-covered continent of Antarctica is bare and empty due to its harsh climate. It was first seen by Captain Cook in 1773, but it was not until the 20th century that Roald Amundsen (1911) and Robert Scott (1912) reached the South Pole. In the 1950s a land expedition crossed Antarctica and today there are scientific bases used by visiting scientists to study the climate, geology and wildlife. Antarctica is protected from exploitation by an international treaty, deeming it to be a 'continent for science' only.

Antarctica

Facts and statistics

Key dates

c. 30,000 BC Aboriginal peoples live in Australia.

c. 4000 BC People sail to settle Pacific islands.

c. 1550 BC Ancestors of Polynesians arrive in west Pacific from southeast Asia.

AD c. 400 First settlers on Easter Island.

c. 850 Ancestors of Maoris reach New Zealand in canoes.

1300s Second wave of Maoris settle in New Zealand.

1400s Malay and Chinese explorers visit northern Australia.

1520 Magellan sails into the Pacific, from Europe.

1606 Dutch explorers reach Australia.

1642 Tasman explores Tasmania and New Zealand coasts.

1768–71 Cook claims New South Wales for Britain.

1788 First British settlement in Australia.

1840 New Zealand becomes British colony.

1851 Gold rush in Australia.

1860–61 Explorers cross Australia.

1901 The federal Commonwealth of Australia comes into being.

1914–18 Australia and New Zealand fight alongside allies in First World War.

1939–45 Australia and New Zealand fight alongside allies in Second World War.

1950s New migration to Australia after Second World War.

1990s Australian aboriginal land rights recognized by law.

Where is Polynesia?

Polynesia is a region in the Pacific Ocean. There are perhaps as many as 30,000 islands in the Pacific, the world's biggest ocean. The three main groups of islands are Melanesia in the west, Micronesia in the north, and Polynesia in the east. Polynesia covers the largest area – the easternmost island in Polynesia is Easter Island, which is more than 6,000 km from New Zealand.

⊕ *Easter Island is famous for its 50-tonne stone heads made between AD 900 and 1600. Why they were made is a mystery.*

What is Ayers Rock?

Ayers Rock is a reddish sandstone landmark in Australia's Northern Territory. It is about 2.4 km long, 1.6 km wide, and 8 km around the base. The rock rises 335 m from the sandy plain in which it stands. Aboriginal people thought the rock was sacred, and made wall paintings in caves there. Europeans first saw the rock in 1872.

Where do people called kiwis live?

The New Zealanders are nicknamed kiwis. The flightless bird of New Zealand called the kiwi has become one of New Zealand's national emblems, and a friendly nickname for its people. With about 60 million sheep and eight million cattle, New Zealand is one of the major exporters of wool, meat and many dairy products. as well as the main producer of the kiwi fruit.

⊕ *The aboriginal people of Australia call Ayers Rock Uluru, which means 'great pebble'.*

⊕ *About 10 per cent of New Zealanders are Maoris, whose ancestors came from the eastern Pacific in about AD 850. The Maori culture is still very much alive in New Zealand, with their traditions and language being upheld.*

Vital statistics: **Oceania**

Area	8,547,000 sq km
Population	More than 30 million
Major cities	Auckland (New Zealand), Melbourne (Australia), Perth (Australia), Sydney (Australia)
Largest country	Australia – 7,686,843 sq km
Highest mountain	Mount Wilhelm, Papua New Guinea – 4,509 m
Longest river	Murray–Darling, Australia – 2,740 km
Largest lake	Lake Eyre, Australia – 9,700 sq km
Largest desert	Australian Desert – 3.8 million sq km
Main religion	Christianity – *c.* 24 million

Vital statistics: **Antarctica**

Area	13,986,000 sq km
Population	Visiting scientists and tourists, but no permanent population
Highest point	Vinson Massif – 4,897 m
Thickest ice	About 4,800 m deep
Most active volcano	Mount Erebus – 3,794 m high
Dangerous hazards	Icebergs at sea, blizzards on land
Coldest spot	Vostok Station, a Russian base where in 1983 a record temperature of –89°C was recorded

Every society needs a structure to make laws, defend its citizens, fix taxes and spend money for the good of all. That is why governments exist. The first governments were headed by powerful rulers, such as a king. The ancient Greeks had the first democracy – or rule by the people – though neither women nor foreigners could vote. Democracy in various forms is practiced across the world, though ideas differ as to what 'democracy' really means.

What is the difference between a republic and a monarchy?

In a republic, a parliament or assembly are elected by members of the public who vote: in a monarchy, even though the government can still be elected, the unelected king, queen, emperor or empress is the head of state. The crown (the symbol of monarchy) is hereditary and so passes through a royal family, from parent to child. Today, they are not usually elected (though Malaysia's kings are). A president is either the head of the government (as in South Africa) or the head of state (as in France), or both. The President of the USA is head of both state and government and acts like chief executive.

◀ The Capitol building in Washington is the seat of the United States Congress, the law-making body for the nation. The President's home is nearby, in the White House.

What is a dictatorship?

A dictatorship is a type of government in which a person or group of people rules a country with absolute power. There are often no legal restrictions over a dictator's power and they govern by decree rather than by election. Dictatorships can be established through violence and maintained through physical force and a limitation of people's freedom of speech and behaviour. For example, curfews can be imposed, whereby citizens must not leave their homes after a certain time of day. Dictators often control the media, allowing only their message to be broadcast or published.

Facts and statistics

Key dates

c. 3500 BC First local governments: kings become first rulers.

c. 3000 BC Kings of Egypt and Chinese emperors are believed to have god-like powers.

c. 400s BC Greek city-states have democratic assemblies to make laws – though women are not allowed to take part.

100 BC Roman Empire starts to expand over much of Europe, North Africa and Middle East.

AD 800s In Europe, assemblies of nobles advise kings.

1500 New ideas of the Renaissance start to challenge royal power.

1649 English Parliament executes King Charles I.

1776 American Revolution, leading to the creation of the United States of America (USA).

1789 French Revolution overthrows the monarchy.

1900s Women in most countries win the right to vote (enfranchisement).

1945 The United Nations (UN) is set up as an international governing body in an attempt to prevent further world war.

2004 Enlarged European Union (EU) of 25 members has a Parliament and Courts of Justice, which can overrule some member states' laws.

Which is the world's biggest communist country?

China is the world's largest communist country, though in recent years it has embraced a capitalist economy. China has had a communist government since 1949. The communist leader Mao Zedong tried to destroy 'old China' with a cultural revolution in the 1960s, but today's Chinese leaders are less revolutionary and more interested in economic growth. Communism allows only one political party, the Communist Party, and tries to control most aspects of people's lives.

⬇ *Statues in Beijing's Tiananmen Square mark the scene of a student-led pro-democracy movement in 1989, which was violently crushed by the government.*

⬆ *In a free election, such as those held in some African countries, voters mark a ballot paper, which is then put into a box. Electronic and postal voting is also sometimes allowed.*

Why do people vote?

People vote to elect a head of state, government or local councillor (someone to represent their views at council level). In a democracy, people over a certain age are allowed to vote. Some non-democratic countries do not allow their citizens the right to vote: instead, these people are told who will govern them. People across the world have had to fight for their right to vote, in particular women. Known as suffragettes, women fought for equal voting rights with men and had to overcome fierce opposition in order to win. Even today many countries will not allow women to vote.

What does a prime minister do?

In many countries the prime minister is the head of a government but not the head of state. He or she is usually chosen by the political party that wins a national (general) election and forms a new government. The prime minister appoints other ministers to run government departments. In Britain there is no fixed term of office for the prime minister, though a parliament must be elected at least every five years. In some countries women have only been encouraged to enter into politics at a high level relatively recently. India had a woman prime minister, Indira Ghandi, elected in 1966.

➡ *The world's first woman prime minister was Sirimavo Bandaranaike of Sri Lanka. She first took office in 1960. Her husband had also been prime minister but was assassinated in 1959. When her daughter, Chandrika Bandaranaike, became president of Sri Lanka in 1994, she reinstated her mother as prime minister.*

⬆ *The Supreme Court, located in Washington DC, has nine judges. They rule on whether the federal, state or local governments of the nation are acting according to the Constitution of the US.*

Amazing **facts**

- The world's biggest national assembly is China's National People's Congress. However, China is not a democracy: almost 3,000 assembly members belong to the Communist Party.

- The use of the word 'parliament' in England dates from 1241, but 400 years earlier, Saxon kings had a council of advisers, known as the witan.

- The first country in which women had the same voting rights as men was New Zealand, in 1893.

- The European Union (EU) has its own law court, and its rulings apply to all member states.

- The idea of 'one person, one vote' dates from the 1800s.

- Left-wing or socialist governments champion the good of the majority over that of the individual. At the extreme left-wing of the political spectrum is communism: shared public ownership and the means of production, distribution and exchange.

- Right-wing governments offer greater support to the individual. At the extreme right-wing of the political spectrum is fascism: a type of movement that supresses democracy and promotes the supremacy of the state over the individual. Examples of fascists are Hitler and Mussolini, who tried to create societies bred from one single race.

The world's many religions teach various beliefs about the creation of the world, the afterlife, why evil exists and good behaviour. The religions with the greatest number of followers are Christianity, Islam, Judaism, Buddhism, Confucianism, Hinduism, Shinto and Taoism. Other world religions include Sikhism, Jainism Baha'ism and Zoroastrianism.

⊙ The Wailing Wall in Jerusalem is the last remnant of the ancient Temple of Solomon, and is a special, holy place for Jews who come from across the world in order to pray there.

Where did Christianity begin?

Christianity is based on the life and teachings of Jesus Christ, who was born in about 4 BC in Palestine and crucified by the Roman governor of Palestine in about AD 30. Jesus' teachings were spread by his followers or disciples, who established the first Christian churches. Christianity was spread to every continent by European explorers. There are Christians across the world today and most belong to Roman Catholic, Protestant or Eastern Orthodox churches.

Why do pilgrims travel to Mecca?

The most sacred place for Muslims is Mecca, in Saudi Arabia, because this was the birthplace of the Prophet Muhammad, who founded Islam in 622. It was from Mecca that Muhammad began his journey to Medina. Millions of Muslims travel to Mecca every year, as they are expected to make a pilgrimage, or *hajj*, once in their lifetime, if they are able.

⊙ *Muslims are called to prayer from the mosque five times a day and turn to face towards Mecca as they pray.*

Which was the first religion to teach about one God ?

The first main religion to teach that there was only one supreme God was Judaism, the religion of the Jews. Christianity and Islam are also 'monotheistic' or 'One God' faiths. Early religious beliefs were based on the worship of many nature-gods, such as the Sun, Moon, trees, rocks, and animals. The ancient Greeks had a large family of gods, headed by Zeus the King of the Gods. Hinduism too has many gods.

World **religions**

Big and small
Christianity is the most widespread of the world religions, with nearly two billion followers in more than 200 countries. One of the least widespread is Mandaeanism, which has about 38,000 followers in Iran and Iraq.

❍ *The Pope is the head of the Roman Catholic Church, the largest branch of the Christian church.*

Origins of **religion**

Religion	Founder	Date founded
Buddhism	Based on the teachings of Siddhartha Gautama	c. 500 BC
Christianity	Based on the life and teachings of Jesus Christ	c. 30
Hinduism	No known founder	c. 2500 BC
Islam	Prophet Muhammad	c. 610
Judaism	Based on the laws of Moses and Abraham	c. 1650 BC
Sikhism	Guru (teacher) Nanak	c. 1480

⬆ *Angkor Wat has five central towers within a moated enclosure. The tallest tower is 70 m high.*

Who was the Buddha?

The Buddha was a prince in Nepal around 500 BC, called Siddhartha Gautama. When he was about 30 years old, the prince became disillusioned with the material world and sought spiritual enlightenment through meditation. He travelled through India for about six years and finally attained 'enlightenment' and became known as 'Buddha', meaning 'enlightened one'. Buddha taught that by detachment from the material world and possessions, humans could achieve *nirvana*, a state of eternal peace.

What is Angkor Wat?

Angkor Wat is a Hindu temple built by the Khmer people, in what is now Cambodia. Built in the early 1100s, in honour of the Hindu god Vishnu, it is the largest religious building in the world. It was also used as an observatory and later housed the tomb of the Cambodian king who commissioned the building. Though Angkor Wat was later abandoned, it was rediscovered in the 1860s by a Frenchman named Henri Mouhot and was restored by archaeologists.

➡ *Statues representing Buddha are found all over parts of Asia. These Buddha statues in Japan are made from gold-leaf.*

Most **followers**

Christianity	almost 2 billion
Islam	more than 1 billion
Hinduism	c. 800 million
Buddhism	c. 356 million
Traditional beliefs	c. 225 million
Sikhism	c. 23 million
Judaism	c .14 million

➡ *Sikhs have five important symbols, known as the ks. The first is kesh (uncut hair). All Sikh men have beards and wear their hair inside a cloth turban.*

⬇ *The other four ks are kaccha, kara, kirpan and kangha.*

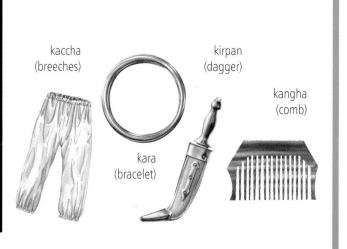

kaccha (breeches)

kara (bracelet)

kirpan (dagger)

kangha (comb)

There are at least 4,000 languages in the world. People who speak the same languages may also share the same customs, but other customs (such as New Year or birthday celebrations) are common to people all over the world. In all human societies, people mark the seasons, growing up, and events, such as marriages and deaths, in certain ways. Each culture or group has its own festivals.

⬆ *Hieroglyphs are picture symbols that represent ideas and sounds. The Egyptians used hieroglyphics for more than 3,000 years for inscriptions on temple walls.*

How can customs change?

Some customs and festivals are very ancient and their original meaning has sometimes been forgotten. Hallowe'en was an ancient festival associated with the onset of winter and darkness. Medieval Christians turned it into a religious festival called All Saints' Day (November 1) and this is still celebrated by Christians in the USA and UK today. However, Hallowe'en has also become a night for young people to dress up as ghosts and play 'trick or treat'. However, in Catholic Mexico, Hallowe'en is still a religious day.`

⬅ *The Chinese celebrate New Year in January and February with fireworks and parades by people carrying colourful dragon models. Dragons in China are associated with good luck. The Chinese calendar, used for more than 4,000 years, has years named after animals: rat, ox, tiger, rabbit/hare, dragon, snake, horse, sheep/goat, monkey, rooster, dog and boar/pig.*

Which is the most spoken language?

More people speak Standard Chinese or Mandarin than any other language, though the language spoken in the most countries is English. English has spread to every continent. Languages change and grow as they are spoken and new words are added. If a language is no longer spoken, it is extinct. Latin, the language of the ancient Romans, is rarely spoken though people still study and read books that were written in it. Language originally developed very slowly from basic sounds. Grammar, vocabulary and sound-patterns all change with the structure of languages. Different languages evolve with common usage and local dialects.

Customs and **meanings**

Alphabets
The term alphabet derives from 'alpha' and 'beta', the first two letters of the Greek alphabet. The 26-letter English version of the Roman alphabet, which is what this text is written in, was continually evolving for many years before the Romans finalized it. Most English-speaking people use about 5,000 words in speech, and about 10,000 words when writing. There are more than one million words in the English language and this grows each year.

⬇ *Not every word or sign can be translated. The per cent sign is universal, and so are some numbers, but Arabic, Hebrew and Chinese numbering is different.*

Language **facts**

Longest alphabet – Cambodian (74 letters)
Most common vowel – a (in every known language)
Most concise language – Japanese (the longest word has only 12 letters)
Most common place name – Newton ('new town') name in English
Word with most meanings – 'set' (about 200)
Most languages spoken in one country – Papua New Guinea (more than 800 local languages)
Longest speech – 22 hours
Most spoken artificial language – Esperanto

Where is tea drinking a polite ceremony?

Tea drinking is an important ceremony in Japan that is taken very seriously. Known as 'cha-no-yu', it is a formal occasion with strict rules, often taking place in a special room. The tea is prepared using special utensils and is served in a bowl from which each guest drinks in turn. Everyone keeps very calm and still, the aim being to find beauty and meaning in simple, ordinary acts, like drinking tea.

➔ *A tea ceremony in Japan, can often be a formal occasion, such as a state banquet for an important foreign visitor, or even part of a wedding feast. People wear their best clothes, and after the eating and drinking, speeches may be made.*

Are languages related?

Most languages belong to families, but there are exceptions, such as Basque, which is spoken in a northern region of Spain. Korean was once thought to be unrelated to any other language but it is often argued that it falls within the Altaic family. English evolved from the Indo-European 'parent' language and belongs to the Germanic branch of the family, along with German, Dutch and Swedish. Welsh belongs to the Celtic branch, and French and Spanish belong to the Romance branch.

When did people first write down words?

The earliest known writing is Sumerian cuneiform, which dates from about 6,000 years ago. The oldest known alphabet comes from the ancient city of Ugarit, Palestine, and dates from 1450 BC. An alphabet is a collection of letter-signs standing for the sounds we make when we speak.

Do customs vary across the world?

Customs vary from one country or culture to another. In some parts of the world, such as Thailand, crossing your legs in someone's house is considered insulting. In Brazil, it is offensive to local people to make an 'o' with your thumb and forefinger – elsewhere this is a sign of satisfaction.

Special **days**

Date	Celebration	Date	Celebration	Date	Celebration
1 January	New Year's Day (except some Southeast Asian countries)	3 May	World Press Freedom Day	24 October	United Nations' Day
		5 June	World Environment Day	31 October	Hallowe'en
late Jan – mid Feb	Chinese New Year	20 June	World Refugee Day	11 November	Armistice Day
14 February	St Valentine's Day	4 July	Independence Day (USA)	20 November	Universal Children's Day
21 March	World Poetry Day	14 July	Bastille Day (France)	2 December	International Day for the Abolition of Slavery
22 March	World Day for Water	8 September	International Literacy Day		
1 April	April Fool's Day	21 September	International Day of Peace	3 December	International Day of Disabled Persons
7 April	World Health Day	5 October	International Teachers' Day		
1 May	May Day	16 October	World Food Day	10 December	Human Rights Day
				25 December	Christmas Day

ARTS, SPORTS & ENTERTAINMENT

People have played and listened to music ever since Stone Age cave-dwellers banged drums and shook rattles. Throughout the centuries, instruments were refined and developed, and the skills needed to play them were taught to others. Music has been written down only since about 1800 BC. A huge variety of different musical styles has been developed across the world, including classical, opera, folk, reggae, jazz, soul, rock and pop.

What are the four main groups of instruments?

The main groups of instruments are wind, stringed, percussion and brass. Wind and brass instruments are played by blowing down a hollow tube with holes in. Stringed instruments have strings stretched tight across a hollow box; the strings are vibrated with a bow (violin) plucked with the fingers or a plectrum (guitar). Percussion instruments such as drums and cymbals make sounds when struck by hammers, sticks or the hands.

French horn

Violin and bow

Guitar

Conga drums

⬆ These are examples from three of the musical instrument groups: French horn (brass), violin and guitar (strings) and conga drums (percussion).

Who are the greatest composers?

People may never agree on 'the greatest-ever composer', but many music-lovers place Wolfgang Amadeus Mozart (1756–91), Ludwig van Beethoven (1770–1827) and Johann Sebastian Bach (1685–1750) among their favourites. Notable works by these musical geniuses include Bach's *Brandenburg Concertos*, Beethoven's *Ode to Joy* and *5th Symphony*, and Mozart's *Eine Kleine Nachtmusik*.

J. S. Bach

Mozart

Beethoven

⬆ All three composers wrote music for small groups of musicians as well as for full orchestras.

Making **music**

Key **dates**

Invented

C. 4000 BC	Flute, harp, trumpet
3500 BC	Bells
AD 1500	Trombone
C.1545	Violin
1709	Piano
1821	Harmonica
1822	Accordion
1832	Modern flute
1840	Saxophone

➲ The grand piano (1709) was a development of earlier keyboard instruments. The grand piano (1855) is normally used in orchestral concerts. Upright pianos and electronic keyboards are used for other types of music.

Star **performers**

Name	Nationality	Music
Maria Callas (1923–77)	Greek	soprano singer
Enrico Caruso (1873–1921)	Italian	tenor singer
Ella Fitzgerald (1918–96)	American	jazz singer
Madonna (born 1958)	American	popular singer
Luciano Pavarotti (born 1935)	Italian	tenor singer
Elvis Presley (1935–77)	American	rock'n'roll singer
Frank Sinatra (1915–98)	American	popular singer
Stevie Wonder (born 1950)	American	popular singer

Who were the first successful rock stars?

The first rock superstar was Elvis Presley, who had 94 gold singles and more than 40 gold albums. Then in the 1960s, the Beatles began their career, which made them the biggest-selling group of all time. The first solo singer to sell one million records was the opera singer Enrico Caruso. Until the 20th century, popular songs were only heard when people sang or played them 'live'. Recorded sound, which dates from the 1880s, changed the way people listened to music, and radio and the record industry combined to create the 'pop' industry, which began in the 1940s with the creation of the first popular hit charts.

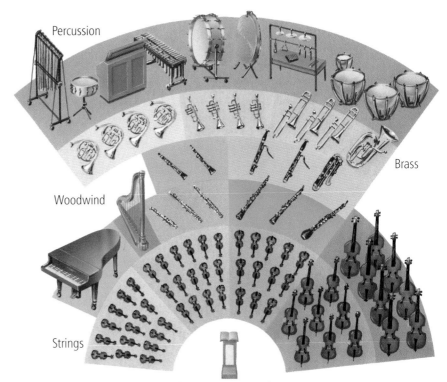

Percussion

Brass

Woodwind

Strings

Conductor's position – the rostrum

↑ *The instruments of the symphony orchestra are arranged in groups in an arc in front of the conductor – strings at the front, then wind, and percussion at the back.*

↑ *The Beatles from left to right: Paul McCartney, Ringo Starr, George Harrison and John Lennon.*

Who wrote the longest opera?

The five longest operas (all lasting more than five hours) were written by the 19th-century German composer Richard Wagner. The longest of Wagner's operas is *The Twilight of the Gods*. An opera is a play in which the actors sing as they act, and in which music plays a much more important part than plot, dialogue or set. Operas were first staged around 1600 in Italy.

How many instruments make up an orchestra?

The modern orchestra has about 100 musicians. Orchestras have four main sections: woodwind (clarinets, flutes, oboes and bassoons), brass (horns and trumpets), percussion (drums, cymbals and bells) and strings (violins, violas, cellos and double basses). The biggest orchestra of all time had 987 instruments and was assembled in 1872 in Boston, USA.

Great **composers**

Johann Sebastian Bach (1685–1750) – German baroque composer.
Ludwig van Beethoven (1770–1827) – German classical composer.
Johannes Brahms (1833–97) – German romantic composer.
Benjamin Britten (1913–76) – British 20th-century composer.
Frederick Chopin (1841–1904) – Polish romantic composer.
Edward Elgar (1857–1934) – British classical composer.
George Gershwin (1898–1937) – American 20th-century composer.
Edvard Grieg (1843–1907) – Norwegian 19th-century composer.
George Frideric Handel (1685–1759) – German/British baroque composer.
Joseph Haydn (1732–1809) – Austrian classical composer.

Wolfgang Amadeus Mozart (1756–91) – Austrian classical composer, who wrote more than 40 symphonies.
Franz Peter Schubert (1797–1828) – Austrian classical and romantic composer.
Igor Stravinsky (1882–1971) – Russian 20th-century modernist composer, most celebrated work, *The Rite of Spring*.
Peter Ilyich Tchaikovsky (1840–93) – Russian romantic composer, famous for symphonies and ballet scores.
Giuseppe Verdi (1813–1901) – Italian 19th century opera composer.
Richard Wagner (1818–83) – German romantic composer.

The earliest art was made by Stone Age people, who painted pictures on walls and made figures from stone and clay. There are many kinds of art – from famous paintings sold for many millions of pounds at auction to clay pots made by children in school. Art can puzzle as well as astound. Some artists have wrapped cliffs in plastic, covered buildings in cloth, displayed a bed with dirty washing, put a dead animal in a case and cut away half a mountain in their efforts to create a unique piece.

What does a sculptor do?

Sculptors are artists who make models, such as figures carved in wood or stone, or cast in metal.
The two most common techniques in sculpture are carving and moulding. Modern sculptors also create art from assembling pieces of scrap, plastic or even paper. A figure of the native Indian known as Crazy Horse being cut into the rock of Thunderhead Mountain in South Dakota, USA (still not finished after over 50 years) will be 172 m high when it is completed.

Who was Picasso?

Picasso was one of the most successful painters of the 20th century. His full name was Pablo Ruiz y Picasso; he was born in Spain in 1881 and died in 1973. He began by painting in a traditional, realistic style but then began depicting figures as fragments of geometric shapes – this style became known as Cubism. One of his most famous pictures is called *Guernica* and portrays the suffering of people during the Spanish Civil War in the 1930s.

➔ *Picasso was a prolific artist who worked on canvas in several styles. Unlike many other artists, Picasso also earned a lot of money from his work.*

← *The* Venus de Milo *is one of the most famous sculptures. This Roman copy of the Greek original is in The Louvre museum in Paris.*

What is ceramics?

Ceramics is the art of making fine pottery, using clay. Potters have made everyday items such as beakers and plates for more than 5,000 years. Examples of pottery are earthenware bowls, Greek and Chinese vases, and terracotta heads and figures. Painted and glazed porcelain (the most delicate form of pottery) was first made in China about 1,300 years ago.

↑ *Porcelain vases were made in China during the period known as the Ming dynasty (1368–1644), when the arts flourished.*

World of **art**

Key **dates**

1266–1337 Giotto, Italian, his pictures showed people in a more lifelike way.
1452–1519 Leonardo da Vinci, Italian, painter, sculptor and architect, famous for the *Mona Lisa*.
1475–1564 Michelangelo Buionarotti, Italian, painted Rome's Sistine Chapel ceiling.
1483–1520 Raphael, Italian painter who also worked in Rome.
1541–1614 El Greco, Spanish, painted many religious scenes.

↑ *Self-portrait by Rembrandt.*

1606–69 Rembrandt von Rijn, Dutch, master of portraits.
1775–1851 J. M. W. Turner, English, painted mostly landscapes.
1776–1837 John Constable, English, famous for his landscapes.
1840–1926 Claude Monet, French, Impressionist, famous for paintings of his garden and various landscape scenes.
1853–90 Vincent van Gogh, Dutch, landscapes and portraits.
1881–1973 Pablo Picasso, Spanish, styles included abstract Cubism.

What is Sutton Hoo?

Sutton Hoo is a site in East Anglia, in England. Here in the 1930s, archaeologists dug into a grave-mound and unearthed the ship-tomb of a king of the East Angles who lived and died in the 8th century. Among the treasures buried with the dead king was a magnificent iron helmet, decorated with animals and scenes from mythology. A replica made by metalworkers shows what a magnificent helmet it must have been.

🔼 *Modern reconstruction of the Sutton Hoo helmet, showing the fine decorative work.*

🔄 *Wall paintings like this are found in the tombs of Egyptian kings and queens. This picture shows a hunting scene beside the River Nile. Cave paintings depict life at the time of their creation, more than 15,000 years ago.*

What is a fresco?

A fresco is a painting on a wall. The Egyptians loved wall paintings and, during the Middle Ages and the Renaissance, frescoes were a favourite form of decoration in Europe. Fresco artists paint on fresh plaster while it is still wet, so they have to work fast. They begin by drawing a sketch, from which they trace the outline on the plaster, and then brush in the colours. As the plaster dries and hardens, the colours are bonded to the wall.

What kind of paints did cave painters use?

The paints used by cave painters, more than 12,000 years ago, were made from everyday materials, such as coloured soil, clay, animal fat, soot and charcoal from their fires and the roots of plants. They painted the animals they hunted, such as ibex, wild ox and deer. The artists did not use brushes but painted with their fingers, sometimes leaving an impression of their hands, perhaps as a signature.

🔽 *This drawing of a wild ox was made by one of the cave painters in Lascaux, France.*

Modern **artists**

Alexander Calder (1898–1976) – American sculptor of mobiles.
Christo (born 1935) – Bulgarian-born Belgian, famous for wrapping buildings and sections of coastline in plastic.
Salvador Dali (1904–89) – Spanish Surrealist painter.
Barbara Hepworth (1903–75) – British sculptor.
David Hockney (born 1937) – British painter.
Roy Lichtenstein (1923–97) – American pop artist.

Henry Moore (1898–1986) – British sculptor.
Piet Mondrian (1872–1944) – Dutch painter of abstracts.
Gilbert and George (Gilbert Proesch born 1943 and George Passmore born 1942) – British avant-garde artists known for their 'Performance Art'.
Andy Warhol (1928–87) – American painter and graphic artist famous for prints of soup cans and Marilyn Monroe.

Salvador Dali

Andy Warhol

Design involves planning, and a designer's job is to create something new, either from brand new materials or by reassembling existing ones. Designers often have to be part-artist, part-engineer and part-salesperson. Some of those whose work includes design are architects, engineers, fashion designers, gardeners, graphic artists (who design books and magazines), interior decorators, stage- and movie-set designers and shop-window dressers.

⬆ *The design of any aircraft involves careful mathematical calculation, not simply 'artistic' design. However, stealth aircraft and warplanes often need a camouflaged design so that they cannot easily be recognized in a dangerous combat situation.*

Who designed the pyramids?

The Egyptian architects who built the pyramids were scribes, astronomers and government officials, the most famous of whom was Imhotep. He lived in the 2500s BC and one of his many jobs was court physician to King Djoser (see page 72). He designed the Step Pyramid at Saggara in Egypt, as a tomb for the king. Architects design buildings by making drawings and doing calculations, but today they also use computers to picture the finished design, to see the inside, and to show how any changes will alter the product.

⬇ *The people who designed the pyramids of ancient Egypt relied on thousands of labourers to heave the heavy stones into position.*

What makes a good design?

There are several principles of design, including balance, repetition, rhythm and unity (overall effect). Design is the basis of every manufacturing process, but however much fun it is to design a complex object, it will not be a success unless it can be manufactured and sold. Design involves arranging materials for a particular or desired effect – either for pleasure or to fulfil a particular function, such as a commission. If a design looks good and works efficiently, people will want to use it. The design of a warplane involves careful mathematical calculation, not simply 'artistic' design. Their strength and safety are just as important as their appearance, which is often camouflaged.

Shaping up **for design**

Craft and design
The term 'designer' dates from the 1600s. Before then, a craftsman who made a chair was both designer and maker. By the 1800s, workers in factories were mass-producing chairs to designs drawn up by specialized designers. The poet and designer William Morris rebelled against factory-produced goods, and started an 'Arts and Crafts' movement in the 1880s, to return to handmade craftsmanship. The first electrical appliances such as vacuum cleaners were unattractive to look at. Today we expect household appliances not only to work well but also to look good in our homes so design is an important feature of manufacturing such products.

➡ *The penny-farthing bicycle of the 1870s was an awkward shape, but the bike was actually very fast – even if tricky to get on and off.*

⬆ *Egyptians designed and crafted artefacts with bright symbols and colourful designs.*

⊙ *A Victorian sitting room was designed for people to sit, read, and amuse themselves in.*

Who first used furniture?

The first people to use furniture were the ancient Egyptians – we know this because they put chairs, stools and tables in their tombs. Thomas Chippendale wrote the first catalogue about furniture in England in 1754. It had drawings of the pieces he offered for sale, and his designs for chairs, tables and cabinets were widely imitated.

A great deal of furniture made in the late 18th century is often described as 'Chippendale', because it describes a style, even though in most cases Chippendale himself was not involved.

⊙ *Furniture designers copied styles of each other, such as Chippendale, as well as from designers abroad.*

⊙ *In the 19th century, the clothes worn by wealthy women were copied by new fashion houses, who supplied cheap clothes to poorer people.*

What was Victorian style like?

The Victorians were the first people to have factory-made curtains, chairs, carpets and household gadgets and so the style of their homes often looks cluttered to modern eyes. People liked lots of pictures and ornaments, and filled rooms with chairs, tables, lamps, bookcases and shelves. Victorian clothes look thick and heavy to us, and sombre colours were preferred. Queen Victoria's reign lasted from 1837 to 1901, so Victorians lived during a new industrial age.

When did the fashion industry begin?

When factory-made clothes went on sale in the 19th century, poorer people were able to buy cheap copies of fashionable clothes. Previously, wealthy people had always bought elegant clothes and set styles for others to copy. In the 20th century, fashion designers such as Coco Chanel and Christian Dior set up fashion 'houses', designing exclusive designs. In the 1960s–70s, youth fashion became the rage, and today designers and super-models rival pop and movie stars as world-famous celebrities.

⊙ *The Petronas Towers in Kuala Lumpur, Malaysia, were designed to impress people with their grand height. The tower was built 88 storeys high and the designers shaped each of the floors like an eight-pointed star. At the 50th floor is a glass-covered bridge. Though no longer the world's tallest building, the Petronas Towers did hold the record for a number of years.*

⊙ *Indonesian long-houses are designed and built in a traditional style.*

Bagless vacuum

James Dyson, who trained as a furniture designer, invented the bagless cleaner. He first had the idea in 1978 and spent five years making and testing more than 5,000 prototypes. Dyson's factory started making bagless cleaners in 1993.

⊙ *The dyson is designed for use without a reusable bag.*

Architecture is the art and science of designing and constructing buildings. The architect has to consider the look, the technology, the site and the cost of the building. Much of early architecture comprised monumental temples, tombs and palaces. The Greeks introduced 'classical' rules of proportion and, ever since, architectural style has reflected the tastes of the age in which it is used.

⊕ *Many skyscrapers, like these in Hong Kong, China, have more than 200 storeys. Plans are continually made to build higher and higher.*

When did the Greeks build temples?

Greek architecture began to take shape about 600 BC. The beauty of the Parthenon temple (see page 77) on the Acropolis hill in Athens typifies Greek architecture. The Greeks loved harmonious proportions. The roofs of their graceful buildings were supported by columns built in three main styles, known as Doric, Ionic and Corinthian, which became more decorative over time.

⊕ *The Parthenon was built between 447 and 432 BC, using classic principles of geometry.*

Where were the first skyscrapers built?

The first skyscrapers were built in the American city of Chicago after a fire in 1871 had destroyed many of its old wooden buildings. The very first skyscraper was the Home Insurance Building, which had ten floors. New technology meant that builders could use steel girders to support a high building internally, rather than relying entirely on the outer walls. The electric lift had been invented, too, so people did not have to walk up stairs to reach the upper floors.

Skyline **shapers**

Key **dates**

Architectural styles		
600s–100s BC	Greek.	
400s–1453	Byzantine.	
600s	Islamic.	
800s–1100s	Romanesque.	
1100s–1400s	Gothic.	
1400s–1600s	Renaissance.	
1600–1750	Baroque.	
1700s	Rococo and Georgian	

1890–1910	Art Nouveau.
1920s	Functionalism.
1950s	Brutalism.
1970s	Post-modernism.

St Paul's Cathedral, London, UK

St Peter's, Rome, Italy

What is the world's most impressive building?

Many would suggest the Taj Mahal in India. The Mogul ruler of India, Shah Jahan, built the Taj Mahal for his favourite wife, Mumtaz Mahal, when she died in childbirth in 1629. He wanted her to have the most beautiful tomb in the world. More than 20,000 labourers and artists worked on the Taj Mahal, which took 20 years to complete. The domed building is made of white marble and rests on a sandstone platform.

⊕ *Each of the Taj Mahal's four minarets is 40 m high. The top of the dome is nearly 61 m above the floor, under which is the vault where Shah Jahan is buried with his wife.*

Where is the world's most famous opera house?

Sydney Opera House in Australia has been a world-famous landmark in Sydney Harbour since it was first opened in 1973. An opera house is a theatre, usually devoted to operatic production. Sydney Opera House is used for other events, such as performance art, and has a distinctive design, with a shaped roof that makes it look as if the building is about to set sail across the water. The building was designed by Danish architect, Jorn Lutzon.

When was Stonehenge built?

Stonehenge is a group of huge stones, set in a circle on Salisbury Plain in England, built in stages between 2800 and 1500 BC. The heavy stones were dragged and positioned in alignment with the rising and setting Sun at midsummer. Stonehenge was probably a gathering point and religious centre for local tribal groups.

What is the Louvre?

The Louvre is the national museum of France. It is located in the centre of Paris, and was originally a palace, used since the 1500s by the kings of France to house their art collections. It was first opened to the public in 1793 after the French Revolution. One of the modern features of the Louvre is the steel-and-glass pyramid entrance in the central courtyard, designed by American architect I.M. Pei. It now houses some of the world's finest paintings and works.

⊕ *The glass pyramid in the courtyard of the Louvre adds a new dimension to an old building.*

◐ *The ancient stones of Stonehenge: some stones have fallen or been removed since the circle was first erected.*

The Duomo, Florence, Italy

Famous **architects**

Gianlorenzo Bernini (1598–1680) – Italian, rebuilt St Peter's, Rome.

Filippo Brunelleschi (1377–1446) – Italian, designed the dome of the Duomo in Florence.

Norman Foster (born 1935) – English, designed the Millennium Bridge in London.

Antoni Gaudi (1852–1926) – Spanish, Barcelona structures.

Walter Gropius (1883–1969) – German, refounded the Bauhaus (School of Building).

William le Baron Jenney (1832–1907) – American, designed the first iron-framed skyscraper in Chicago.

Sir Christopher Wren (1632–1723) – English, designed St Paul's Cathedral and Greenwich Hospital.

Frank Lloyd Wright (1869–1959) – American, known for office buildings and his 'prairie houses'.

The performing arts include performances by dancers, musicians, singers, actors and even puppets. Through these varied art forms, storytellers have long thrilled audiences, who have enjoyed the emotional experience of a 'show', whether it be comedy (humour) or tragedy (serious) or a mixture of the two.

Which country is most famous for its ballet?

Russia, as it has produced many fine dancers, including Vaslav Nijinsky, Rudolf Nureyev and Anna Pavlova, as well as famous ballet companies, who perform all over the world. However, ballet did not begin in Russia. It was first recognized as an art-form in the 1600s in France, and it was then that the five basic ballet positions were devised. Famous ballets include *Giselle*, *Swan Lake* and *Sleeping Beauty*.

➔ *Steps in classical ballet use turn-out (feet pointing sideways) and pointe-work (dancing on tip-toes). Ballet dancers' must be very fit and their muscles extemely strong.*

How old are puppet performances?

Puppets are one of the earliest forms of performing entertainment. String puppets, also known as marionettes, have been popular for centuries. One of the traditions of the English seaside resort is the Punch and Judy show, performed by an entertainer who is concealed inside a cubicle using just his hands (inside glove puppets) and his voice. Other puppets have become famous as television celebrities in their own right, and some of the computer-generated figures have become almost life-like. In Indonesia people watch plays performed by 'shadow-puppets'.

↑ *The modern circus clown developed from 'buffoons' who performed in Greek and Roman plays, sometimes throwing items such as nuts at the audience!*

When did the first circus appear?

In ancient Rome a circus was called a stadium. In the 1700s, showmen used the name 'circus' for horse shows in Europe. Philip Astley put on shows of trick-riding in the 1770s in London. Travelling circuses, which often included horses, wild animals, acrobats and clowns, became popular in the 1800s. The most famous circus is Ringling Brothers and Barnum and Bailey's (the two shows combined in 1919), which had the biggest ever Big Top (tent).

Writer and **players**

Backstage at the theatre

To perform a play in a theatre, it takes more people than the actors. Behind the scenes a team of backstage technicians work hard to ensure that every theatre performance is well-organized and seamless. Set-designers, costume organizers, lighting technicians, sound monitors, curtain technicians – even ticket sales staff are all crucial to the success of a performance.

↖ *George Bernard Shaw wrote witty plays such as* Heartbreak Hotel.

↑ *William Shakespeare's plays were first performed in the original open-air Globe Theatre, which has been recreated beside the River Thames in London.*

➔ *Anton Chekhov is Russia's most celebrated dramatist. He is best known for his tragedies.*

Who was the most famous silent comedian?

One of the most famous cinema stars was Charlie Chaplin (1889–1977). He was was also one of the first movie-stars. Chaplin learnt his craft as a comedian on the music-hall stage in London but then went to America where he made his name as a comic actor in silent movies. His success as a comedian has made him synonomous with silent movies.

⬅ Charlie Chaplin's character 'little man' in baggy trousers, with a bowler hat and cane, became known all over the world.

➡ Greeks sat in open-air theatres to watch one of two types of play: tragedies or comedies. Tragedies were serious plays and included a sad end, an unhappy love affair, a crime or a disaster. Comedies were humorous plays. Traditionally, tragedy and comedy were never mixed.

⬇ Fancy dress and masks are a feature of the carnival in Venice.

What is a carnival?

The original carnival was a religious holiday and feast, celebrated before the beginning of the Christian fasting period of Lent. The modern carnival is a huge outdoor theatre and parade, with dancers, decorated floats, entertainers and marching bands. Famous carnivals are held in Brazil, the USA and the UK.

Who went to the first theatres?

The first theatre-goers were the ancient Greeks, who gathered in hundreds and sat on hillsides to watch tragedies and comedies. Greek theatres were bowl-shaped arenas, surrounding a circular stage, called an orchestra. The Romans built stone theatres that could seat 40,000 to watch raucous comedies. The most successful playwright in the world is the English bard William Shakespeare (1564–1616), whose plays are staged all over the world and whose Globe Theatre has been recreated in London.

Famous playwrights

Aristophanes (c. 445–385 BC) – Greek, wrote comedies such as *The Frogs*.
Alan Ayckbourne (born 1939) – British, prolific author of successful comedies of modern life, including *The Norman Conquests*.
Samuel Becket (1906–89) – Irish, wrote *Waiting for Godot*.
Anton Chekhov (1860–1904) – Russian, wrote *The Cherry Orchard*.
William Congreve (1670–1729) – English, author of *The Way of the World*, a comedy.

Johann Wolfgang von Goethe (1749–1832) – German, playwright and scientist, his most famous work is *Faust*, in which a scholar sells his soul to the devil.
Henrik Ibsen (1828–1906) – Norwegian, wrote *A Dolls House* and *Hedda Gabbler*.
Molière (Jean-Baptiste Poquelin) (1622–73) – French, wrote comedies including *The Misanthropist* and *The Miser*.
Eugene O'Neill (1888–1953) – American, wrote *The Iceman Cometh* and other plays.
William Shakespeare (1564–1616) – English, greatest dramatist whose plays include tragedies (*King Lear*), comedies

(*Much Ado About Nothing*) and histories (*Julius Caesar*)
George Bernard Shaw (1856–1950) – Irish, wrote *St Joan, Major Barbara* and other plays, usually from a satirical viewpoint.
Richard Brinsley Sheridan (1751–1816) – Irish, wrote *The Rivals*, one of the most enduring comedies.
Sophocles (about 496–406 BC) – Greek, wrote tragedies, including *Oedipus the King*.
Tom Stoppard (Thomas Straussler, born 1937) – Czech-born British writer, whose plays include *Travesties* and *Jumpers*.

Cinema was made possible by the invention of the camera obscura and lantern slide, which projected pictures onto a screen. By the 1930s, millions of people visited the cinema every week. The advent of television in the 1950s, however, enabled more people to stay at home to watch TV and video movies on 'the box'. Now DVD (digital versatile disc) provides us with home entertainment unimagined by early pioneers of screen entertainment.

How did 'movies' develop?

Moving images, known as 'movies' developed in the early 1900s, after experiments with 'kinetoscope' peepshows. The first big movie was D. W. Griffith's epic *Birth of a Nation* in 1915. Early movies were silent and dialogue appeared as words printed on the screen. Often a pianist played appropriate music in the cinema. 'Talkies' appeared in the late 1920s.

The Lumière brothers pioneered cinema shows in France, in the 1890s.

↑ *John Logie Baird was a pioneer of television.*

When did people first watch TV?

The first TV pictures were produced in 1924 by John Logie Baird, but a more effective electronic system was used for the first BBC TV service in 1936. When the television age began, very few people owned sets, and pictures were in flickering black-and-white. Today, satellite and cable networks provide hundreds of channels around the world, with thousands of hours of viewing.

Where is the centre of the movie industry?

Although the cinema was a French invention, thanks largely to the Lumière brothers, it was America that gave birth to the international movie industry. Movie-makers found that sunny California was an ideal place to shoot movies, and by the 1920s Hollywood had become 'the capital of the motion picture world', with large studios full of technicians, writers, make-up artists, costume designers, set-builders, producers and directors.

← *Modern TV cameras work in any conditions. Today, TV is the world's biggest medium for information and in-home entertainment.*

Movie **magic**

Marilyn Monroe

Audrey Hepburn

Elizabeth Taylor

Boris Karloff (as Frankenstein's Monster)

Rudolf Valentino

Movie **terms**

Dubbing – Adding words to pictures.
Flash-back – Interruption in the story to recall a past event.
Long shot – A picture taken from a distance.
Prop – Short for 'property', an object used by an actor, such as a weapon or a mobile phone.
Rushes – Shots taken during a day's filming, before editing.
Shooting – Filming a scene.
Take – Part of a scene, with words and action, shot without interruption.

⬆ *The Hollywood sign on the hill tells visitors they have reached the heart of 'movieland'.*

Where would you find someone using a clapperboard?

A clapperboard is used in a movie or TV studio to mark the beginning or end of a 'take' (a short section of movie). Movies are not usually made in the order of a story. Director, scriptwriters, camera crew and actors work on the scenes in whatever order is convenient. This might be when the star is available or when the weather is right. Several takes may be needed before a scene is filmed properly. The final takes are put together in order by an editor and, if necessary, cut to create the finished movie.

➡ *Details of each take are filled in on the clapperboard, which is held up in front of the camera before filming begins.*

What is the difference between a producer and a director?

In the movie industry, a producer raises money to make a new movie and organizes the financial side, while the director is in charge of filming. The director tells the camera crews how to set up their cameras, and directs the actors to act the way the script is written. In TV, however, the producer may also act as the director: the money comes from the TV company who is making the series or programme.

➡ *Alfred Hitchcock, director and master of suspense, made a cameo appearance in most of his movies.*

⬇ *Special effects, such as those used in the* Matrix *(US 2000), create excitement in a movie and allow scenes to be created that would otherwise be difficult, dangerous or impossible.*

The Oscars
Oscars are the gold-plated awards presented each year by the US Academy of Motion Picture Arts and Sciences. Katharine Hepburn (1907–2003) is the only actor to have won four Oscars.

Nicole Kidman

Tom Cruise

Nicholas Cage

Samuel Jackson

George Clooney

Oscar-winning **movies**

Date	Movie
1994	*Forrest Gump*
1995	*Braveheart*
1996	*The English Patient*
1997	*Titanic*
1998	*Shakespeare in Love*
1999	*American Beauty*
2000	*Gladiator*
2001	*Crouching Tiger, Hidden Dragon*
2002	*The Lord of the Rings: the Two Towers*
2003	*Chicago*
2004	*The Lord of the Rings: the Return of the King*

The earliest literature was oral (spoken word or song) not written. The oldest hand-printed book dates from the AD 800s, but books were not available cheaply until the invention of steam-powered printing machines in the 1800s. Paperbacks were produced from the 1930s. The most quoted writer is William Shakespeare, and the most widely read children's books of today are the adventures of Harry Potter, by British author, J. K. Rowling.

What is an illuminated manuscript?

A manuscript, or hand-written book, was either hand-printed (using a wood block) or copied by hand by monks, who decorated the pages with beautifully coloured illuminations. Often the monks began a page with a decorated letter. Before the printing press with movable type was invented in the 1440s, monks did most of the book copying in Europe. Today, ancient illuminated manuscripts, such as the *Book of Kells* and the *Lindisfarne Gospels*, are priceless treasures.

Who was the most famous fictional detective?

Sherlock Holmes, the pipe-smoking master-sleuth, created by British writer Sir Arthur Conan Doyle (1859–1930). Holmes and his friend Dr Watson solved mysteries involving mysterious dogs (*The Hound of the Baskervilles*), venomous snakes (*The Speckled Band*) and numerous robberies and murders. He was eventually 'killed off' in a final contest with his arch-enemy, the criminal genius Professor Moriarty, but was then 'reborn' by popular demand.

→ *Sherlock Holmes uses a combination of science and outstanding logic to solve cases that baffle the police.*

← *Medieval illuminated manuscripts took such a long time to make, because they were hand-written, that they had to be treated with great care.*

Which famous novelist gave public readings of his work?

Charles Dickens (1812–70), a talented amateur actor, gave public performances of scenes from his best-selling novels. Dickens is considered one of the greatest British novelists, writing a succession of masterpieces including *Oliver Twist* (1838), *Nicholas Nickleby* (1839), *David Copperfield* (1850) and *Great Expectations* (1861).

↑ *Dickens endured hard times as a child, which he never forgot, even when he became a successful author.*

Books, authors and **characters**

Key **dates**

1340–1400 Geoffrey Chaucer, English poet, wrote *The Canterbury Tales.*

1547–1616 Miguel de Cervantes, Spanish novelist, wrote *Don Quixote.*

1608–74 John Milton, English poet, wrote *Paradise Lost.*

1667–1705 Jonathan Swift, Irish author, wrote *Gulliver's Travels.*

1770–1850 William Wordsworth, English poet, lead Romantic Movement.

1775–1817 Jane Austen, English novelist, wrote *Pride and Prejudice.*

1788–1824 Lord George Byron, English poet, wrote *Don Juan.*

1795–1821 John Keats, English poet, wrote *Ode to Autumn.*

1805–75 Hans Christian Andersen, Danish, wrote many fairy tales.

1821–81 Fyodor Dostoyevsky, Russian novelist, wrote *Crime and Punishment.*

1835–1910 Mark Twain, American author, wrote *Tom Sawyer* and *Huckleberry Finn.*

1840–1928 Thomas Hardy, English novelist, wrote *Tess of the D'Urbervilles.*

1850–94 Robert Louis Stevenson, Scottish author, wrote *Treasure Island.*

1882–1941 James Joyce, Irish author, wrote *Ulysses.*

↗ *In Lewis' imaginative story-telling, Alice meets the Mad Hatter, the March Hare and the Dormouse at a very strange tea party.*

What was Lewis Carroll's most famous work?

Alice in Wonderland. Lewis Carroll (Charles Lutwidge Dodgson 1832–98) had a shy exterior, but this English mathematician at Oxford University had a wild imagination and delighted in word play. He enjoyed telling stories to friends' children, and wrote two classic children's books: *Alice in Wonderland* (1865) and *Alice Through the Looking Glass* (1872).

➡ *Anne Frank died in a concentration camp in 1945. Her father, who survived the death camps, published her diary after the war.*

Which teenage girl kept a wartime diary?

Anne Frank, a German teenager living in hiding and in fear of her life, wrote a diary that is regarded as a moving testament to those who died in the Holocaust during World War II **(1939–45) (see page 94).** Anne's family were Jews who fled Germany to escape persecution by the Nazis. They moved to the Netherlands, but after the Germans invaded in 1940 were in peril once more. Anne, her sister, parents and four friends hid in a secret annexe at the back of an office building. She kept a diary, recording her thoughts until 1944, when the Franks and their friends were discovered and arrested.

Who were Britain's most famous literary sisters?

The Brontës were three sisters who grew up in the village of Haworth, in Yorkshire, with their brother and father, a clergyman. All three became novelists, at first sending in their work under men's names. Charlotte Brontë (1816–55) wrote *Jane Eyre*, about a governess; Emily Brontë (1818–48) wrote a passionate romance, *Wuthering Heights*, while the youngest sister Anne (1820–49) was the author of *The Tenant of Wildfell Hall*.

↗ *The Brontë sisters (left to right): Anne, Emily and Charlotte.*

Famous **authors and characters**

Author	Character	Author	Character
James Barrie	Peter Pan	Hergé	Tintin
L. Frank Baum	The Wizard of Oz	Rudyard Kipling	Mowgli
Enid Blyton	Noddy	C. S. Lewis	Aslan
Raymond Briggs	The Snowman	A. A. Milne	Winnie the Pooh
John Le Carré	George Smiley	Beatrix Potter	Peter Rabbit
Agatha Christie	Miss Marple, Hercule Poirot	J. K. Rowling	Harry Potter
Roald Dahl	The BFG	R. L. Stevenson	Long John Silver
Ian Fleming	James Bond, 007	J. R. R. Tolkien	Frodo the Hobbit
Kenneth Graham	Toad, Rat, Mole and Badger	Jules Verne	Captain Nemo

Wells

Christie

Verne

Hardy

Myths are stories about gods, supernatural beings and the origins of the world. Legends are stories about heroes, strange animals and adventures, which, while not perhaps true in every detail, may be based on real events. Such stories, some very old, are told all over the world.

Who hid inside a wooden horse?

Greek warriors. The story of the wooden horse is found in the *Iliad*, a long poem by Greek poet, Homer. It tells how the Greeks and the Trojans went to war following the abduction of Helen, the wife of a Greek king, by Paris, Prince of Troy. Troy was besieged for ten years, until the Greeks brought about its downfall by a trick. They built a gigantic wooden horse, inside which warriors were concealed. They left the horse outside Troy, and the unknowing Trojans dragged it into their city. At night, the Greek warriors climbed out, opened the city gates and led the invasion on Troy.

➡ *Greek soldiers hid inside a wooden horse as a deception to overthrow the Trojans.*

⬆ *According to legend, Romulus and Remus were cared for and fed by a female wolf.*

Who were Romulus and Remus?

Roman legend tells of twins named Romulus and Remus, who founded Rome in 753 BC. As babies, they were thrown into the River Tiber by a wicked uncle, but they were rescued by a she-wolf. Later, a shepherd brought them up. Remus was killed but Romulus became the first king of Rome. The Romans liked legendary explanations; the historical truth is that Rome grew from several village settlements on the seven hills upon which the city stands.

Which people told stories about Ragnarok?

The Vikings and other Norse peoples of Europe. Ragnarok, according to Norse mythology, was a battle between gods, giants and monsters who brought the end of the world. The leader of the gods, one-eyed Odin, led his warriors against his evil enemies from his great hall of Valhalla. In the slaughter, everyone died and the gods' realm of Asgard was destroyed by fire. Yet from this 'twilight of the gods' a new world was born. Two humans who hid in the branches of the World Tree, Yggdrasil, crept out to begin the life-cycle again.

➡ *The enemies of the gods rode in a ship with the terrible serpent to the last battle that ended the world.*

Mythological **creatures**

➡ *Greek poet Homer wrote the* Odyssey, *about the eventful journey of a man called Odysseus, returning home from The Trojan Wars.*

⬆ *The Amazon warriors also performed rain dances.*

Mythological **terms**

Amazons – A race of women warriors, according to Greek legend.

Aphrodite – Goddess of Love, said to have risen from the sea near Cyprus.

Dragon – Fabulous winged, fire-breathing animal, usually fearsome in Western mythology, but wise and good in Chinese.

Gorgon – Snake-haired monster of Greek myth, whose glance turned people to stone.

Heracles (Hercules) – Famous for his strength, he had to perform 12 'impossible' tasks or labours.

Who led the Argonauts?

The Argonauts, a band of 50 sailors and heroes from Greece, were led by Jason, son of King Aeson. Jason set sail on his ship, the *Argo*, to find the fabulous Golden Fleece – a golden ram's skin hung from a tree and guarded by a fearsome dragon. The Argonauts had many adventures before the arrival of Jason, with the aid of the witch Medea – they defeated the dragon and returned home with the Golden Fleece. The adventures of the Argonauts may have been based on tales told by Greek sailors, exploring the Mediterranean and Black Sea.

➲ *One hazard encountered by Jason and the Argonauts on their voyage was the Symplegades – these were rocks that clashed together, crushing everything that passed between them.*

Who is Rama?

Rama is one of the gods in Hinduism, the predominent religion of India. He is the hero of an epic poem called the *Ramayana*, written about 2,300 years ago, in Sanskrit (an ancient Indian language often used to write scriptures). It tells how prince Rama wins Sita as his wife, but then has to rescue her from the demon-king, Ravanna, who has kidnapped her and taken her to Lanka (now Sri Lanka). Rama is helped by his brother Laksmana and an army of monkeys.

Why is Anansi the spider so popular?

Anansi is the cunning hero of West African folk tales. He is a 'trickster', living on his quick wits and duping his enemies. Slaves taken from Africa to the United States took Anansi with them, and the stories of the crafty spider probably inspired Brer Rabbit, the hero of the Uncle Remus stories.

➲ *Hindus believe that the hero Rama was one of the ten human forms (avatars) of the god Vishnu.*

Hiawatha – Mohawk Native American hero, said to have united the tribes and learned the secret of the wilderness.
Lancelot of the Lake – Bravest of the knights of King Arthur.
Mermaid – Sea creatures that looked like beautiful women with tails of fish.
Phoenix – Fabulous bird that was born again from the ashes of its funeral pyre.
Robin Hood – Hero of medieval stories. An English outlaw famous for his skill as an archer.

➲ *Legend says that the phoenix was reborn in fire, rising from the flames.*

➲ *In mythology, the unicorn could only be caught by a maiden.*

Unicorn – Mythical animal with a horse's body, a lion's tail and a single horn protruding from its forehead.
Valkyries – Winged maidens in Norse mythology who decided which heroes should die in battle.

Culture is the way of life of a group of people who share certain customs, beliefs, technology and ideas. People who speak the same language may share the same culture (the Japanese, for example), but not necessarily – English is spoken by people from different cultural backgrounds. Every society has its own culture, and throughout history cultures have borrowed from one another and ideas have been communicated, shared and developed.

When was writing invented?

The earliest form of writing was created some 5,000 years ago in the ruins of Uruk, a city in Sumeria (modern Iraq). It was made by pressing a pointed tool into soft clay. The Sumerians wrote in pictograms (stylized drawings of objects). The ancient Chinese also developed a form of symbol writing using characters to stand for words. By the 1700s, there were over 40,000 Chinese characters! Compared to the 26 letters of the western alphabet, Chinese and its variants are extremely complex.

Which African people were sculptors?

The Nok people of Nigeria, in West Africa, created incredibly detailed and intricate terracotta figures more than 2,500 years ago. The Nok people and the sculptors of Benin (also in West Africa) used a method known as 'lost-wax' to cast bronze. During this process, a wax model is first made, then it is encased in soft clay or wet plaster, which hardens around it to form a mould. The mould is then heated, and the melted wax runs out of a hole, leaving a hollow inside that can be filled with molten bronze. When the bronze has set, the mould is taken apart to reveal the bronze sculpture.

A carved head from West Africa, where craftworkers still make traditional items for the tourist trade.

Which saint became Father Christmas?

St Nicholas, a 5th-century bishop, of whom very little is known except that he probably lived in the area of Asia Minor (modern Turkey). Legends about St Nicholas and tales of his miracles spread and he became a popular saint and Russia's patron saint. In Dutch, Nicholas was known as 'Sinter Claes', and Dutch migrants to America turned him into 'Santa Claus'. In Germany, he became 'Father January' or 'Father Christmas'.

One of the most common legends tells of Father Christmas (Santa Claus) arriving by a sleigh that is drawn by reindeer.

Cultural **history**

Key **dates**

c. 20,000 BC	Cave art and first sculptures.	**500 BC**	Nok culture in Africa.	**1826**	Joseph Niepce takes the first photograph, in France.
c. 10,000 BC	First towns, encouraging a settled way of life.	**AD 105**	Chinese invent paper.	**1876**	Alexander Graham Bell demonstrates the telephone.
		700	Beginnings of Islamic art. Monastic art in Christian Europe.	**1885**	Benz drives the first car.
c. 5000–3000 BC	Art and writing developed in Egypt, Mespotamia and China.			**1906**	Reginald Fessenden demonstrates radio broadcasting.
		1300s–1500s	Renaissance or 'rebirth' of art, learning and new science in Europe.	**1927**	First 'talkies': cinema films with recorded sound.
2000 BC	Greek and Mycenean art at its height.	**c. 1440**	Invention of printing with movable type.	**1936**	BBC starts world's first public television service.
400s BC	Golden age of Greek art.	**1600s**	First newspapers published in Europe.	**1946**	First electronic computer, made in the USA.
				1956	Videotape recording introduced.
				1960	First communications satellite.

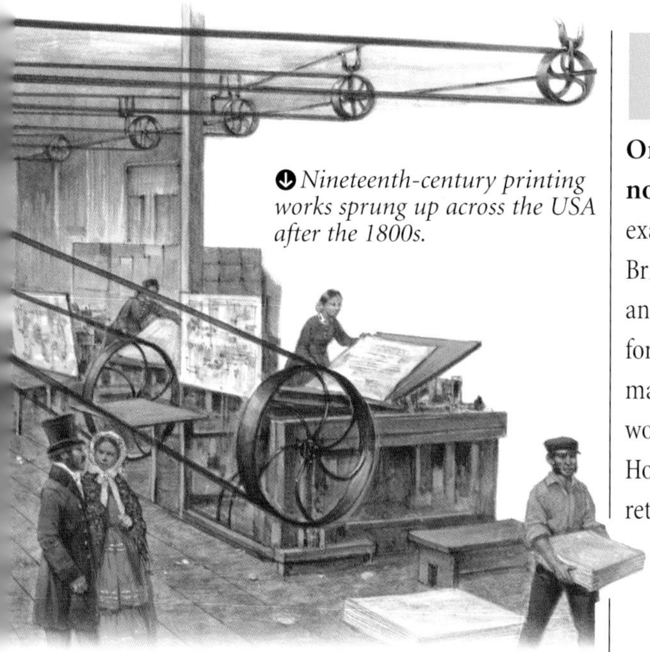

Nineteenth-century printing works sprung up across the USA after the 1800s.

What is oral culture?

Oral culture is passed on by speech, not by being written. In this way, for example, the Celtic people of pre-Roman Britain passed on their history, folk stories and religious beliefs. There was no written form of their language. Oral cultures exist in many parts of the world, and many of the world's epic tales were told in this way. Homer's *Iliad* and *Odyssey* were told and retold by generations of Greeks before they were written down.

Bards or Celtic poets sang to their lord, passing on history, and creating tales about the deeds of current heroes.

How did printing revolutionize culture?

In the 1440s, Johannes Gutenburg invented a screw-press that could print on paper sheets using movable pieces of type, arranged to make words. Printing made books cheaper, but it also brought in standard spellings and punctuation. Books were printed in vernacular (everyday) languages such as English, French and German, and not just in Latin. Novels, magazines and newspapers, even mail-order catalogues were all printed on machines. Knowledge was thus made more widely available to everyone.

It took 700,000 workers 40 years to build the Chinese emperor's tomb and its army of clay soldiers.

Which emperor had clay soldiers in his tomb?

The first emperor of China, Shih Huang-di, who died in 210 BC, was buried with an army of terracotta soldiers and horses. The pharaohs of Egypt were also buried with treasures as well as everyday items. The more important the person, the more splendid the tomb. In many ancient cultures it was the custom to bury 'grave goods' with a dead person for use in the afterlife.

1980s CDs begin to replace magnetized tape for information storage.

1990s Spread of home computers, laptops and World Wide Web via the Internet.

2000s Rapid growth of multi-channel, digital TV and radio and mobile phone networks.

Early alphabets

The use of an alphabet was a key stage in the development of written language. This document in the form of a scroll (an early form of book that rolled up) shows some alphabets. The term alphabet comes from the first two letters of the Greek alphabet, *alpha* and *beta*.

ABCDEF
АБВГДЕ
人月子水雨木

Phoenician
Classical Greek
Roman
Cyrillic
Modern Hebrew
Modern Arabic
Ancient Egyptian
Chinese
Japanese

In many countries culture is preserved in folk dance, music and songs.

Snow sports originated in lands where winter snow was prevalent – skiing in Scandinavia, ice-skating on frozen canals in the Netherlands and tobogganing in the Alps. Although ancient Greeks, Romans and Polynesians swam and sailed for pleasure, organized water sports, including swimming and yacht-racing did not develop until the 19th century. Today, winter sports and water sports are included in the Olympic Games.

↑ *The surfboard's profile or cut determines how it surfs on the wave.*

Who first stood on a surfboard?

Surfing was first enjoyed by the Polynesian islanders of the Pacific Ocean. The earliest description of someone surfing was written in Hawaii in 1779. Hawaiians used wooden boards more than 5 m long. Interest in surfing was revived in Australia and the United States, and world championships were first held in 1964.

Which is the fastest swimming stroke?

Of the four strokes in competitive swimming (breaststroke, backstroke, crawl and butterfly), the crawl is the fastest, followed by the butterfly. In competitive swimming, some races are designated 'freestyle', but all the top swimmers choose the crawl. The most widely used strokes by 19th-century swimmers were the breaststroke and sidestroke. Butterfly was officially recognized for use in racing in 1952.

What is a trimaran?

A trimaran is a sailing boat with three hulls. Trimarans and the twin-hulled catamarans were developed from the outrigger canoes used in the Pacific. Their appearance would have startled competitors in the first yacht race, between King Charles II and his brother James, Duke of York in 1661 on the River Thames. The original yachts were Dutch sailing boats.

➔ *The centre hull of a trimaran has the mast and crew compartment; the two other hulls provide extra stability at high speed.*

⬇ *All swimming strokes call for strong use of arm and leg muscles. This swimmer is using the butterfly stroke.*

On snow and **in water**

Skiing and snowboarding
The two main forms of ski-racing are Alpine and Nordic. Alpine skiing is done on a downhill slope, sometimes with gates to twist through (a slalom event). Competitors set off one at a time and are timed to see who is fastest. Nordic skiing takes place across country, and includes ski-jumping, where skiers zoom down a slope and leap off the end of a ramp. Snowboarding combines skiing, surfing and skateboarding on a stubby board that flips across the snow, enabling the rider to perform stunts in the air.

↑ *Many aerial manoeuvres achieved in snowboarding are inspired by skateboarding techniques.*

Skiing **terms**

Basket – ring at the end of the ski pole.
Bindings – fastenings holding ski boot to the ski.
Fall line – direct route down a slope.
Mogul – a bump in the slope.
Schussing – skiing straight down a slope.
Traversing – skiing across a slope.
Wedge or snow plough – stopping manoeuvre, bringing the front ends of the skis together in a V-shape.

➲ *A waterskier can skim over the water at speeds of up to 160 km/h.*

What is the difference between a kayak and a canoe?

A kayak paddler uses a two-bladed paddle, whereas a canoeist has a single-bladed paddle. Modern canoes and kayaks originated among the Native Americans and Inuit peoples of North America, who used canoes for transportation. Canoeing as a sport dates from 1866 and has been an Olympic event since 1936. In a modern canoe it is possible to turn upside down and roll upright again without coming to any harm.

➦ *The kayak paddle must hit the water at such an angle as to provide the correct stroke to propel the kayak forward.*

Who was the first waterskier?

The first waterskier was an American named Ralph Samuelson who gave the first exhibition of ski jumping from a ramp in 1925. Waterskiers hold on to a tow-rope and are pulled along on water skis, which are wider than snow skis, by a motorboat. The skier does stunts, slalom turns in and out of obstacles or jumps up a sloping ramp.

⬆ *Skiers hold long sticks, called ski-poles, to help them to steer and control.*

When were snow skis first used?

Ancient skis over 4,000 years old have been found in Scandinavia, where people made wooden skis to get around on during the long, snowy winters. In 1843, the first skiing competition was held in Norway. Modern skis are made of plastic, metal or fibreglass, but the basic principles are unchanged: the novice skier has to learn how to start, turn, and stop. At top speed, a downhill skier can whizz along at up to over 240 km/h.

Safety rules **for swimmers**

- Never swim alone in a lake or the sea.
- Beware of currents in the sea.
- Obey 'no-swimming' signs, warning flags or advice from lifeguards.
- Never dive into water without knowing how deep it is.
- Never dive into a pool close to other swimmers.
- Avoid swimming straight after eating.

⬇ *Most swimming races start with a dive from one end of the pool.*

Key **dates**

36 BC Japan is the first country to stage swimming races.

1888 First World Championships (unofficial) are held in Australia.

1896 Swimming is one of the events in the revived Olympic Games.

1900 Water polo introduced to the Olympics.

1904 Diving (for men) introduced to the Olympics.

1973 First swimming world championships.

1984 Synchronized swimming is admitted to the Olympics.

People probably first played ball games thousands of years ago. Inflated pigs' bladders were used as balls in the Middle Ages, and children used curved sticks for early versions of cricket and golf. Schools and colleges began organizing ball games as part of formal education in the 19th century, leading to the amazing growth in professional ball-sports across the world today.

Baseball catchers wear protective clothing to shield against the impact of the ball.

Which team sport attracts the most spectators?

The world's most popular spectator sport is soccer, which is played and watched on every continent. Only in the USA is professional soccer not the leading team game. Soccer originated from violent medieval football games, but was organized with rules, leagues and professional teams in the 19th century. The World Cup, held every four years, is the biggest international soccer tournament. The international governing body, FIFA, was set up in 1904.

Soccer is money-making entertainment, especially in Europe and South America.

How fast does a pitcher throw a baseball?

A baseball pitcher can throw the ball (which weighs 148 g) at up to 160 km/h. Baseball was first played by modern rules in New Jersey, USA in 1846, although a similar rounders-like game had been played long before this in the UK. Professional clubs first appeared in 1871 and the national league was established in 1876. The winners of the two main US leagues, the National and the American, meet every year in the seven-game World Series.

Which king played tennis?

The monarch best-known for playing tennis is England's Henry VIII who, as a young man, was an expert at real (royal) tennis, which was played on a walled court. The game later moved outside and rules for 'lawn tennis' were drawn up in the 1800s. The first Wimbledon Championship, the oldest of the 'Grand Slams', was held in 1877. The most successful men's players at Wimbledon are Bjorn Borg (five singles titles, 1976–80) and Pete Sampras (seven singles titles, 1993–2000). Martina Navratilova won her 20th Wimbledon title in 2003, equalling the women's record held by Billie-Jean King.

Ball **facts**

Catching the ball in a net

Lacrosse is a minority game among the world's ball games. First played by Native Americans in Canada, when as many as 1,000 players practically fought one another in a game, it is now played mostly in schools and colleges.

Lacrosse players wield a netting pocket on the end of a stick (the crosse), with which to catch and throw the ball.

Fastest **balls**

Name	Speed
Pelota ball	300 km/h
Golf ball	270 km/h
Tennis ball	220 km/h
Baseball / cricket ball	160 km/h

The speed of a cricket ball depends on how it is bowled: it can be bowled fast or spun slowly.

⬆ *Players grapple for the ball during American football, which requires them to wear padding.*

Where was golf first played?

The earliest mention of golf is in a Scottish law of 1457, banning the game. Golf-like games were played much earlier, using crooked sticks and balls. The oldest golf championship in the world is Britain's 'Open', first played in 1860. Since 1892, it has been a 72-hole championship (four rounds of 18 holes). The objective of golf is to get the ball into a small hole on the 'green' in as few putts as possible.

⬆ *One of the most successful player of modern times is American Tiger Woods.*

Which game is played on a grid-iron?

The grid-iron is the pitch on which American football is played. Developed by university students in the 19th century, the game is a spin-off from soccer and rugby. The pitch contains lines that cross the field every 4.6 m from one sideline to the other. Two teams of 11 players compete for the Super Bowl, which is played each year by the champions of the two main leagues: the National Football Conference (NFC) and the American Football Conference (AFC).

In which sport does it help to be exceptionally tall?

Basketball, because very tall players can more easily send the ball into the net or basket to score points. Basketball was invented in the USA in 1891 as an indoor team game for winter. Two teams each of five players try to score points by tossing the ball into the opposing team's basket. Players must not run with the ball and have time limits for passing the ball.

➡ *The basket is fixed on a backboard that can also bounce the ball into the net.*

Playing pelota

Pelota is a ball game that originated in northern Spain. It usually involves two players (known as pelotari) or two teams each comprising two players, who use either their bare hands, a racket or a cesta (curved wooden basket) to hit the ball onto the opposing side's wall. There are seven forms of the game in total, each with differing rules.

➡ *Pelotari can hit the ball using a cesta, which is made from chesnut and willow.*

Soccer **records**

The first World Cup, held in Uruguay in 1930, was won by Uruguay. Brazil is the only country to have appeared in every World Cup final. Brazil are the only team to have won the World Cup five times.

Record	Answer
Most famous soccer player	Pelè of Brazil
Britain's first soccer knight	Sir Stanley Matthews
Biggest soccer tournament	World Cup
Oldest tournament	FA Cup
First women's world championship	1991
Highest score in UK	36–0 (Arbroath v Bon Acord in 1885, a Scottish Cup Match)

The first people to take running seriously and compete against one another were the ancient Greeks. Track and field athletics as we know them began in the 19th century in schools and colleges in Europe and North America. These events play a big part in the Olympic Games, and there are also regular world and regional championships. Track races and some field events can also take place indoors.

● As sprinters cross the finish line, they push their heads forward so that the winner is clearly visible.

How fast can a sprinter run?

A male sprinter can speed down the 100-m straight in about 9.8 sec – a speed of just over 40 km/h. This is slower than a horse, which can sprint at 56 km/h, or a greyhound (67 km/h), but faster than a swimmer (about 8 km/h). The 100-m sprint is the shortest outdoor race in athletics; indoor sprints are 60-m dashes.

How many hurdle races are there?

In track and field events, three races involve runners jumping over barriers called hurdles. The shortest is the 110-m hurdles race (100-m for women) in which competitors aim to stride over hurdles, which measure 107 m high for men and 84 m high for women. For both men and women, in the one-lap 400-m hurdle race the hurdles are lower. In the steeplechase, which is more than 3,000 m, athletes jump over a wooden hurdle and leap over a waterjump.

Which long jumper astonished the world?

Bob Beamon (USA) set an amazing world long jump record in 1968 at the Mexico City Olympics. The high altitude caused thin air (a lack of oxygen), making Beamon's leap of 8.9 m even more amazing. Beamon had shattered the previous world record and no jumper had ever jumped more than 8.5 m. Beamon's record lasted until 1991 when Mike Powell (USA) broke it by 5 cm.

● A male hurdler must jump clear of a barrier at least 1 m high.

On your marks...

● Carl Lewis, winner of ten world championship medals.

● Jesse Owens was the star of the 1936 Olympics, winning long jump, sprint and relay.

Amazing track facts

• Jesse Owens (USA) won four gold medals at the 1936 Olympics and held seven world records.

• Emil Zátopek (Czech Republic) won four gold medals at Olympic Games and held ten world records.

• Al Oerter (USA) won the Olympic discus gold medal four times.

• Roger Bannister (UK) was the first man to run a mile in under four minutes, in 1954.

• Raymond Ewry (USA) won a record ten Olympic medals between 1900 and 1908 for jumping.

↑ *A javelin thrower runs about 12 very quick strides and accelerates to 7 m/sec, gaining momentum for the throw. A throw is only valid if the javelin touches the ground with the tip first. Javelin throwing has featured in the Olympic Games since 1908.*

What is a relay race?

Relays are team races, played by four runners in each team. Each runner carries a baton, which must be passed to the next runner at a changeover point. The most common relays in track athletics are the 4 x 100 m and the 4 x 400 m, for both men and women. In a baton relay race, dropping the baton means the whole team is disqualified from the event.

What are field events?

Field events include throwing and jumping. There are four throwing events: javelin, discus, shotput and hammer. The four jumping events are long jump, triple jump, high jump and pole vault. Pole vault athletes use a fibreglass pole to help lift themselves over a bar, which is more than 6 m high.

↑ *In a baton relay race the next team member must start running before the previous runner has handed the baton to him. It is the baton, not the runner, that is timed. The baton is made from wood or metal and weighs about 50 g.*

↓ *The triple jump involves three stages: a hop, a step and a two-footed jump.*

1 Gaining height

2 Gaining momentum

3 Gaining speed

4 Landing on sand with both feet as far forward as possible

• Paavo Nurmi (Finland) won five gold medals for running, in the 1925 Olympics.

• Irena Szewinska (Poland) won medals at four successive games from 1964 to 1976.

• Barbara Jones (USA) was just 15 years old when she won a gold medal in the 4 x 100 m relay at the 1952 Olympics – the youngest track gold medallist.

• Carl Lewis (USA) won ten world championship medals, eight of them gold. His events were long jump, 100 m and 4 x 100 m relay. He also won eight Olympic gold medals between 1984 and 1992.

← *Top distance runners like Britain's Paula Radcliffe put in many hours and kilometres of training.*

The earliest sport on wheels was chariot racing (see page 70), which was enjoyed by ancient Egyptians and Romans. In the 19th century, bicycles were raced, and from 1885 the motorcar and motorcycle were soon used for racing. Today, motorsport in its various forms, on purpose-built racing circuits and on roads, is followed avidly by fans across the world.

British racing champion Stirling Moss drove 84 different vehicles during his career.

Where was the first motor race?

The first race for cars was in France in 1895. Emile Levassor won, driving his car at an average speed of just over 24 km/h. The race from Paris to Bordeaux and back covered 1,178 km. Grand Prix racing began in 1906, also in France, and is now held at circuits across the world. Today's Grand Prix cars travel more than ten times faster than in 1895.

Competitors take part in events such as indoor sprints, pursuit and time trials on steep tracks and outdoor road races.

Which is the most famous cycle race?

The Tour de France, which was first raced in 1903. It is the biggest event for racing cyclists and takes 21 days to complete. Each stage has a separate winner but the overall winner receives the coveted yellow jersey. Cycle racing began in 1868 and the first world championships were staged in 1903. Cycling has been an Olympic sport since the first modern Olympics in 1896.

Speedway bikes have no brakes so riders must use their feet as they slide around bends, sending up showers of dirt.

What is speedway?

Speedway, also known as dirt-track racing, is a form of motorcycle racing. Modern speedway dates from the 1920s in Australia and the first world championships were held in 1936. Unlike other forms of motorcycle racing, such as scrambling or motocross, which take place on 'natural' outdoor circuits, speedway riders compete around an oval track. During each race, which lasts for four laps, the four riders taking part slide into the tight bends.

Motorsport **facts**

Cyclo-cross riders have to negotiate hills, water and mud.

Key **dates**

1895	First organized car race in France.
1906	First Grand Prix race, at Le Mans, France.
1911	First Indianapolis 500 in the USA.
1920	Grand Prix races first held outside France.
1923	First 24-hour race for sports cars at Le Mans.
1936	First organized stock car races in the USA.

1960s Rear-engined cars take over from front-engined cars in Grand Prix races.

Motorcycle racers compete over winding circuits.

Motocross riders become airborne on a 'scramble' over bumps and bends.

What is the difference between a rally and a race?

During a car rally, cars set off at intervals and are timed on each section. During a race, a number of cars start in ranks from a grid and race around a circuit with bends and straights. Rallies cover several thousand kilometres and take several days to complete. They are often held across wild country: one rally is held in East Africa, another across the Sahara. The most famous rally is the Monte Carlo Rally. Car races include the Grand Prix races held in various countries, the Indianapolis 500 in the USA and the Le Mans 24-hour race in France.

⊙ *Stock cars look like wrecks but keep going at full speed.*

⊕ *Drag racers have huge rear wheels to get them moving, and aerofoils to keep the wheels on the ground as the car accelerates.*

⊙ *A rally car is a modified production car, which can be driven over extremely challenging terrain, such as muddy hillsides, that tests both machine and driver.*

What are stock-car and drag racing?

Stock cars are known as hot rods or old bangers, which have been modified for a crash-and-bang race around a large, speedway-sized track. Drag cars are designed to speed down a 400 m long track, at speeds of up to 500 km/h. A race lasts less than 10 sec and only two cars compete each time, until one car is left victorious. In both stock-car and drag racing, collisions are frequent and many of the cars end up looking like battered wrecks.

Amazing **facts**

- The oldest motorcycle races are the Isle of Man TT races, first held in 1907.

- Specially modified cycles have been pedalled at more than 268 km/h – behind a windshield provided by a car in front.

- More than 31,000 people took part in the London to Brighton bike ride in 1988.

- The oldest world motor racing champion was the Argentinian Juan Manuel Fangio, who won the last of his five titles in 1957 at the age of 46.

- The longest car rally was in 1977 from London to Sydney – a distance of 31,107 km.

- Skateboarding is fairly new, in wheely-sport terms, and fairly slow. Even so, skateboard experts can put on a startling show of acrobatics on wheels.

⊙ *A GT car is a faster-than-normal version of a standard model.*

Grand **Prix drivers**

Name	Nationality	Number of wins
Michael Shumacher	German	53
Alain Prost	French	51
Ayrton Senna	Brazilian	41
Nigel Mansell	British	31
Jackie Stewart	British	27
Jim Clarke	British	25
Niki Lauder	Australian	25
Juan Fangio	Argentinian	24
Graham Hill	British	2
Damon Hill	British	1

People have always enjoyed playing games. As town life began to develop more than 5,000 years ago, people played board games and games of chance, using dice or marked pieces, such as dominoes. The ancient Egyptians enjoyed chariot racing and wrestling, and Greek athletes took part in the Olympic Games more than 3,000 years ago. Rules for many modern games such as tennis, rugby, football and baseball were established in the 1800s. Some professional sports stars today are among the highest-paid people in the world.

How did the Marathon race get its name?

The Marathon race takes its name from a battle in 490 BC between the Greeks and Persians on the Plain of Marathon, in Greece. After the Greek victory, a runner named Philippides ran 24 mi (38 km) to Athens, gasped 'Rejoice, we have won' and died of exhaustion. The Marathon has been set at its present distance of over 26 mi 385 yd (43 km) since 1908, and is run in various cities. Thousands of amateurs as well as top athletes take part in popular races, such as the London Marathon.

Why did Romans flock to the Colosseum?

Crowds flocked to the Colosseum (see page 201), a stadium in ancient Rome, to watch 'the games'. The games were not sports in the modern sense but lavish shows, during which animals and people met bloody deaths. People came to watch fights between gladiators (specially-trained fighters) or between men and wild animals. There were even mock hunts and mock sea-battles, for which the arena was flooded.

➔ *Philippides ran from Marathon to Athens, then collapsed and died.*

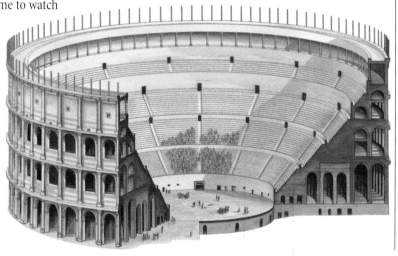

🔽 *In Rome's Colosseum, the spectators sat in circular tiers that rose in height around the arena, which was built like a circus ring. The structure itself was made of concrete, which was invented by the Romans.*

When were the first Olympic Games held?

The first Olympic Games were held in ancient Greece, in 776 BC and continued to be held there until AD 393. In 1896, the first modern Games were held in Athens, Greece, with just nine events. The Winter Olympics began in 1924. The Olympics have been held every four years since 1896, except during wartime (1916, 1940 and 1944).

All about **games and sport**

🔽 *Greyhound racing is a modern version of ancient contests, such as hare-coursing, between hunting dogs. The mechanical hare was first used in 1919.*

Key **dates**

1299	Bowling club recorded in Southampton, England.
1330	First known references to, and pictures of, hockey.
1544	Earliest mention of billiards.
1620	*Mayflower* pilgrims play darts.
1657	Earliest known golf match played between Scotland and England.
1744	First cricket rules were formed.
1846	First recorded baseball game under modern rules.
1860s	Badminton first played.
1863	English Football Association (FA) formed.
1865	Queensberry Rules for boxing were established.
1874	Lawn tennis invented, as 'sphairistike' (Greek for 'ball').
1875	Earliest mention of snooker.
1898	First international cross-country race.

Which country has the fattest wrestlers?

Japan, where sumo wrestling is practised by wrestlers of huge body weight, up to 267 kg. Sumo is at least 2,000 years old, and has strict rules and ceremonies. Being very fat is an advantage, since the object of the wrestler is to push his opponent out of the circular ring. Any hold is permitted, unlike Greco-Roman wrestling, where the wrestler cannot seize his opponent below the hips or use his legs. In freestyle wrestling, almost all moves are permitted.

⊙ *The goaltender is heavily padded during an ice-hockey game to prevent serious injury.*

⊙ *The heavier the sumo wrestler, the more strength they have to push their opponent.*

Which is the fastest team game?

In a game of ice hockey, the rubber puck can whizz over the ice at more than 160 km/h. A form of hockey on ice was played in the Netherlands in the 1500s, but modern ice hockey has its origins in 19th-century Canada. Each ice hockey team is made up of six players, and substitutes are allowed during the game, which has three periods each lasting 20 minutes.

Who first played polo?

Polo began among the horsemen of central Asia and Persia (now Iran) some 4,000 years ago. The polo 'ball' was sometimes the head of a slain enemy! Modern polo dates from the 1860s, when British army officers saw the game played in India. Polo is played on a field 274 m long by riders who wield mallets whilst mounted on ponies. The aim of the game is to score a goal by hitting a ball through the opponents' goal posts.

⊙ *Training a polo pony to twist and turn at speed takes about six months.*

Amazing **Olympic facts**

⊙ *An early 20th-century golf championship player preparing to drive, watched by attentive spectators in the Open Championship, which was first played in Britain in 1860, at Prestwick in Scotland.*

Record	Date	Place
First modern Olympics	1896	Athens, Greece
First women medallists	1900	Paris, France
First Winter Games	1924	Chamonix, France
First Olympic village built	1932	Los Angeles, USA
First torch-lighting ceremony	1936	Berlin, Germany
Mark Spitz wins seven gold medals	1972	Munich, Germany
Carl Lewis wins eight gold medals	1984 / 1992	Los Angeles, USA and Barcelona, Spain
Marion Jones wins five medals	2000	Sydney, Australia
Most events ever held (300)	2000	Sydney, Australia

Now's your chance to test your knowledge on what you have learnt! Use this quiz to find out how much you know about space, geography, history, nature, wildlife, the human body, science and technology, the world of entertainment and much more. This quiz will ask questions about what you have learnt from this book (grouped into sections as found in the book), as well as asking questions about subjects that you may have studied already.

The Universe

1 How long ago is the Big Bang thought to have taken place?
2 What do stars generate other than light?
3 What shape is the Milky Way?
4 What did the first astronauts to land on the Moon bring back with them?
5 What is the temperature of the Sun's surface?
6 How many planets are in our Solar System?
7 How long does Saturn take to travel around the Sun: two years, 20 years or 29 years?

Planet Earth

8 How long does it take for the Earth to revolve around the Sun?
9 What is made during the process of cartography?
10 Is there more land or more water making up the Earth's surface?

11 The tectonic plates of India and Asia have pushed together over the last 40 million years to create which mountain range?

12 What is the name given to a small warning shock delivered by an earthquake?
13 What ocean separates Europe from North and South America?
14 What is the second most common element in the air?
15 Meteorology is the study of what feature of Earth?

World History

16 Odin was the chief god of which people?
17 Pizarro conquered which empire?
18 Which Greek philosopher founded the Academy in Athens?
19 Which female East Anglian leader rebelled against Roman rule in Britain in AD 122?
20 What were the Crusades?
21 Which explorer, who discovered America, sailed in the *Santa Maria*?
22 At which battle did the Indians defeat General Custer?

23 A giant tortoise, which can grow up to 1.2 m long, comes from which group of islands in the Pacific Ocean?

The Natural World

24 Is an animal that eats meat called a herbivore or a carnivore?
25 What does a sygnet grow into?
26 Which furry animal flies on wings of skin?
27 What baby reptile squeaks inside its egg: a lizard, crocodile or snake?
28 Which sea creature usually has five limbs?
29 Was the dodo a type of bird or deer?
30 Which vegetable does not grow underground: carrot, pea or potato?

The Human Body

31 What is the science of the body and its parts called?
32 How many bones make up the skeleton?
33 What carries blood from the heart?
34 Which part of the throat tightens across the airway and vibrates in order to produce sound?
35 What are the five senses?
36 The optic nerve leads to the brain from where?
37 What part of the mother does a baby grow in?

Science & Technology

38 What happens to water at 0°C?

39 What is the name for a machine made of ropes and wheels used to lift heavy loads?

40 What is an example of natural electricity?

41 Does a conductor let energy flow, or stop it flowing?

42 What navigational device uses a magnet suspended or floating in liquid?

43 What did Thomas Edison invent to create light in 1879?

44 How many hours are there in a day?

45 Who developed the first hot-air balloon, launched in 1783?

46 In which Australian city is the famous opera house?

Around the World

47 Which continent has more people: South America or Africa?

48 In which country would you find the Ural mountains?

49 Nairobi is the capital city of which African country?

50 Name the Scandinavian countries.

51 In which Asian country would you find Mount Fiji?

52 What does the abbreviation EU stand for?

53 Botany Bay is an ex-convict settlement in which country?

Arts, Sports & Entertainment

54 Of what type of instrument are the violin, cello and guitar examples?

55 In which century was the artist Michaelangelo born?

56 Which Shakespeare play is often referred to as the Scottish play?

57 Who is the Greek goddess of love?

58 From which art gallery was the Mona Lisa stolen in 1911?

59 Which American sprinter set a world record for the 100 m in 1999?

60 Which country hosted the 2002 Winter Olympics?

Answers

1 15 billion years ago
2 Heat
3 Spiral shaped
4 Moon rock
5 6,000°C
6 Nine
7 29 years
8 One year
9 Maps
10 More water
11 The Himalayas
12 Foreshock
13 Atlantic
14 Oxygen
15 Its atmosphere and weather
16 Vikings or Norsemen

17 Inca empire
18 Plato
19 Boudicca
20 Religious wars against the Turks
21 Christopher Columbus
22 Battle of Little Bighorn
23 The Galapagos Islands
24 Carnivore
25 Swan
26 Bat
27 Crocodile
28 Starfish
29 Bird
30 Pea
31 Anatomy

32 206
33 Arteries
34 Vocal cords
35 Sight, hearing, smell, touch and taste
36 The eyes
37 Womb
38 It freezes
39 Pulley
40 Lightning
41 It lets it flow
42 Magnetic compass
43 The light bulb
44 24
45 The Montgolfier brothers
46 Sydney

47 Africa
48 Russia
49 Kenya
50 Denmark, Finland, Iceland, Norway and Sweden
51 Japan
52 European Union
53 Australia
54 Stringed instruments
55 15th century
56 *Macbeth*
57 Aphrodite
58 The Louvre in Paris
59 Maurice Green
60 USA

The publishers would like to thank the following artists who have contributed to this book:
Lisa Alderson, June Allan, Richard Berridge, Syd Brak, John Butler, Chris Buzer/Galante Studio, Steve Caldwell,
Martin Camm, Vanessa Card, Jim Channell, Kuo Kang Chen, Mark Davis, Peter Dennis, Richard Draper, Nick Farmer,
Fiammetta Dogi/Galante Studio, Wayne Ford, Nicholas Forder, Chris Forsey, Terry Gabbey, Luigi Galante, Shammi Ghale,
Peter Gregory, Terry Grose, Alan Hancocks, Peter Harper, Alan Harris, Ron Hayward, Sally Holmes, Richard Hook,
Ian Jackson, Rob Jakeway, John James, Stuart Lafford, Mick Loates, Kevin Maddison, Alan Male, Maltings, Janos Marffy,
Angus McBride, Doreen McGuiness, A.Menchi/Galante Studio, Andrea Morandi, Chris Odgers, Rachel Phillips, Terry Riley,
Pete Roberts, Steve Roberts, Eric Robson, Martin Sanders, Peter Sarson, Mike Saunders, Rob Sheffield, Guy Smith,
Roger Smith, Sarah Smith, Graham Sumber, Gwen Tourret, Rudi Vizi, Steve Weston, Mike White, Paul Williams,
Colin Wolf, John Woodcock

The publishers wish to thank the following sources for the photographs used in this book:
Roger Ressmeyer/CORBIS p48 (c/r); Michal Heron/CORBIS p142 (b/r);
JEAN-CHRISTOPHE VERHAEGEN-PIG/AFP/GETTY IMAGES p147 (b/r); Lester Lefkowitz/CORBIS p151 (b/r);
EDELMANN/SCIENCE PHOTO LIBRARY p152 (t/c); Norbert Schaefer/CORBIS p153 (c/l); Robert Essel NYC/CORBIS p166 (c/r);
Apple Computers p170 (b/l); Richard T. Nowitz/CORBIS p171 (t/r); Sony Computer Entertainment p171(b/c);
SAM YEH/AFP/GETTY IMAGES p177 (c/r); Trek Aerospace p179 (b/r); AFP/GETTY IMAGES p182 (c/l);
FRANK PERRY/AFP/GETTY IMAGES p183 (t/r); Sony Computer Entertainment p185 (t/r); Warren Morgan/CORBIS p188 (c/l);
Nik Wheeler/CORBIS p188 (t/r); David Ball/CORBIS p189 (t/r); Wally McNamee/CORBIS p190 (b/l);
Alexander Nemenov/AFP/GETTY p192 (c); Gerard Vandenberghe/AFP/GETTY IMAGES p195 (c/l);
Joe McDonald/CORBIS p197 (t/l); Charles and Josette Lenars/CORBIS p197 (c/l); Roger Wood/CORBIS p197 (b/l);
Jonathan Blair/CORBIS p199 (b/l); Alan Schein/CORBIS p203 (b/r); Dennis Degnan/CORBIS p207 (t/r); Argos p223 (b/r);
AFP/GETTY IMAGES p226 (b/r); Pictorialpress.com (b/r); Pictorialpress.com p227 (b/r); Volkwagen p229 (b);
Warners/Pictorialpress.com (b/r); Pictorialpress.com p230 (c/r); Jim Sugar/Corbis p239 (b); Corr/AFP/GETTY IMAGES p240 (b/c);
Damien Meyer/AFP/GETTY IMAGES p241 (b/r); Joel Saget/AFP/GETTY IMAGES p242 (c/r); Neil Brake/AFP/GETTY IMAGES p243 (b/c)

All other photographs are from:
Castrol, CMCD, Corbis, Corel, Digitalvision, John Foxx, ILN, NASA, Photoalto, PhotoDisc, STOCKBYTE